James Macaulay

Ireland in 1872

A Tour of Observation

James Macaulay

Ireland in 1872
A Tour of Observation

ISBN/EAN: 9783744717304

Printed in Europe, USA, Canada, Australia, Japan

Cover: Foto ©Andreas Hilbeck / pixelio.de

More available books at **www.hansebooks.com**

IRELAND IN 1872.

IRELAND IN 1872:

A TOUR OF OBSERVATION.

WITH REMARKS ON

IRISH PUBLIC QUESTIONS.

BY

JAMES MACAULAY, M.A., M.D., Edin.,

Author of "Across the Ferry."

LONDON:
HENRY S. KING & CO.,
65, CORNHILL, & 12, PATERNOSTER ROW.

1873.

PREFATORY NOTE.

"IRELAND in 1872" is a wide theme, upon which one might expatiate through many volumes. I confine myself to points which now most occupy public attention, and to matters which seem chiefly to determine the existing social and political situation.

We are always hearing about the improved state of Ireland. In its material wealth there are proofs of prosperity and progress, yet its government remains the difficulty of statesmen. Are the disturbing elements social, political, or religious? I endeavour to show how far each of these classes of questions affect the general condition of the country. I have only a few prefatory remarks to make.

In speaking of the Catholic influence, I am careful to distinguish between the Irish Catholics and the

Italian Catholics or Ultramontane party. To understand this distinction, it is necessary to consider the change that has been gradually made in the constitution and administration of the Catholic Church in Ireland. When the struggle for Emancipation was going on, several of the leading prelates of that Church were examined before a committee of the House of Commons. Dr. Doyle was the principal witness, then the most distinguished and most representative man among Irish Catholics. Being asked as to the authority of the Pope, Dr. Doyle said it was purely spiritual, and that "his power was limited by decrees of council and also by usage." Being asked as to the mode of electing bishops in Ireland, Dr. Doyle said, "The Pope does not at present, and he could scarcely presume to, nominate any one except such person as we recommend." In fact, the usage was for the bishops to send to Rome a list of three, *dignus, dignior, dignissimus*, and the Pope invariably appointed the person thus recommended as the worthiest and fittest.

But all this is changed now. In the conspiracy for increasing the Papal power in Ireland, the first step was to disregard the recommendation of the bishops in filling a vacancy. It was first done in the case of Dr. Cullen, known to be a trusty agent of the Vatican, who had lived many years in Rome, and is far more an Italian than an Irishman in spirit. Ever since, the appointments have been made of men who would be subservient to the same policy, and now the whole of the bishops, with, I believe, two exceptions, are Ultramontanes. The appointment of parish priests and of curates is in the hands of the bishops, and they take care to appoint men who will be most under their control. If any parish priest shows symptoms of independence, a curate coadjutor is planted beside him. The well-organized power of the hierarchy prevents outspoken protest, or effectual resistance to the crafty power by which the liberties of the Irish Church are being crushed. The new doctrine of Papal Infallibility has removed the former limits to the Pope's power, imposed by "decrees of council, and also by usage." His authority is now supreme, not only as the head of the Church, but it extends to every diocese and to every parish. The independence of the Irish Catholic Church is thus destroyed; and, not content with this, the Ultramontane power is attempting to limit the civil rights of the Irish clergy. The well-known O'Keeffe case, now before the Courts, will show the extent and direction of the attack on the laws and constitution of the nation. It is the restless and aggressive policy of this faction which causes the most serious difficulties in Irish affairs, and most retards the peaceful progress of the country.

In affirming that Popery is the main cause of the troubles and woes of Ireland, the statement is made on grounds of history and experience, without touching on theological controversies. I give the result of my own observation, in many countries besides Ireland. In confirmation of my statements, I have quoted the opinions of men like Sydney Smith and Charles Dickens, of Sismondi and De Tocqueville, as being free from suspicion of religious bigotry or prejudice. The social results of the system may be examined, without any unkind or uncharitable feeling towards its adherents. I bear testimony to the exemplary character of many of the Irish Catholic clergy, and I so admire John Banim's ballad, "Soggarth Aroon," that I wish every "priest dear" had a wife, as St. Peter had, and so double his happiness and usefulness. Of the natural piety and devoutness of the poor Irish Catholics, no one can speak without respect. To them may be applied the complimentary epithet which St. Paul used to the men of Athens, that they are full of reverence, or as we mistranslate it, "too superstitious." The Irish Catholic Church in early ages gained for Ireland the name of "the Isle of Saints," and it may yet regain the brightness it had in the days of St. Patrick and St. Columba. It has not lost the ancient truths, although they are now overlaid with Romish errors and innovations.

CONTENTS.

CHAPTER		PAGE
I.	IRELAND IN TRANSITION	1
II.	SOME STATISTICS OF PROGRESS	17
III.	PARADOXES AND PROBLEMS	31
IV.	DECREASE OF POPULATION.—EMIGRATION	38
V.	ABSENTEEISM	53
VI.	VISIT TO MR. BIANCONI	63
VII.	IRISH POLITICS	77
VIII.	HOME RULE	89
IX.	A CHAPTER ON IRISH HISTORY	115
X.	THE QUESTION OF RACE	133
XI.	CATHOLIC AND PROTESTANT CONTRASTS	143
XII.	ROMAN CATHOLICS AND IRISH CATHOLICS	167
XIII.	THE O'KEEFFE CASE	183
XIV.	THE KEOGH JUDGMENT	231
XV.	IRISH AGRICULTURE	249
XVI.	LAND TENURE AND THE NEW LAND ACT	268

CHAPTER		PAGE
XVII.	IRISH FISHERIES	285
XVIII.	THE ROYAL IRISH CONSTABULARY	291
XIX.	IRISH PRISONS AND PRISONERS	301
XX.	PARTY PROCESSIONS	311
XXI.	THE NEWSPAPERS OF IRELAND	319
XXII.	THE DUBLIN EXHIBITION	344
XXIII.	STATE PURCHASE OF IRISH RAILWAYS	350
XXIV.	IRISH NATIONAL EDUCATION	355
XXV.	IRISH UNIVERSITY EDUCATION	383
XXVI.	EVANGELICAL AND PROTESTANT AGENCIES	404

IRELAND IN 1872.

CHAPTER I.

IRELAND IN TRANSITION.

An Irish Funeral—Wakes—Fairs—Ireland of Last Generation—Since the Famine—Social Changes—National Progress.

I WAS sauntering one day in Killarney, watching the Kerry peasants at their marketing, when a great crowd was seen moving up the long main street of the town. As it drew near it proved to be a funeral, and I heard what, from description, I knew to be the "keen" or wail of mourners. There were about a dozen elderly women, in two rows, walking in front of the hearse. They had the long cloaks and the hooded shawls or kerchiefs of the country. One woman seemed to be the chief keener, leading the dirge, the others joining in the melancholy wail. In an Irish car following the hearse were four women, relatives of the deceased. Every now and then they also uttered cries, the natural and unchecked expressions of passionate grief, less formal than the keen of the old women in front, but in the same minor key of plaintive tone. Ten or twelve cars, carts, and various vehicles followed with female mourners, and a dense crowd on foot closed up the procession. The burial was to be at a rural churchyard some miles off. Shutters were put up in the shops of the town, and every mark of respect paid as the funeral passed by.

In reply to enquiries, I learned that the deceased was a tradesman of the town, an O'Donoghue, "come of dacent people." "Was he an old man?" "No, he was only a boy," which might denote any age from ten to fifty or more. "Were these keeners paid?" "No, they attend only out of respect to the family." The use of professional keeners or hired mourners is going out. These old women, however, were experienced performers, and the "keening" will not soon be a thing of mere tradition. The women will continue to be paid, in kind if not in coin, for there is always hospitable supply in houses between the time of death and burial. A "dacent funeral" implies many guests, though not necessarily with the scandalous scenes of former times.

In Mr. and Mrs. S. C. Hall's "Ireland" the writers say, "We followed, in 1858, a funeral to Aghadoe; there were attendant keeners, who chaunted the death song nearly all the way. The 'keen' is not often heard now-a-days, and the ceremonies connected with death have of late lost much of their earlier, more picturesque, but more barbarous accompaniments." Hundreds of tourists have visited Ireland without hearing the "keen," and I was told that I might be many years without seeing a funeral such as I had witnessed at Killarney. It was a strange and unexpected incident, and as the wild wail echoed in my memory, the whole scene seemed representative of the transition state of Ireland, and of a time when many "old things are passing away."

Wakes, with their strange medley of mourning and merry-making, are becoming rarer, even in rural districts. The clergy, greatly to their credit, discountenance and even from the altar denounce them, on account of the irreverence and immorality to which they gave occasion. There was never a death in a house but the place was for two or three days and nights made a common resort for the friends and neighbours of the deceased. Among the poor peasants the guests brought their own supplies of drink and tobacco, but in a farmer's house all comers were entertained at the host's expense The original intention of watching and bewailing the dead became a very secondary affair to the gossiping and revelry that brought disgrace on the ancient usage.

Does the reader remember the scene in "Castle Rackrent" where Sir Condy took it into his head to know what the people would say of him after he was gone? "Thady," says he, "as far as the wake goes, sure I might without any great trouble have the satisfaction of seeing a bit of my own funeral." So Thady and his "shister" contrived a sham sickness and sham death, and he was laid out properly. There came a throng of men, women, and childer, "till the house was as full and fuller than it could hold." The joke had very nearly a tragic end, for what with the heat and the smoke and the noise, Sir Condy was nearly stifled under the bed-clothes, on the top of which many frieze great-coats had been piled. When he could lie still no longer, and sat up, there was a great surprise; but the night was duly finished with more whisky from the shebean-house. These death wakes lasted down to the famine-time with little diminution. But in the dark days of fever that followed, the fear of infection brought sanitary motives into play, and wakes were often omitted. More recently, during the small-pox epidemic, they were prohibited, and it is to be hoped that the custom may pass gradually into disuse.

The Irish fairs are also fast losing their barbarous character, and reverting to the original purpose of buying and selling. There was never a fair that did not end with a savage faction-fight, or if there were no faction-feud at the time, with a general fight and skrimmage. Some lives were almost invariably lost, and the list of maimed and wounded was always large. The alpeens, ash saplings loaded with lead, were murderous weapons, not to speak of the missiles which darkened the air in the thick of the *mêlée*. Women joined in the affray, and in the drunken madness of the combatants not even the priest's interference was of any use. The faction-feuds are not extinct yet, for last year there were fatal encounters in various counties, especially in Limerick, where a poor fellow was brutally murdered by some members of a hostile faction, a woman taking part in the foul deed. The ruffians, tried for murder, were convicted of homicide. The unusual public notice attracted to the case proved that these disgraceful scenes are becoming rarer. At no distant period many such murders, quite as deliberate and savage, passed unnoticed; although the continuance of faction-feuds reveals a spirit as barbarous as the Corsican Vendetta. Both at fairs and at "patrons'" or saints' *fêtes*, the kermes of Ireland, the fun now-a-days is of a less sanguinary kind, an improvement due partly to the increase of education, partly to the influence of power and of law, and partly to the better example of the higher classes, who were not so very long ago just as reckless in their way as the unlettered peasantry.

Donnybrook Fair is gone, like our own St. Bartholomew, and the Irishman is no more to be seen there in all his glory, with his sprig of shillelagh, "his heart soft with whisky, and his head soft with blows." There is a peaceful "Citizen omnibus" starting for Donnybrook every twenty minutes from College Green, by which the tourist can go to the scene of which Irishmen used to be proud, but are now mostly ashamed. On the way to Glendalough and the Vale of Avoca we are also shown the oak plantations whence the shillelaghs were cut for battle in the eastern counties, as alpeens were in other parts of the island. But Donnybrook Fair is only a symbol of many other things that are passing into history.

It is not so long since "Harry Lorrequer" and "Charles O'Malley" were accepted as faithful portraitures of Irish life and character. The rollicking, reckless, fighting, fox-hunting squire or squireen; the half-pay captain of dragoons, professional duellist, gambler, and scamp; the punch-imbibing and humorous story-telling priest; the cringing tenantry and lawless peasantry; how unreal and unrepresentative all these characters seem now! Before Charles Lever died last year most of his pictures were out of date. It is Ireland of the past that he depicted. The intemperance, the improvidence, the reckless jollity, the duelling, the fighting at the dinner-table, or at funerals, in short, the savagery of Ireland, in the upper classes quite as much as in the lower, is becoming a tradition. Yet Charles Lever was a true artist of days not long gone by. I have met with men who have fought duels, and assisted in abductions, and hunted bailiffs, and taken part in scenes which would now seem strange in the wildest book of fiction.

Carleton's sketches of Irish peasant life are equally out of date. The hedge schoolmaster, the bare-headed and bare-footed scholars, the swarms of troublesome beggars, and the lunatics at large, are all becoming dissolving views. We want an Irish Dean Ramsay to gather up the traditions and stories of the past generation. We can scarcely imagine the Munster bar, or as many of them as remained above the table, singing the lewd ballad of "The Rakes of Mallow," or an Irish judge singing his own song of "A bumper, Squire Jones," or a parish priest chanting "An Cruiscin Lán, the love of my heart is my little jug, An Cruiscin Lán." (Cruiskeen Lawn).

The "Monks of the Screw" were not so indecent and discreditable a set as our English "Monks of Medmenham Abbey," but even that noted Irish club could scarcely now be joined by the statesmen and judges and gentlemen of Dublin, any more than the chiefs of the Parliament House at Edinburgh could now take part in the high jinks and drunken revelries described by Sir Walter Scott.

All these things and many more are passing away. The Fairy Mounts are being fast levelled, and the mysterious sounds of the Banshee are seldom heard. The tithe-proctor is gone, and the bailiff or process-server can no longer with impunity be made to swallow his parchment writ, and be shut up in the Keep, as was done by "Dick Martin" of Galway at Ballinahinch. If these functionaries are ever now interfered with, or if violence is done to constables, or to land agents, or others of higher grade, it is by hired assassins that the deeds of crime are perpetrated. There may not yet be the general respect for law which marks a highly civilized people, but there is at least a wholesome fear of its penalties. The presence of the constabulary force throughout the country has had a good moral effect, as representing everywhere public order and law, an effect far beyond the actual service rendered in the detection or the repression of crime.

The growing respect for law among all classes of Irishmen is one of the most sure tests and hopeful signs of progress. It may surprise some to hear this affirmed in the face of the frequent reports of violence and lawlessness, especially agrarian outrages. But it must be remembered that every such case is now made public, and attracts universal notice when circulated through the press. They are rare in comparison with times not very remote. In this as in many other matters the example of the richer classes is now not against but on the side of law. Few proprietors would venture to interfere with legal proceedings, or to disregard legal decisions, even in questions touched by the Land Act, which some landlords seem to regard as a statute of confiscation. They read the law reports, and know the consequences of resisting authority. But among the lower classes a lawless spirit is more frequently shown, not so often in defiance as in ignorance of the consequences. We must not be impatient, nor expect too sudden a transition from the long period of comparative anarchy, of which Ribbonism and other crimes were the fruit. When the power of law is made to be felt in many separate localities, the peasantry will gradually learn what the upper classes have learned more promptly. A curious case in point occurred at an early period of the Land Act operation. An Englishman had purchased property in county Galway, where landlords such as Mr. Martin used to keep all law at bay. Some tenants, refusing to pay rent, were to be served with notices. But the bailiffs were so mauled that they positively refused to venture their lives again in the district. Application was made to Mr. Justice Keogh, and that firm and upright judge gave an order that it should be deemed sufficient service to put the notices in a public place in Ballygar, the nearest town, and to send a letter by post to each of the defendants. If all administrators of the law had the decision and firmness of Judge Keogh, the people would learn respect for legal authority with more promptness. The same Judge Keogh has since read a lesson of respect for law to the priests of the same county, in his judgment on the Galway election case, with results to be presently noticed.

Sir Robert Kane tells how " in Ovoca, on pay-days, where two thousand men were employed when he wrote, five hundred gallons of whisky used to be bought by the miners, and drunk upon the works. The men spent the night in fighting, whilst their wives and children begged in vain that some of their wages should go for provisions and for clothing. There is now upon pay-days no whisky whatsoever sold. The wives of the workmen receive their wages for them, and quarrelling is unknown." Of another village he says, "On pay-day it presented a scene of strife and drunkenness, which always required the intervention of the police, and often rendered the position of the superintendents dangerous. At present nothing of the sort is known. There is a temperance hall for quiet social meetings, and extensive schoolrooms for the education of the children, and the same workmen are able to earn £300 per month more than they formerly received, by the greater steadiness and attention to their work which accompany their improved domestic habits." It was in referring to these and similar cases which had come under his notice that Sir Robert Kane used words which have often been quoted, and which cannot be too widely known: "I do not hesitate to assert that the existing generation in this country is half a century in advance of that which is dying off, and that the generation now at school will be a century in advance of us. We were reckless, ignorant, improvident, drunken, and idle. We were idle, for we had nothing to do; we were reckless, for we had no hope; we were ignorant, for learning was denied us; we were improvident, for we had no future; we were drunken, for we sought to forget our misery. That time has passed away for ever."

It is difficult to realise the condition of the greatest part of Ireland only a few years back, when the houses of country gentlemen required to be barricaded like fortresses in an enemy's country, when agrarian outrages were so common as to excite little surprise or attention, and when landlords and their agents went in daily peril of their lives. Twenty years ago this was still the normal state of too many districts, but the time of the famine marks a broad division in the general history of the island. No one who knew Ireland before this latest period of her "long agony," and knows her now, will dispute the greatness of the revolution that has taken place. With the exception of occasional outbreaks, the result of political agitation, the whole tone of national feeling is changed. Material prosperity is steadily progressive. A spirit of enterprise is abroad among the people. The arts of peace are flourishing, and the great body of the nation are engaged in quiet pursuits of agriculture and commerce. The spirit of discontent is kept up chiefly by professional agitators, who require only a firmer hand to keep them from their mischievous work. In most parts of the country life and property are as safe as in England.

The Lord-Lieutenant, Earl Spencer, during his "progress" through the north of Ireland last autumn, had a pleasant tale to tell in his speeches. He told that the deposits in Government Funds and Joint Stock Banks, in Trustee and Post-office Savings' Banks, had increased year by year in the last five years at the rate of a million sterling. The total aggregate of such investments is now above £67,000,000 in Ireland. The bank-note circulation had shown a continuous increase during the same period. He told how railway returns and the prices of all commercial stocks and funds were steadily rising. He told of the progress of education, and the prosperity of agriculture and trade, especially in Belfast, where he went officially to open the agricultural show and the magnificent new docks. He spoke of the diminution of the number of indictable offences in all parts of the country, and, what was most gratifying and hopeful, the number of political and agrarian crimes had been greatly reduced.

This prosperity was everywhere manifest in Ulster. At Lurgan, for instance, the Chairman of the Town Commissioners, in his address to the Lord-Lieutenant, said that "the population of the town had increased thirty per cent., and the property seventy per cent., since the visit of Lord Carlisle eleven years before."

Having followed this vice-regal progress, as a good opportunity for observation, I can bear testimony, not only to the signs of healthy prosperity in Ulster, but to the demonstrations of loyalty among all sections of the community. I saw demonstrations of another kind, very soon after, both in Lurgan and Belfast, but the turbulent factions that then brought disgrace upon Ulster were in numbers and character contemptible, contrasted with the crowds of orderly and peaceable and industrious people, poor and rich, Catholic and Protestant, who gave hearty welcome to the Queen's representative in the festival week of the Lord-Lieutenant's visit.

If the same visible proofs of prosperity and of demonstrative loyalty are not found in other parts of Ireland, there is at least good ground for congratulation on the decrease of many evil and discouraging signs of the national condition. For this I am happy to give the testimony of one of the oldest law officials, Mr. Seed, who has been for upwards of forty years Crown Solicitor. Mr. Seed says, " The spirit of the country is more peaceable; the administration of justice is becoming more respected and more feared than it ever yet has been; the people being taught that the law is more powerful than themselves, and that in upholding it they find the surest protection for their lives and properties. I firmly believe that crime will decrease, and the improved and improving condition of the country and the people under recent legislation, and the present firm and impartial enforcement and administration of the law, will yet restore it to perfect tranquillity and peace. Even at the present time I believe Ireland is, as a whole, freer from serious and aggravated crime than any other country in Europe."

In an article in the *Times* on the condition of the country at the close of 1872, the same hopeful strain was expressed :—" Ireland is prosperous; her trade and her wealth are increasing together, crime is steadily on the decline, and public order is undisturbed. The improvement of affairs has been diffused through all classes of society. Farmers and shopkeepers are making money alike; labourers have demanded better wages, and obtained them without difficulty; while everywhere there are signs of enterprise, activity, and confidence in the mercantile community. Our correspondent who transmits this intelligence looks round him in vain for the signs of poverty and embarrassment only too visible in former years—lists of bankruptcies and failures, notices of sales, closed shops, and tenantless houses. Few of these once familiar objects are now to be seen. Industry thrives and is well remunerated, commerce is rapidly expanding, and the trade of Dublin is growing at such a rate that a large increase in the dock accommodation is urgently required. In short, Ireland begins the year now opened with a material prosperity little inferior to that of England. In all that makes, or should make, a nation rich, she is evidently flourishing."

This improvement is not all due to political causes, or to better government. Many social changes have been quietly and steadily going on amidst the more noisy and conspicuous public agitations. The increased communication with England by steam navigation; the improvement of roads, and the formation of railways; Mr. Bianconi and his cars; Father Mathew and the Temperance movement; the introduction of the Poor Law; the organization of police and of the constabulary; the Encumbered Estates Act, and other measures for helping Irish property out of the slough of past neglect; the cheap post and the money-order system; the establishment of the National Schools and of the Queen's Colleges; the Landlord and Tenant Act; the constant flow of emigration; the progress of agriculture and commerce;—these and many other social movements, apart from political and religious questions, have helped to make the Ireland of our time different from the Ireland of other days.

CHAPTER II.

SOME STATISTICS OF PROGRESS.

Dr. Hancock's Judicial Statistics — The "Idle Assize of 1872" — Sanitary and Economic Progress—Outward Civilization.

UNWILLING to repel at the outset by too many statistics, I select only a few facts as authority for the general statement in the opening chapter as to the hopeful progress of the country. If any one is inclined to take too sanguine a view, he will soon meet enough to check his hopes and modify his opinions. The recent progress has been great—for Ireland. The present prosperity is promising—for Ireland. It was a country so long stationary, if not retrogressive, and, as some thought, relapsing into barbarism, that the onward movement is the more surprising. What we now see is not so much a proof of national health as of recovery from a condition which seemed without remedy. And the questions still recur, Is the improvement general or local? Is it seen in all parts of the country, or in some parts only? Is it due to internal changes, or external influences? Is it permanent or temporary? But let us have the bright side of the subject first.

Dr. W. Neilson Hancock's annual report on criminal and judicial statistics is the most authentic record of the social and political state of Ireland. In 1864 this statistical department was organized, and Dr. Hancock appointed as its superintendent. He has official apartments in the building of the Four Courts, where the returns for every part of the country are deposited and tabulated. The reports contain a mass of valuable information as to the condition of the people and the administration of the law. Year by year, with the exception of some extraordinary periods of special disturbance, the progress has been marked and satisfactory. The register of crime for 1871, the latest I have seen, is more favourable than for any year since these records commenced. As compared with the previous year it shows a decrease of 14 per cent. in the number of indictable offences. This improvement was marked in those classes of crime which are dealt with summarily, drunkenness, theft, and wilful or malicious destruction of property. A large per-centage of criminals in Ireland, as elsewhere, are habitual drunkards. The record of treasonable offences is scanty, showing the disappearance of Fenianism as a dangerous influence. In 1866 and 1867 these offences exceeded 500 in number; in 1870 they had fallen to thirty-seven; and in 1871 there were only seven cases. Treason is for the present almost extinct, for the Home Rule agitation is a peaceful strife. Agrarian crime, the most inveterate disorder of the Irish body politic, is also declining. In 1867 there were 767 cases reported by the constabulary; in 1870 the number had increased to 1,329. In 1871 there were only 368 cases.

The improvement has been still more marked in the first half of 1872. The numbers then were 116 as compared with 1,219 in the first six months of 1870. A few years previously, the whole number in the year 1866 had been only eighty-seven cases of agrarian outrages. The increase subsequently was no doubt due to the agitation that preceded the public discussion of the Land Act, and the remarkable decrease now exhibited attests the beneficial result of recent legislation.

Of the offences classed as agrarian outrages, a large number originated in disputes about rights of way, rights of pasturage or fishing, questions of title and holding of property between families or tenants and small proprietors, questions with which the Courts under the Land Act are not empowered to deal. The offences arising out of disputes about improvements, or compensations, or disturbance of holding, have diminished in marked proportion, showing the confidence in the equitable administration of the law.

The Peace Preservation Act has worked successfully, there being seventy-two proceedings less in 1871 than in 1870 in the proclaimed counties. In Mayo alone there is a slight increase, ten more in 1871 than in the previous year.

A detailed examination of the returns gives even more satisfactory results as to the condition of the country. While the total average of serious crime is only fifteen per 10,000 of population, in the Dublin police district it is 130 per 10,000, or nearly nine times the average. The amount of crime in the towns, as compared with the rural districts, is remarkable. In Dublin it is 89 per cent. more than in the adjacent country, in Cork 72 per cent., in Waterford 55, in Belfast 49, in Limerick 42 more than in the surrounding country districts. Of 8,155 indictable offences, not disposed of summarily, 4,401, or more than one-half, were committed in the Dublin metropolitan police district. The most orderly counties and most free from serious crime are the parts of Down and Antrim outside of Belfast. The proportion of criminals in these counties was only three in 10,000, and Carrickfergus had the distinction of presenting only one in 10,000.

Even in the places giving the worst returns in

previous years the improvement is observable. In Dublin the decline has been twenty-three in the 10,000, and in Westmeath eleven decrease in the 10,000, falling from twenty-six in 1870 to fifteen, the average of the whole island, in 1871.

The returns afford many interesting points of comparison with the criminal statistics of England, Scotland, and other countries, showing what classes of offences prevail, and so throwing light on national or local habits and social condition. But to these comparisons it is not necessary to advert here. The general conclusion from Dr. Hancock's important Blue Book is that, in regard to crime of every form, Ireland can compare favourably with any portion of the empire, and that the condition of the country in this respect is steadily progressive.

The comparative absence of ordinary crime throughout the island was never more conspicuous than in the records of the circuits for 1872. In a characteristic article of the *Nation*, headed "The Idle Assize," this was referred to with justifiable pride. "From county to county, from province to province, the Irish judges dart in rushing trains to appal the evil-doers by the vision of avenging justice, and the number and severity of their sentences. In all respects the performance has been provided for—in all respects save one. The grand jurors, bursting with inflated importance, and purple with zeal, are ready to find bills without number; the *petit* jurors, discreetly selected, are not averse to the contemplated work; the police are at hand with witnesses to swear anything that may be required. Above all and beyond all, the judges—solemn, stately, and severe—are at their posts, and the whole machinery of the law, in its most impressive and awful character, is in readiness for operations. But still the business hangs fire, and business is slow almost beyond precedent. The fact is simply this—that the judge can find no one to try, and the jurors discover no one to convict. The bench and the jury-box are full, but the docks are empty. The calendars are blank, and there are no criminals to be had. . . . To the mass of the people, however, the remarkable absence of crime throughout the land, as exemplified by the present assizes, will be a source of unmingled satisfaction. It is a proof that British 'civilization' has not yet triumphed over Irish virtue; and to the labourers in the cause of the country and the people it affords a new cause of encouragement and a new guarantee of success. ' 'Tis righteous men shall make our land a nation once again,' sings the poet of Irish nationality; and in deserving the character which 'The Idle Assize' has obtained for them, our countrymen are showing themselves the possessors of the first essential of freedom."

Of the health and sanitary state of Ireland ample details are given by the Registrar-General in his quarterly reports and annual returns. The poverty of the people, and the squalid dwellings, still too common, cause epidemic diseases to prevail. *Since the famine the sanitary returns have shown constant improvement*, but there have been occasional epidemics which have swelled the per-centage of deaths. During last year small-pox and scarlatina were both very fatal in Dublin and other towns, and fevers are always breaking out in various localities. In the reports of local registrars we find frequent entries, such as the following: "The prevalence of epidemic diseases may well be attributed to the extremely filthy condition of the wretched houses of the people, which have been saturated by the rains and the overflowing cesspools by which they are surrounded." "It is a common occurrence to see pigs in the houses of some families, and the registrar has seen in the kitchen of a house the horse standing in one corner and the family eating in another." Manure heaps are common at the doors of the houses of labourers and farmers. Cattle and people often live and sleep in the same apartment. There was an article last year in an Ulster paper denying, in a tone of virtuous indignation, some statements that had appeared in an English book about the cabins of the peasantry. It is not worth while quoting either the statements referred to or the northern editor's sturdy denial of the facts. I can only say that in various parts of the south and west, last year, I have been in cabins where cow and pig and dog and bipeds, both feathered and unfeathered, were living in contented company. The open door and the wholesome "peat-reek" made the atmosphere less perilous than it might have been; but the surroundings of some of the houses were even worse than the interiors. While such things are not exceptional but frequent in many parts of Ireland, the wonder is that the registrars' returns are not worse than they are. Too large a per-centage of the deaths are due to "preventible diseases," and we may hope that this excess will be diminished as education increases, and as the general civilization of the people advances.

In regard to the improved dwellings of the labourers, some interesting facts are included in the Report of the Commissioners of Public Works. Mr. J. Poe, the Inspector for Clare and Tipperary, reports: "The applications for loans for farm buildings have increased, and I anticipate a progressive improvement and increase. Loans for building labourers' cottages must become more numerous; the difficulty of getting labourers even at 50 per cent. advance on the rate of wages paid ten or twelve years since, unless suitable habitations are provided for them, will increase every year, and landowners who reside any distance from towns must provide houses for their workmen on their lands, and even with this inducement they do not find it easy to get good men." Mr. W. P. Prendergast, the Inspector for the North-Western district, reports: "The applications for new loans have not been numerous, as owners do not, for the most part, feel disposed to expend money on farms in the hands of tenants, and the greater number of resident landlords in these counties had already improved the land in their own occupation; but wherever any ground falls under the immediate control of a proprietor, there is ample proof that drainage and other improvements are far better understood than in former years, and that it is not from any objection to the terms of the Acts, or to the regulations of the Board,* that the fund is not more

---

* The Board of Public Works has been in existence since 1831. During forty years upwards of £11,000,000 have been advanced for public works, of which about £6,000,000 have been repaid, and nearly £5,500,000 remitted, chiefly in times of national distress. In the financial year 1871-72 they made advances amounting to £161,202. Of this sum £85,500 was advanced to proprietors for improving their estates, under the Land Improvements Acts, and £45,830 to tenant-farmers to enable them to purchase their farms, under the provision of the Landlord and Tenant Act of 1870.

frequently resorted to. I find in all quarters more attention paid than hitherto to the question of improved dwelling-houses and offices for farmers and labourers, and the advance of money at 5 per cent., to clear both principal and interest in thirty-five years, has been considered a most useful and liberal provision. . . . The improvement in all newly-constructed country dwellings is accompanied by an equally marked change in dress, furniture, and food among the farming classes; and in the smaller towns, supported altogether by the agricultural population, there are now permanent shops with meat and bread, where such supplies were only to be procured once a week, on market days, when I first acted for the Board in this part of Ireland. The consumption of tea, coffee, and sugar is so much increased in the farming districts that a great portion of labourers' wages is expended on them, and shops with modern imported articles of dress are now well supported in the same towns and villages where no such things were seen prior to the potato failure. New banks have also been established in numerous towns, frequented exclusively by farmers, and which have not increased in size, but derive their business from the agricultural profits brought in. The breed of live stock of all kinds—cattle, sheep, pigs, and poultry—has vastly improved. Prices for all farming produce, especially what is sold by the smaller farmers in this district, such as butter, pigs, eggs, and poultry, have risen so much that the rewards for exertion are felt to be quite different from what were formerly known; and the use of money is better understood by the rural population, so that while higher wages are demanded than employers ever before paid—and some check is said to be given to works of drainage and land improvement from this cause—it can only be considered as a temporary stoppage, similar to what occurs in manufacturing enterprise."

Earl Spencer, in his speech at Belfast, at the Agricultural Meeting last August, said that, notwithstanding the unwonted temptation from high prices, the number and value of live stock showed an increase on the previous year, in fact, had reached higher figures than ever before. I noted the remark specially, from the statement being an unexpected one. Shortly before, I had been talking to a farmer about the high prices horses were fetching: "There is not a horse left in the country," was his answer, in Hibernian exaggeration. "Oh, but you will breed plenty more, with such a demand." "Sure, they've taken over the brood mares, too," he replied. Judging by prices, and the numbers constantly bought for England and the Continent, I fancied that the farmer's broad assertion implied a great diminution in number.

But Lord Spencer was speaking by the book, for, according to the Report of the Irish Registrar-General, there were actually 2,250 more horses in the country than at the corresponding time of 1871. The estimated value of the horses in Ireland is not far short of five millions sterling. With the exception of pigs, of which there was a slight decrease of number, due probably to the lessened population, there was an increase in every other live stock. The increase in cattle was 80,250 over 1871, and the increase of estimated value £521,625. The total value of Irish cattle was set down by the Registrar, for 1872, at £26,368,045, but this is much below the real amount, as the value is still taken the same as thirty years ago, "in order to facilitate comparison." In Thom's Statistical Directory the value is given, for 1871, at £35,114,828. The increase of value of all live stock, cattle, sheep, and pigs, has been rising steadily ever since 1865, when it was estimated at £41,278,331. In 1868 it was £44,234,313, and in 1871, £46,955,529.

There is scarcely a single department of Irish statistics which does not afford similar proof of progress. The average amount of property which paid duty on passing under probate and administration, annually, during the years 1846-1850, was £2,534,611; during the years 1856-1860 it was £4,222,395; in 1871 it was £5,014,795.

Some Statistics of Progress.

I reserve for separate consideration the most important of all conditions of progress—those of education and of religion. The few facts cited in the present chapter are only connected with the domain of civil government and political economy, with things common to countries Catholic or Protestant, Pagan or Christian. Law, police, public health, dwellings, food, property, and all such matters, can be tabulated in statistics, and show progress, or the reverse, without looking closely at the political, still less the religious life of a nation. The connection between the material and moral condition is important, but these can be viewed separately, and are so viewed generally by the mere statistical reporter and political economist. Looking at the records of all that is commonly taken to constitute "the wealth of nations," the condition of the country is good and hopeful.

No one who visits Ireland after a few years' absence will hesitate to admit that there has been improvement. The report will be most favourable from superficial observers or holiday tourists. Leaving London in the morning by the North-Western Irish express, and making a swift passage in the splendid Holyhead boats, it is pleasant to arrive the same evening at the Gresham, or the Shelburne, or other of the comfortable hotels for which Dublin is famous. To any part of the island the railways convey us with as much comfort as on the best English lines. At the remotest towns and villages the post arrives with laudable regularity, and the electric-telegraph wires reach to every corner where there are English-speaking inhabitants. At the railway stations there are bookstalls, with newspapers and miscellaneous literature; and the traveller, whether commercial or non-commercial, will notice no great differences from what he has been accustomed to in provincial journeys in England. In some things, and these not unimportant—such as police, primary schools, workhouse buildings and management—he will even be forced to admit superiority in Ireland. If he asks no questions about church and chapel, and reads no local newspapers, he would hardly feel that he was in a strange country, and cannot realize all he has heard about Irish wrongs and Irish wretchedness, and about the hopeless difficulty of governing a country apparently so civilized and prosperous.

CHAPTER III.

PARADOXES AND PROBLEMS.

Analysis of Irish Progress—Is it Chiefly Imperial or National?—Improvement rather of the Country than of the People—The True Key to the "Irish Difficulty."

HITHERTO we have been looking at the brighter side of the "Condition of Ireland" question. If satisfied with this surface view, it would prove as delusive as the treacherous verdure that clothes some of the horrible bog-holes in the "green island." These external signs of civilization attest the improvement of the country more than of the people. Ireland has shared and is sharing the prosperity of Great Britain, to which it is united. It is not by Irish enterprise and Irish money alone, that those roads and docks, railways and telegraphs, schools and poor-houses, and other visible works of civilization, have been planned and constructed. To British capital and British enterprise more is due than Irishmen care to admit, though of late years they have borne their share in the patriotic work. The names of Dargan and Guinness, and many more, may be bracketed with the most enterprising and liberal strangers who have risked their capital, whether in land or manufactures or commerce. In the country especially, Irish and English proprietors appear in the honourable rivalry of agriculture. The old generation of landlords, most of them absentees or oppressors, has given place to men many of whom understand that "property has its duties as well as its rights," and who possess land on other conditions than extorting as much money as possible, to be spent out of the country. Good landlords make good tenants, as good masters make good servants, and the improvement tells upon the labourers, who are now getting higher wages and better employment, and live in greater comfort than at any former time.

But still, the improvement of which we have been speaking is chiefly material and external. Even in regard to Dr. Hancock's wonderful statistics, we cannot tell how much is due to improved law and police, to prosperous conditions in agriculture and trade, and other temporary and mutable causes. The strange social phenomenon of Ireland is, that under or alongside of the prosperity which everyone observes, there is a mass of poverty and mendicancy, of wretchedness and discontent, upon which the progress of the country seems to make little or no impression. The people may be peaceable and law-obeying one year, and the next there may be a new Irish insurrection. Agrarian outrages may be reported as few, but the next season may require an Arms Act, or Peace Preservation Act, in several counties. With all their fine natural qualities and their quick wit, the people in the largest part of the island are the slaves of the grossest superstition, and are as backward as in the least advanced countries of southern Europe.

Ireland is peaceful: yet nearly a fifth of the British army has to be quartered there, as in a hostile country.

Ireland is loyal: yet it sometimes returns as members of Parliament disloyal traitors and even convicted felons, as a defiance and insult to the English nation.

Ireland is entering upon a social millennium, if we are to believe Dr. Hancock's statistics: yet there seems little abatement of rags and wretchedness, of ignorance and superstition.

Ireland is prosperous: yet it remains the difficulty and the despair of British statesmen.

How are these paradoxes to be explained? How can we reconcile the reports of progress, with the facts of social disorder and of political disaffection?

There are other questions still more perplexing. What becomes of the vast multitudes of Irish youths who pass through the National Schools? Many have emigrated, and it is to be hoped have benefited by their education. But how is it that so few out of the hundreds of thousands of Catholics go on to intermediate schools, far less to College? They mostly belong to the poor classes, and it might be said that chill penury represses the "noble rage" and laudable ambition of scholarship. But this is not the case in Scotland or in Prussia, where a large number of the poorest lads work their way to a higher education. The truth is, that in all those parts of the country where Romanism prevails, education ends with what is obtained in the National Schools. They get the three R.'s—reading, writing, and arithmetic; or rather the four R.'s, religion of a sort being appended. Until the new agitation began about a Roman Catholic University, there was no attempt to obtain for the people any higher education. In fact, Cardinal Cullen not long since told the Royal Education Commissioners, that "the poor ought to be educated with a view to the place they hold in society. Too high an education will make them oftentimes discontented." No wonder the mass of the people are left ignorant and untrained, the ready prey of priestly deluders and political agitators.

> "Hereditary bondsmen! know ye not
> Who would be free, himself must strike the blow?"

This was one of O'Connell's favourite appeals; but he did not tell his poor dupes that the chains to be struck off were not those of "Saxon oppressors," but the chains of ignorance and superstition, and other evils which enslaved their spirits. A more recent political leader, John Francis Maguire, had the courage to speak on one occasion some words worth recalling, now that he is gone and his memory is held in respect. It was when inaugurating the Cork Industrial Exhibition. "Let industry," he said, "be preached as a new gospel to the Irish people, by word, by example, by influence, so that it may reach the hearts and understandings of young and old, and drive into the sea the twin devils of idleness and mendicancy, which have long possessed a noble but afflicted nation." Poor Maguire! he gave the best advice he could in those days, but he was only a blind leader of the blind. He did not see that idleness and mendicancy are only among the many evil fruits springing from the same bitter root—evils which have degraded Spain and other "noble but afflicted nations" to the same level as Ireland.

It was to the prince of agitators, Daniel O'Connell, that Sydney Smith said, "What trash to be bawling in the streets about 'the Green Isle,' 'the Isle of the Ocean,' the bold anthem of 'Erin-go-Bragh'! A far better anthem would be 'Erin go bread and cheese,' 'Erin go cabins that will keep out the rain,' 'Erin go pantaloons without holes in them.'" The people must help themselves, and not be always calling on others to help them. "A stout constable, an honest justice, a clear highway, and a free chapel"—these are some of the things that Government can secure, and has secured for Ireland. Sydney Smith was one of the most earnest and eloquent advocates of Catholic emancipation. He was not a man of deep feeling on matters of religion, and his one grand panacea for securing peace was the endowment of the Romish priests. But when he was considering the influence of that Church on the condition of the people, here is his deliberate and clearly-expressed judgment: "The Catholic religion contributes to the backwardness and barbarism of Ireland. The debasing superstition, childish ceremonies, and the profound submission to the priesthood which it teaches, all tend to darken men's minds, to impede the progress of knowledge and inquiry, and to prevent Ireland from becoming as free, as powerful, and as rich as the sister kingdom."

This is the true key to "the Irish difficulty." But before entering into the subject which it opens up, let us dispose of some other questions which bear upon the condition of Ireland.

CHAPTER IV.

DECREASE OF POPULATION. EMIGRATION.

Census Returns—Depopulation—Subdivision of Land—Small Proprietors—The Irish in England—Emigration to America.

THE decrease of population at first glance seems at variance with the alleged prosperity of Ireland. It is disheartening to look at the population returns in every census return since 1841. The total of Ireland in that year was 8,196,567. The estimated population at Midsummer, 1845, was 8,295,061, the highest reached. In 1851 it was 6,574,278; in 1861, 5,798,967; in 1871, on the census-night, April 2nd, 5,402,795. The decrease between 1861 and 1871 has been, in every province, in the following ratio: in Leinster, 8·35 per cent.; in Munster, 8·14; in Ulster, 4·38; in Connaught, 6·83.

The population of the four provinces in 1871 stood thus: Leinster, 1,335,960; Munster, 1,390,402; Ulster, 1,830,398; Connaught, 845,913. The only county in all Ireland showing an increase since last census is Antrim, the population of which rose from 378,588 in

1861 to 419,782, an increase of 41,194. In each of the thirty-one remaining counties there has been decrease. From the town returns I select the following items: Belfast rose from 121,602 to 174,394, or 43·41 per cent.; Londonderry (city) rose from 20,873 to 25,242, or 20·92 per cent.; Carrickfergus shows an increase of thirty persons; Waterford an increase of forty, probably from the steam line to Milford Haven. The Dublin suburban townships showed an increase of 4,459, or 2·87 per cent.; but Dublin city a decrease of above 9,000, or 3·50 per cent. Almost every town and county in Ireland showed decrease.

It is sad to see everywhere the deserted villages, and ruined homesteads, and roofless cabins. But these ruined houses are in reality marks of the country's progress, as much as the ruined castles and fortresses are marks of the "bad old times" which have passed away. In the times when "every rood of ground maintained its man" it was a poor and precarious maintenance at the best, and always on the verge of starvation by famine, which did come at last. The emigration, which then began to flow in earnest, saved the country. The famine year, with all its calamities, has proved the dawn of a better era, and that by compelling the "depopulation," of which Oliver Goldsmith spoke sentimentally in the Dedication to Sir

Joshua Reynolds of his "Deserted Village." Not many years ago Mr. Gladstone expressed his anxiety to get rid of "the frightful and monstrous evil of emigration." He knew as little about the matter when he said that, as the poet did. "To complain of emigration, and to endeavour to devise some means which shall induce the peasant to struggle against nature, to toil on in improving barren surface, where his earnings will be perhaps a few pence a day, while he is within a short sail of a country where he can earn five shillings, is surely sadly to mislead him." These are the words of the late Earl of Rosse, one of the wisest and best friends of the Irish peasantry. In the same pamphlet where they occur, Lord Rosse combats the speculations of Mr. John Stuart Mill in favour of multiplying peasant proprietors. In the Channel Islands, to which Mr. Mill pointed as a "crucial instance," Lord Rosse found that his statements were wholly erroneous. "The agriculture of the islands maintains," Mr. Mill had said, "besides cultivators, non-agricultural populations, respectively four and five times as dense as those of Great Britain." Lord Rosse went to examine for himself, and found this statement directly contrary to fact. There is a very large importation into the islands of wheat, cattle, and sheep. "So soon," he says, "are fables dissipated by statistics."

Of the impossibility of raising wages without diminution of population, and the possibility of this being made plain to the labourers, an amusing illustration is given in Mr. Nassau Senior's "Irish Journals." "When I began to reclaim my mountain farm, I employed 100 men, at wages varying from 8d. to 1s. a day, the average being 10d., and the weekly expenditure £25. After this had gone on for about three months, my clerk wrote to me in Tipperary, where I was staying on business, that the men had struck, and demanded that the *minimum* payment should be 1s. 2d. a day, and that the wages of the better men should be raised in proportion. We were in a critical period of the work, and my clerk thought the matter serious. In my answer I said to him, 'I am ready to accede to the men's demands. I am willing to give a *minimum* price of 1s. 2d. and a *maximum* price of 3s. a day. Of course, at that rate of wages I cannot continue my present expenditure. You will reduce it to £12 10s. a week. You will select the best men, beginning by the highest wages. In this matter you will follow out, not your own opinion, but my instructions, and you will read this letter to the men.' The men assembled next day to hear my answer. It was read to them, and highly approved. My clerk then said, 'Now, boys, I must choose my men,' and he began by selecting a dozen of the best.

'And what wages must you have?' he asked. 'Oh!' they said, 'we'll take the top price, the 3s.' 'Very well,' he answered, '18s. a week for 12 men makes £8 8s. a week; there is only £4 2s. left of the £12 10s.; at that rate I can only have four more; then there will remain 10s. for one other. I can, therefore, take 17 of you; the remaining 83 may go.' This did not suit the 83. They began to talk together in knots, to abuse the greediness of those who had demanded 3s., to threaten to break their heads—first, if they took more than 1s. 6d., then if they took more than their *minimum* of 1s. 2d., and at last, finding that even at that price more than half of them would be thrown out of employ, they broke up their combination and returned to work at the old prices. 'The master,' they said, 'is too many for us.'"

Nothing but emigration can meet a state of things like this. The multiplication of peasant proprietors, as proposed by Mr. Stuart Mill and, partly, by Mr. Bright, would not lessen but rather increase the pressure. The country is overpeopled still, not only in the ratio of cultivators to the land under cultivation, but in a more extended sense in the ratio of population to capital. This necessary capital is what small tenants cannot bring. The subdivision of land into a multitude of small holdings has been the most serious hindrance to agricultural progress. Tenants have rarely been able to do more than subsist, nor has there been often inducement to better farming, as improvement would only involve increase of rent from the exacting middlemen or agents. Having no money to start the sons as they grow up, or to portion the daughters, a patch of ground was given to them. The result has been calamitous. A teeming population sprang up, living a mere animal life, in sordid contentment while food could be obtained to hold body and soul together, but left in helpless misery when the potato famine came. The moral and social evils of these small tenures were worse if possible than the physical. There was no effort at improvement, but the old squalid mode of living continued. No prosperous, independent yeoman class could exist, and the grinding middlemen formed the only link between the gentry and the peasantry. The blame of this subdivision is not to be wholly laid on the poverty or improvidence of the people. The prosperity of some of the finest districts in Ireland was crushed by the political ambition of the landowners. To obtain votes for Parliament, a miserable race of freeholders was created. The qualification of a freeholder was an interest in property for life, to the annual amount of forty shillings. To get rid of the small holdings has been always a necessary step towards any improvement of property, and this was possible on a large scale after the famine, when the poor tenants were glad to emigrate in order to flee from fever and death.

A letter of Mr. Cobden, written nine or ten years ago, has been lately republished by Mr. Bright, which raises the often-discussed question of great or small holdings of land. The occasion of the letter being first written was a speech of the Hon. Wm. Cowper, at Romsey, who had said that to make labourers the owners of land would be a retrograde movement in agriculture. "The great progress in agriculture of late years has been due to the concentration and application of capital to an amount of land which is sufficient to justify the favourable employment of the capital; and it would be going back to times of less prosperity—it would be following the example of countries less prosperous than England in agriculture, if we were to aim at such an absurd and impossible object." Lord Palmerston gave utterance to similar opinions in the House of Commons, and deprecated any change which should reduce the occupiers of the Irish soil to the condition of the French peasant proprietors. It was this position which Mr. Cobden set himself to assail. He began with a sentence from Niebuhr, who says, "All ancient legislators, especially Moses, grounded the success of their ordinances concerning virtue, justice, and morality upon securing hereditary estates, or at least, landed property, to the greatest possible number of citizens." Mr. Cobden affirms that, "on the moral aspect of the question, it is indisputable, that the possession of landed property by a body of men imparts a higher sense of independence and security, greater self-respect, and supplies stronger motives for industry, frugality, and forethought, than any other kind of property." Passing to the economical view of the question, Mr. Cobden quotes many French authorities, and especially M. Passy, peer of France under Louis Philippe, and afterwards Minister of Finance. M. Passy affirms that the subdivision of land, as practically carried out in France, has been exaggerated and even caricatured in English descriptions of the system; that the landed properties are not increasing in proportion to the population; that arrangements are generally made in a family, on the death of a proprietor, by which the land is not subdivided, at all events to an extent that would be wasteful and thriftless. Within this limit, M. Passy affirms that the system of small farms, *la petite culture*, yields the greatest produce, and is on the whole to be preferred on economical as well as on moral grounds. Mr. Cobden[*] quotes, besides M. Passy, the testimonies

---

[*] Mr. Cobden's letter was printed in the *Times* and *Daily News* of January 7 of this year.

of M. de Tocqueville, the Duke de Broglie, and M. de Lavergne. Dr. Chalmers went to France prejudiced by Mr. McCulloch's predilections against the division of landed property, but his views were modified after his conversations with M. de Broglie. An American special commissioner, Professor Coleman of Massachusetts, also gave a good report, though he had thought he should find nothing in French agriculture worthy of much attention. But Mr. Cobden lays most stress on the work of M. Leonce de Lavergne "On the Rural Economy of France since 1789." Considering all the terrible catastrophes and revolutions of France, and the enormous disadvantages in every way, it is wonderful how the peasantry can bear any comparison with that of England on economical ground. Yet they are certainly as industrious and frugal, as temperate and peaceable as our peasantry. And small farms do pay, not in France alone, but in Flanders, Switzerland, and many parts of the Continent. Small proprietors need not imply what is understood by small farming. By co-operation, several neighbouring proprietors may purchase or may hire the expensive machinery which it is supposed only larger farmers can make use of. There is no reason why lesser machines than the steam-plough or the threshing-machine should not be used by several farmers. The principle of association is applied in cheese-making and other branches of agriculture on the Continent, and if brought into play in England or Ireland, would remove the theoretical objections to small proprietorships.

Whatever may be the result of the discussion on grounds of agricultural progress and political economy, there is much to be said on moral and social grounds for the small farm system. In the days when there were ten farmers in a parish where now there is only one, they lived respectably, maintained their families decently, and inured them to habits of industry. If they grew less corn they reared more stock, and the supply of poultry, butter, and other produce was more plentiful than it is now. The opportunities are fewer now-a-days for a young industrious couple to stock a small farm, and bring up a family, with comfort and independence. A check is thus put upon matrimony, and temptation to licentiousness increased. A broader separation has also taken place between farmers and labourers, who on small farms used to work together. The English farm-labourers are often merely hirelings, little above the condition of serfs, earning hardly enough to keep body and soul together. The farmers have too much abandoned their old thrifty, frugal ways, and as for the sons and the daughters of farmers, their education, dress, habits, and ways are as much removed from those of other days, as is their position in the political system. They are often as much the servile dependents of the great landowners as are the liveried servants at the Hall, while to the poor clodhopper labourers they are obliged to be hard taskmasters. Where are the representatives of the independent freeholders of other days? or of the sturdy yeomen-farmers of the English Commonwealth? In the New England States the yeomen-farmers are the strength of the commonwealth, and an increase in the number and influence of the rural middle-class—yeomen freeholders, not mere "*peasant* proprietors," would be an immense gain both in Great Britain and in Ireland.

Much has been said about Irish emigration to America and to our colonies, but the emigration to England and Scotland has been also of enormous extent. The Irish population of Manchester, Liverpool, Glasgow, and other great towns, with London, amounts to some millions. A large proportion of them are quiet, hardworking, and respectable. They form the bulk of the lower grades of workmen in the building trades and other large branches of labour, and a large proportion of the inferior class of domestic servants are Irish girls. The number of Roman Catholic priests and chapels in all the large towns of England, especially in the great manufacturing centres, bears testimony to the general character of these strangers. We may not approve their kind of religion, but the fact of their supporting so many priests and churches is evidence of their desire to do well, and of their respect for what they think good, even if it be zeal without knowledge. In any case, superstition is more worthy of respect than infidelity. It is not among the Irish so much as among the English that absolute heathenism, with its attendant brutal vices, is to be found. The proportion of Irish working men who attend and contribute to the support of places of worship is, I believe, as large as of English working men of the same class. Any one who has witnessed the annual procession of the Catholic school children in Manchester at Whitsuntide, and the crowds of parents and friends of the poor children who line the streets on that holiday, will speak with respect of the industrious portion of the Irish population of Manchester. And this is a pattern of what is going on in all the large towns, in the way of educating the young, and of saving the adult population from the debasing influences to which the poor in such localities are exposed.

At the same time, it must be admitted that in all these large towns there are dens of wretchedness and vice, which present the worst features of Irish character. The lowest district is generally that where the Irish herd together. Every town has its named or unnamed quarter, notorious like the Seven Dials in London, the Cowgate in Edinburgh, and the Five Points in New York. A police magistrate, trying an assault case last summer in Manchester, took occasion to remark that the worst cases of the kind were those in which the Irish were concerned, and added that something should be done to bring them into a state of civilization. These remarks drew out much protest from the Manchester Irish, who affirmed that the worst classes of crime are those with which Englishmen are concerned. This may be true; but it would be pushing patriotism to the verge of folly to deny that there is much in the condition of the Irish, in the great towns of England and Scotland, to cause sadness of heart. Intemperance is the chief bane and curse of the Irish labourers. The increase of wages obtained for work in England brings temptation. Adult men seldom change their habits and ordinary cost of living. A labourer who in Ireland made three shillings a day and lived on it, gets four shillings in England and lives on three. What does he do with the odd shilling? Very few put it by for a rainy day. It is spent in drink; and when a colony of Irishmen, in a street or court, spend their surplus earnings in drink, there is a scene of violence and madness which brings trouble and disgrace, poverty and disease. One of the Irish journalists commenting on the Manchester magistrate's charge in that assault case, gives wholesome advice to his countrymen. " Of all races that ever existed, the Irish is the one which ought most carefully to avoid heating with stimulants an already too mercurial temperament. To the Irishman at home, drink is a curse; to the Irishman abroad, drink is absolute ruin. Go to America, to England, to Scotland, to any part of the world, you will find there two classes of Irishmen—one is the sober Irishman, happy and prosperous, an honour to the land of his birth, an ornament and prop to the land of his adoption ; the other is the drunken Irishman, a pest and a disgrace. If the emigrating Irishman had one grain of sense he would, as the hills of his native land fade on the distant horizon, fall upon his knees and swear never to taste drink again. But for this one horrible vice the Irish would be among the purest and noblest peoples of the world. But intemperance obliterates their good qualities, and turns their virtues into vices ; converting generosity into folly, courage into combativeness, and high spirit into insane absurdity."

The emigrants who go to America, and pass on beyond the great seaboard cities, are far more protected from this temptation, for the habits of the working classes in the United States are not so sottish as in England. In New York and some other large towns there is plenty of intemperance; but the majority of emigrants are fit for agricultural work, and get to situations where they soon attain a comfort and prosperity undreamed of at home. The large sums of money transmitted to Ireland to fetch out their relatives and friends is a pleasing and practical attestation of this. They get free education for their children also, and many of them become prosperous American citizens. They become so prosperous that the priests hasten after them in increasing numbers. It used to be said that half the Irish who settled in the States were lost to the Church of Rome. It is not so now, so much the worse for them, as they are more sharply followed and "shepherded" by the well-organized Popish agencies.

CHAPTER V.

ABSENTEEISM.

Edgeworthstown—Statistics of Absenteeism—The *Times* on Absenteeism.

ABSENTEEISM has always been one of the stock grievances of Ireland. Dean Swift used to inveigh against the evil, asserting that a full third of the rental of Ireland was transmitted to landlords resident in England, besides large sums carried out of the country by other Irishmen of the upper classes. From the time of Sir William Petty to that of Arthur Young, Absenteeism was always prominent in every report of "the condition of Ireland." In the year 1730 a list of absentees was published, giving the yearly value of their estates and incomes spent out of the country. Other lists, both general and local, were from time to time published. While the penal laws were in force, and while the country continued in chronic disorder and disturbance, there was much excuse for English proprietors, who declined to risk their own lives and the lives of those dear to them by residing on their Irish estates.

That these fears were often groundless, the experience of such landlords as Richard Lovell Edgeworth demonstrated. A touching memorial of this is given by Maria Edgeworth in her memoir of her father, in which she describes the results of his life at Edgworthstown. When Mr. Edgeworth closed his own too brief autobiography, his accomplished daughter thus commenced her portion of the memoir: "With the manuscript of my father's memoirs I found, on the next page to that where his narrative broke off, in his handwriting, the following memorandum: 'In the year 1782 I returned to Ireland, with a firm determination to dedicate the remainder of my life to the improvement of my estate, and to the education of my children; and further, with the sincere hope of contributing to the melioration of the inhabitants of the country from which I drew my subsistence.'" In the thirty-five years that remained of his life Mr. Edgeworth had many difficulties to meet, and witnessed perilous times, but his patriotic spirit and lofty sense of duty found ample reward in the end. "As he advanced in years," says Miss Edgeworth, "my father had the very great satisfaction of seeing himself surrounded by a respectable, independent, attached, grateful tenantry. He endeavoured to be of use not only to his tenantry, but to all within his influence as a country gentleman; not merely relieving the wants of the poor, but by protecting them as a magistrate from injustice and oppression, by instructing them as to their real interests, showing them the consequences of their bad habits, and exciting and encouraging them by approbation and assistance to improve. In this point of view his residence in Ireland succeeded beyond his hopes .... The residence of well-educated landed proprietors contributed to improve not only the pecuniary circumstances, prudence, and moral conduct of the lower classes, but refined and elevated the tastes and manners of all the middle and intermediate classes of gentry. In the course of a quarter of a century, even in our own memory and observation, in our own county and neighbourhood, the whole style and tone of society altered. The fashion has passed away of those desperately tiresome, long, formal dinners, which were given two or three times a year by each family in the country to their neighbours; where the company had more than they could eat, and twenty times more than they should drink; when the gentlemen could talk only of claret, horses, or dogs, and the ladies only of dress or scandal: so that in the long hours when they were left to their own discretion, after having examined and appraised each other's finery, many an absent neighbour's character was torn in pieces merely for want of something to say or do in the stupid circle. But now the gentlemen and ladies are not separated from the time dinner ends till the midnight hour, when the carriages came to the door to carry off the bodies of the dead; or, till, just sense enough being left to find their way straight to the tea-table, the gentlemen could only swallow a hasty cup of cold coffee or stewed tea, and be carried off by their sleepy wives, happy if the power of reproach were lost in fatigue.

"No doubt in other parts of Ireland where gentry have settled, similar improvements in society have appeared. The residence of great English landed proprietors, wherever it has been, must have operated advantageously, by bringing to Ireland, by their intermarrying and wide-spread connexions, numerous visitors, and increasing the much-wanted reciprocal knowledge of each other in both countries."

The changes described by Miss Edgeworth have increased immensely in these later times of ready communication between the two countries. The two nations are now even more united by social than by political ties, and the habits and modes of life in the upper classes are the same in all parts of the kingdom.

Irish absenteeism, however, is still sometimes a topic of unmeasured censure and popular declamation. An official return, recently laid before the House of Commons, gives authentic and accurate information as to the owners and occupiers of land in each province, and county by county. It was prepared in 1870, when the Government was collecting evidence on everything directly bearing on the land question, and was based on the valuation-books of 1869. The inquiry did not include the holdings of property in cities, towns, or townships, but showed the nature, extent, and value of the property held in the rural districts over all Ireland. The facts as to residence and absenteeism were obtained by the poor-law department of the Irish Government, from information supplied by clerks of unions, poor-rate collectors, and other persons possessing local knowledge. No return has equalled this in completeness and accuracy.

The total number of proprietors, holding in fee-simple, in perpetuity, or on long leases at chief rents, was 19,547. Their holdings amounted to 20,046,182 statute acres, and the valuation of the property was £10,180,434. Of these 19,547 rural or landed proprietors 5,892, holding 236,873 acres, of the value of £257,100, held less than 100 acres each. Those having 100 acres and upwards were 13,565 in number, and they held 19,809,309 acres, the valuation of which was £992,334.

Now, as to the statistics of residence or absenteeism. Of the whole proprietors, the vast bulk of the holders of less than 100 acres, nearly six thousand in number, are resident. Of the remaining 13,565, it is known that 5,589 are resident on or near their estates. There are also 4,465 proprietors of 100 acres and upwards who reside constantly in Ireland, though not on their estates, and 377 who usually reside elsewhere in Ireland, and occasionally on their estates. Only 180 are returned as "resident usually out of Ireland, but occasionally on the property." These 180 constitute less than one-hundredth of the whole Irish proprietary, though owning between them nearly one-fifteenth of the whole acreage. Those "rarely or never resident in Ireland" are stated at 1,443— between one-thirteenth and one-fourteenth of the whole number, but owning together between one-sixth and one-seventh of the whole acreage. More than half a million acres belong to 161 "public or charitable institutions or public companies" (as the London city companies, colleges, schools, and various corporations); a somewhat larger amount belongs to owners "not ascertained;" and nearly half a million to the six thousand proprietors of properties under 100 acres. Comparing the classes as returned, we find that constant residents are nearly four times as numerous as constant absentees, while they own nearly thrice as much property in area, and above thrice in value. But this fact by no means represents the real preponderance of proprietors resident in Ireland over absentees, properly so called, spending their money out of the country. There remains to be added for this purpose the large class of Irish proprietors who do not live, indeed, on their properties, but in Dublin or elsewhere in Ireland, falling short of the actual residents by one-fifth only in number, and owning nearly half as much land in area and value. If these be taken into the account, and if Swift's computation be accepted as fairly accurate for his own time, we must needs infer that a vast abatement has taken place in the list of Irish absenteeism. Instead of one-third of the Irish rental going directly into the pockets of "perpetual absentees," never to come back in any shape, it is here clearly shown that little more than one-seventh is thus absorbed, of which it is certain that a very large part is sent back to Ireland to be spent in improvements and otherwise for the benefit of the country. Even if absentees who occasionally reside, and corporations be thrown into the same category, absenteeism cannot be made accountable for so much as a quarter of the Irish rental, and no one who knows Ireland will deny that among the former, at all events, are some of her best landlords and greatest benefactors. Such examples will occur as the Duke of Devonshire and the Marquis of Lansdowne. Nor do we think of absenteeism in connection with statesmen like the late Earl Derby or Lord Palmerston, who had higher duties to perform than those of resident landlords.

"We may still," says the *Times*, commenting on this statistical return, "conclude with some confidence that Irish absenteeism has not increased, but, on the contrary, has rather diminished, since the Union. There is reason to believe that, on the whole, the Encumbered and Landed Estates Courts have promoted the substitution of resident for non-resident proprietors. Whether the Land Act will have the same tendency, by encouraging tenant farmers to bid for estates on sale, or will have the opposite tendency, by weakening a landlord's motives for residing on his property, it is as yet impossible to foresee. However this may be, what cannot be denied, and ought not to be forgotten, is that absenteeism, if it is not so enormous and crying an evil as in the last century, is still, as it has ever been, one of the main obstacles to the prosperity of Ireland. In Great Britain, and especially in Scotland, where it has become much too common, its evil effects are mitigated by the independent spirit of the people. In Ireland there is nothing to supply the place of a resident landlord's example and influence, yet, by a strange fatality, the very circumstances which make this so necessary to the island are the immediate cause of absenteeism. Berkeley asks, in his pregnant style, 'whether a gentleman who hath seen a little of the world, and observed how men live elsewhere, can contentedly sit down in a cold, damp, sordid habitation, in the midst of a bleak country inhabited by thieves and beggars.' After making due allowance for a marked advance in Irish civilization since Berkeley's age, which, however, is partly compensated by a corresponding advance in the Irish squire's notions of comfort, this question of Berkeley's might be put with equal propriety at the present day. The simple reason why so many Irish proprietors reside in England or on the Continent is that life is there more agreeable, more stirring, and, we must add, more secure. In the early part of George III.'s reign it was actually proposed by the Government to counteract the force of this gravitation eastward, by levying a tax of two shillings in the pound on the net income of all Irish landlords who should not reside at least half the year in the island. No one would now venture to revive such a proposal, and it is more than doubtful whether the tenant farmers, on a property like that of Lord Fitzwilliam or Lord Devon, would gain by the forced sale of it to a Dublin landjobber, equally non-resident, but far less generous and indulgent.

"There is, in fact, no heroic or summary remedy for absenteeism, and though home rule might induce some English noblemen to sell their Irish estates, it could not compel the new purchasers to reside upon them, or to abstain from putting them, after the manner of old Irish families, into the hands of middlemen. The agrarian outrages which have so long disgraced Westmeath, and the political terrorism recently exercised by priest-led mobs in Galway, exemplify the causes which swell the number of proprietors 'rarely or never resident in Ireland.' After the Galway election a Roman Catholic gentleman of ancient Irish lineage, whose life had been threatened, signified his intention of leaving the country, and who can blame him if he carries out his resolve? Yet his departure will close one hospitable mansion, and thereby render the neighbourhood less attractive to others, besides involving a direct loss of employment and custom. Those who aspire to guide popular opinion in Ireland will do well to reflect on such considerations as these. Of course it is possible that Ireland is destined to become a community of small proprietors, with no landed aristocracy and few capitalist manufacturers. In that case it will probably exhibit the nearest approach yet realized to what economists call 'the stationary state.' In any other case a resident gentry may be of the utmost service in the social regeneration of Ireland, and no Irishman deserves well of his country who seeks to make the position of a resident gentry less enviable."

CHAPTER VI.

VISIT TO MR. BIANCONI.

Mr. Bianconi's History—Seventy Years' Recollections—Bianconi's Cars—Irish Travelling.

ONE of the most satisfactory pages in my Irish notebook is that which records a visit paid to Mr. Charles Bianconi, at Longfield in Tipperary. His name is familiar in connection with the public car service which he organized and long conducted, but it may not be known to many English readers that he is proprietor of a fine estate, one of the best of landlords, a capital farmer, and a much-respected magistrate. I had on several occasions corresponded with him, and was glad of the opportunity of seeing him in his own home and amongst his prosperous tenantry. He is now in his 87th year. He was born at Tregolo in northern Italy, Sept. 20, 1786, and came to Ireland in 1802. From an accident a few years ago he is lame, but otherwise in excellent health, with memory clear and intellect vigorous. In all that concerns the welfare of his adopted country he takes the most lively interest. It was truly a treat to converse with a man who has such large knowledge and experience, and who has witnessed the progress of Ireland during the last seventy years of its eventful annals.

A brief narrative of the career and public life of Mr. Bianconi will be accepted not only as an interesting piece of biography, but as throwing light on the history and the condition of Ireland. He allowed me to read a manuscript memoir of the early incidents of his life, which he had drawn up at the request of Mr. Drummond, whose intimate friendship he enjoyed. Mr. Drummond was one of the best of Irish secretaries, an enlightened statesman, and a warm friend to Ireland. He knew how to appreciate a man like Mr. Bianconi, and often took advantage of the information and advice which he was able to give. I urged Mr. Bianconi to publish this autobiography, but he declines on the ground that it touches on too many personal matters, and refers to persons whose descendants or relations might take offence, and because "we are yet too little removed from the dark penal times." I must therefore confine my narrative to matters which are of public notoriety, and of which Mr. Bianconi has himself given account. In 1843 he read a short paper at the Cork meeting of the British Association for the Advancement of Science. He read a second paper at the Dublin meeting in 1857; and in 1861 a third paper at the Dublin meeting of the Social Science Association. While these papers chiefly related to his coach and car establishment, incidentally many points were introduced which illustrate the social condition of the country. They have been printed in the proceedings of the Associations, but the substance of them with some characteristic extracts may here attract the notice of new readers.

Let me first give a short notice of Mr. Bianconi's early life, as he narrated it to me, so far as needful to explain the commencement of the enterprise which made his name famous. He was born, as has been stated, in a village in north Italy, not far from the Lake Como. His father was a small proprietor. He had an uncle, an ecclesiastic, who directed his early education. At school he showed little brilliancy, was rather counted dull, but was well grown, and a bold, active boy. In those times the conscription was severe, and youths were in danger even when beginning their teens. His father and two neighbours, in order to save their sons from service and death in the wars, determined to send them to England. A friend arranged this, and young Bianconi and three other youths were shipped for England. He had with him an introduction to the elder Colnaghi the publisher.

But instead of the Thames the ship anchored in the Liffey, and the Italian boys began life in Dublin. Bianconi found employment in a little shop on one of the quays, the chief business of which was the sale of pictures, chiefly such as were suited for the poor devout people. After a time he was sent out on expeditions to the country, with about £2 worth of goods on sale. He liked this life better than that of the city, the vice and misery of which had shocked him, and had confirmed his own good resolutions and moral conduct. Surprise at the prevalence of dram drinking, and at seeing poor women smoking, he mentioned as one of his earliest Dublin recollections. Trudging along the roads at that time was at first rather humiliating, as the proposal on leaving his father was that he was to be a merchant in London, for sale of thermometers, barometers, and other instruments, for which Italians have always been famous; or failing that trade, to be under Colnaghi. The sale of small pictures was humbler traffic. Once he got into trouble, and was actually arrested for selling portraits of Bonaparte.

In 1806 he resided at Carrick-on-Suir, and afterwards went to Clonmel, where he took a shop, and married. Here his business prospered, and through the assistance of some of the leading townspeople he engaged in other profitable transactions. He was a bullion merchant, and contracted for the pay of the troops under Government. Mr. Ryall, banker, and Messrs. Grubb and Isaac Jacob, quakers, were his friends and helpers in these Clonmel days. Through their influence he was appointed one of the visitors of the hospital, in which he reformed some flagrant abuses. Mr. Bianconi's anecdotes of the oppression then endured by the Roman Catholics would hardly be credited in our time. They were treated as an inferior caste, not only in matters set down in the penal code, but in the common relations of life. If a Catholic opened a shop in Clonmel, the Protestants compelled him to pay a tax or fee which they called "intrusion money." Mr. Bianconi in many ways withstood the tyranny, and his character being respected by both parties, he helped to bring about a better state of feeling. "I grew up between them," as he expressed it, "and took my own way."

It was when engaged in business at Carrick and Clonmel that he saw the need of greater accommodation for travellers of the humble class. The public conveyances at that time in Ireland were confined to a few mail and day coaches on the great lines of road. In parts less frequented by wealthy travellers, particularly from the country places to market towns, there were no facilities for speedy or convenient communication. A farmer living twenty miles from his market town would spend the first day in riding to it, a second day in doing his business, and a third in returning. The poorer people had to make the journey on foot with their burdens.

In July, 1815, he started a car for conveying passengers at cheap rates from Clonmel to Cahir, and soon after to Tipperary and Limerick. At the end of the same year similar cars were started to Cashel and Thurles, and from Clonmel to Carrick and Waterford. In the first start there was a great advantage in obtaining a supply of capital horses, intended for the army, and which were thrown on the market by the peace of 1815. They were bought at prices varying from £10 to £15. One of these horses drew a car with six passengers with ease at the rate of seven miles an hour. This was a wonderful improvement on the "ould Irish jaunting car," with its miserable jade of a horse, which the town or village innkeeper let out, with its wild driver, at an exorbitant rate, to the helpless traveller.

Encouraged by the success of his first conveyances, Mr. Bianconi extended his establishment, opening lines in the most remote districts, as from Longford to Ballina and Belmullet, 201 miles north-west from Dublin; from Athlone to Galway and Clifden, 183 miles west from Dublin; from Limerick to Tralee and Cahirciveen, 233 miles south-west from Dublin.

By this time the demand for first-class horses

having diminished, the breeding of them ceased, and it was necessary to put two horses to the cars. The size of the cars was, however, enlarged, so as to hold four passengers instead of three on each side. Gradually the two-wheeled cars were displaced by four-wheeled cars, drawn by two, three, or four horses, according to the traffic on the several roads.

In 1843, when Mr. Bianconi made his first statement to the British Association at Cork, he had on his establishment a hundred vehicles, including mail coaches and cars of all sizes, capable of carrying from four to twenty passengers each, and travelling eight or nine miles an hour, at the low rate of a penny farthing a mile, going over 3,800 miles daily, and calling at 140 stations.

This success brought similar conveyances into the field in other parts of Ireland, and all over the country communication was easy and cheap, often cheaper than the journeys could have been made on foot, not to speak of the enormous saving of time. Fourteen years afterwards, when the second statement was laid before the British Association, the growth of railway communication had necessarily affected and diminished Mr. Bianconi's establishment, but he still had sixty-seven conveyances, travelling daily 4,244 miles, and extending over portions of twenty-two counties, and requiring above 900 horses.

Such in brief are the statistics of the establishment; now for some of the results, which I shall chiefly state in Mr. Bianconi's own words. In the first place, as to the direct commercial and economical advantages, he says: "I found, as communication between different localities was extended, the consumption of manufactured goods greatly increased. The competition of those availing themselves of the facilities of travelling was so great that, instead of buying from local retail shopkeepers, after many profits, they were enabled to obtain the supplies nearer the manufacturer. In the remote parts of Ireland, for instance, on my opening the communication from Tralee to Cahirciveen in the south, Galway to Clifden in the west, and Ballina to Belmullet in the north-west, purchasers who had been obliged to give eightpence or ninepence a yard for calico for shirts, subsequently paid only threepence or fourpence, thus enabling that portion of the population who could previously badly afford only one shirt each, to have two for a less price than was paid for one; and at the same ratio other commodities came into general use at reduced prices. The resources of the country, many of which lay so long unproductive, were opened up. For instance, I enabled the fishermen on the western coast to avail themselves of a rapid transit for their fresh fish, which being a very perishable article would be comparatively profitless unless its conveyance to Dublin and other suitable markets could be ensured within a given time. The amount realized by this valuable traffic is almost incredible, and has, in my opinion, largely contributed to the comfort and independence now so happily contrasting with the lamentable condition the west of Ireland presented a few years since."

There was also direct encouragement given to agriculture as well as to trade. When there were 140 stations for the change of horses, the consumption of hay was from 3,000 to 4,000 tons annually, and of oats from 30,000 to 40,000 barrels, all of which were purchased in their respective localities.

Each of these 140 stations had from one groom to six, and even eight; and there were about 100 drivers for 1,300 horses. The men were paid according to the line, the least pay being given to those on well-frequented lines, where there was more certainty of gratuities from travellers. They were promoted according to their services and conduct. Personal inspection was impossible in so extended an establishment, but the men were put on their good behaviour, and on the whole they were a well-conducted, trustworthy staff. One of the most responsible men had risen from being a poor orphan boy, who was seen by Mr. Bianconi one day on his knees currying a horse with a wisp of straw. He thought a lad who would not spare himself would turn out a painstaking servant, and was not disappointed. On retiring from the superintendence, Mr. Bianconi transferred the various lines on advantageous terms to his employés, and I saw some of the weekly reports which are still sent to him from various parts of the country. He said that his "cars, many of them carrying very important mails, have never once been stopped, even during the time of the Whiteboy insurrection, and when Kilkenny was disturbed. Never, although travelling all hours of the day and night, often in lonely and unfrequented places, and during the long period of forty-two years, has the slightest injury been done to my property, or that entrusted to my care. I repeatedly passed hundreds of people on the road, and no one asked me where I was going, or interrupted the conveyance—a fact which showed the high bearing of the people, and which gives me greater pleasure than any pride I might feel upon the other rewards of my life."

In reply to a question at the British Association whether a horse could be worked economically more than ten hours a day, Mr. Bianconi stated that he found by experience that he could better work a horse eight hours a day for six days in the week, than six hours for seven days in the week. By not working on

Sundays he saved 12 per cent., an experience to be noted by the advocates of Sabbath observance on economical grounds.

Mr. Bianconi also expressed his opinion that the freedom of communication had a good social and moral effect, in aiding the elevation of the lower classes, by their mingling with the better orders of society. "The intercourse in travelling tended to inspire the higher grades with respect and regard for the natural good qualities of the humbler people, which the latter reciprocated by a becoming deference, and an anxiety to please and oblige. Such a moral benefit seems to me worthy of special notice and congratulation." I may add that pensions were secured for those in his employment who had to retire from age, incapacity, or sickness, and the orphan children of grooms or drivers were educated by him, and afterwards filled the situations of their deceased fathers.

This history shows that foreigners may succeed in Ireland as well as natives, and proves that there is nothing in the character of the people of the most Celtic districts of Ireland to prevent the success of any enterprise, however extensive, which is conducted with such energy, ability, good feeling, and sound sense as Mr. Bianconi displayed.

In his retirement on his estate at Longfield, I was struck with the patriarchal life of the worthy proprietor.

His tenants and domestics, most of them born and educated on the estate, look up to him with respect and affection. "We are all one family," he remarked. "I put myself inside of them, and treat them accordingly;" and the kindly relation was apparent as I went with him over the property. He keeps his "pack" with which in early life he travelled as a salesman, and he showed me one of the original "Biancs," with which he started his public career. Among the conveyances in his yard was a hearse, which he had originally purchased for a member of his own family, and which he retains for the use of his tenants and dependents, "to save needless outlay for undertakers' charges." Of his farming he was proud, every modern appliance of farm implements and machinery being used. His special pride seemed to be his stock of Kerry cows, which are purchased in sorry condition, and sold at good profit after improving on the rich Tipperary pasturage. The estate seemed in capital condition, and the house and garden showed every comfort and refinement. A mortuary chapel contains the remains of a favourite daughter, with a beautiful marble monument by an eminent Italian sculptor. He has no son surviving; the heir to the property is the child of Morgan John O'Connell, nephew of the great Daniel O'Connell, who is married to his youngest daughter.

Mr. Bianconi is a Catholic, but liberal in his opinions, and he has proved a true benefactor to his adopted country. I have a pleasant recollection of his courteous hospitality, and trust I may be excused for this public record of what I saw and heard at Longfield. "It does not matter what a man is, native or foreigner, Catholic or Protestant, if he is a good fellow, and if he is just and kind to the people." This was the remark of one of Mr. Bianconi's neighbours in Tipperary, and what I had seen confirmed the truth of the statement. Yet he had difficulty in obtaining letters of naturalization. Sir Robert Peel, when Home Secretary, was unable to procure them for him, and it was not until he had been nearly thirty years resident in Ireland, that in 1831, this recognition of citizenship was granted, during the administration of Earl Grey, the application being supported by the Grand Jury of Tipperary.

What I have narrated is interesting as a piece of biography, the story of "a self-made man," but it is more valuable as throwing light on the national character. Mr. Bianconi speaks well of "the peaceable and high moral bearing of the Irish peasantry, which can only be known and duly appreciated by those who live among them, and who have long and constant intercourse with them." Apart from agrarian outrages, crime is really rare; and the agitation about the land, he thinks, would not have arisen if proprietors had lived among the people, improving their estates, and granting leases to their tenants. His own experience has been that security of tenure gives incitement to industry and maintains good feeling. The landlords have chosen to keep their tenants in subjection, treating them as a servile class, partly for political reasons. He had purchased property where the farms were held by tenants-at-will, the population being poor and indolent, and rents in arrear. Granting leases at an advanced rent, the property improved in value, the rent was always paid, and the tenantry became a prosperous and contented class of yeomen farmers. If all landlords had been like Mr. Bianconi, there would have been no need of any Land Act, nor the wild agitation about "fixity" of tenure, by which the just relations of landlord and tenant are disturbed. It was gratifying to hear the testimony of such a man as to the progress of the country, and the expression of his firm faith in the future prosperity of Ireland.

CHAPTER VII.

IRISH POLITICS.

Imperial and National Parties — A New Political Pale — Cardinal Cullen's Claims for Popish Nationality — Ruling Ireland by Irish Ideas.

IRISH politics seem somewhat confused and complicated, but can be easily explained, so far as analysis of Irish representatives to Parliament is concerned.

The first obvious division is into members who are, in their principles and sympathies, British or Imperial, and those who are Irish or National. The great body of the landowners, magistrates, and members of grand juries throughout Ireland, whether Catholic or Protestant, are associated by education, by family connections, by social ties and political sympathies with English interests, and, however patriotic in personal feeling, they work for Ireland as part of the united empire. The majority of voters, taking the whole of Ireland, have the same British and loyal sympathies, and are opposed to agitations for Repeal or Home Rule, or other schemes for separate nationality. As in other parts of the kingdom, there is division into Liberal and Conservative, the Liberals prevailing in Catholic constituencies, the Conservatives in Protestant constituencies.*

The Irish or National party is at present much identified with the Roman Catholic power, but is not necessarily subject to it, and will remain so only while each can gain its ends by combination. As long as the Romish Church can hope to obtain concessions from the Government, it will disclaim sympathy with the Home Rule movement, which is the present *cheval de bataille* of the national party. If the Government refuses to submit to the dictation of the Romish bishops, the influence of the priests, who are under thorough control of the hierarchy, will be more openly given to the National party.

In the last Galway election this influence was used, and the election was gained by an ecclesiastical terrorism, which revealed the probable result of such power in other parts of Ireland. The power of the landlords, even when Catholic, is weak when in opposition to that of the priests. In other elections, how-

---

* Mr. Robert H. Mair, the Editor of "Debrett," informs me that in the returns received this year from the Irish Members, only five have marked themselves in the schedules as "Home Rulers." These are Butt, Martin, Redmond, Ronayne, and Smyth. The other Home Rule or Nationalist members return themselves under the head of Liberal or of Conservative.

ever, independent National candidates have carried the day, in spite of the opposition both of landlords and priests.

It is a mistake in the Government to show so much deference, and almost servile subjection, to the will of the Romish Church, and to give so little attention to the opinions of the National party, many of whom are disinterested and patriotic, however visionary or mischievous we may consider them to be. The wiser policy would be to conciliate the National party, by considering their alleged grievances, and hearing their proposals, instead of driving them into secret conspiracies, and throwing them into combination with that ultramontane faction whose irreconcileable hatred to England is well known. There is not a country in Europe where the Catholic Church would be tolerated in the attitude assumed by the heads of the Romish Church in Ireland. Even in the most Catholic countries they are excluded from the control of education and patronage, and from the political influence which is wielded by Cardinal Cullen and his satellites.

In Anglo-Norman and early English times "the Pale" was a geographical as well as political expression. The condition and privileges of those "within the Pale" were widely different from the state of those "beyond the Pale." But when English life and law and language spread over Ireland, the local meaning of the word was lost. Long before that time, the ancient characteristics of the two divisions of the island had been worn out. In fact, there had been in some things strange reversal of earlier distinctions. The Irish beyond the Pale had long resisted the rule of Rome, and maintained something of the independence of the ancient Irish Church. The Catholics of the Pale were intensely Papal. Afterwards they became Protestant, while the Church of Rome has no more abject adherents than the once independent Irish beyond the Pale. The English who came over, either at the first conquest or in after settlements, always sooner or later became racy of the soil, *Hibernis Hiberniores*, and but for the religious division perpetuated by the penal laws, the old differences of foreign and native were matters of tradition and history.

I find in Ireland of to-day a duality as marked as in the days of the Pale, only now without any local limits, and wholly social and political. Before the law all are equal, yet this division remains. It is not the division of Protestant and Catholic, or of Celt and Saxon, or of English and Irish speaking. These differences exist, but none of them are coterminous with the division to which I allude. Most of the Irish beyond this modern political pale are Catholic, but not all, nor necessarily any, although Cardinal Cullen wishes us to think that "Irish nationality" and "the Church of Rome" are the same.

"Can he forget that the nationality of Ireland means simply the Catholic Church?" Thus Cardinal Cullen wrote, in his anger against Judge Keogh, because that Catholic layman resists the subjugation of civil rights to ecclesiastical supremacy. In former times it was the policy of Rome to ally itself with despotic kings and governments, in order to obtain the help of the civil power to suppress freedom of thought and liberal opinions. In those nations where despotic power still prevails, happily they are few, the alliance of civil and ecclesiastical authority is sought.

If in France, for instance, it was possible to have a Bourbon restoration, the ecclesiastical influence would reappear, and make itself felt in education and in social life, as it did in the time of Charles X. But in countries under constitutional government, and with free institutions, the policy of Rome is to seek alliance with democracy, and to try to appear as in the van of popular opinion. This is what is going on in Ireland. It would not do openly to espouse the cause of Fenianism or Home Rule, because a fair face must be kept towards the British Government, as long as it can be coerced or cajoled into further concessions and boons. But meanwhile let the people be taught that their best friends are the ultramontane delegates of the Vatican, and "that the nationality of Ireland means simply the Catholic Church."

Can patriotic Irishmen, whether Catholic or Protestant, be deceived by this crafty policy? Let them hear the reply given by one who is a zealous patriot, and who has suffered for his love of Ireland. "The nationality of Ireland simply the Catholic Church!" said John Mitchell, in the *Irish Citizen*, of New York; "we know not what Judge Keogh may say to this statement, but *we* never heard of the fact before. There has been a kind of idea prevailing that Grattan, and Lord Edward Fitzgerald, that Tone, and the Emmets, and Davis, and O'Brien, were advocates of Irish nationality, though they had nothing to do with the Catholic Church. It has even been thought that the Presbyterian clergyman, who was hanged as a United Irishman in 1798, was a better Irishman than Dr. Troy, this Cardinal's predecessor."

I know not whether Thomas Francis Meagher is Catholic or Protestant, but in his speeches there is the ring of true patriotism, and a spirit of toleration widely different from Cullen's intolerant claims. It was in Conciliation Hall, long ago now, that Meagher thus spoke, and was applauded to the echo: "A spirit of brotherhood is abroad, old antipathies are losing ground, traditional distinctions of sect and party are being now effaced. Irrespective of descent or creed, we begin at last to appreciate the abilities and virtues of all our fellow-countrymen. We now look into history with the generous pride of the nationalist, not with the cramped prejudice of the partisan. We do homage to Irish valour, whether it conquers on the walls of Derry, or capitulates with honour before the ramparts of Limerick. We award the laurel to Irish genius, whether it has lit its flame from within the walls of old Trinity, or drawn its inspiration from the sanctuary of St. Omer's. 'We must tolerate each other,' said Henry Grattan, he whose eloquence was the very music of freedom, 'we must tolerate each other, or we must tolerate the common enemy.' After years of social disorder, years of detestable recrimination, between factions and provinces and creeds, we are on the march to freedom. Let us sustain a firm, gallant, and courteous bearing, let us avoid all offence to those who pass us by; and by rude affronts let us not drive still farther from our ranks those who at present decline to join. An honourable forbearance towards those who censure us, a generous respect towards those who differ from us, will do much to diminish the difficulties that impede our progress. Let us cherish and upon every occasion manifest an anxiety for the preservation of the rights of all our fellow-countrymen—their rights as citizens, their municipal rights, the privileges which their rank in society has given them, the position which their wealth has purchased or their education has conferred; and we will in time, and before long, efface the impression that we seek for Repeal with a view to crush those rights, to injure property, or erect a Church ascendancy."

In this strain Meagher followed the teaching of his great master O'Connell, who said, "The real obstacle to the Repeal of the Union is apprehension that it would be followed by religious intolerance and sectarian animosity. Men of Ireland, your duty is to conduct yourselves so as to obliterate every such apprehension. Exert yourselves unremittingly to exhibit kindliness, affection, conciliation, cordiality towards persons of all sects and of every persuasion. Let us leave the settlement of our religious differences to grace, to piety, to the mercies of God, to the merits of our adorable Redeemer. Irishmen, the more Christian charity you display, the more Christian virtues you practise, the more shall you advance the temporal interests and the civil liberties of your native land. Patriotism and religion run in the same channel."

These are noble sentiments, and there is no reason to question the sincerity of this utterance. Let this conciliatory spirit of Meagher and of O'Connell be impressed on Irishmen, and there will be brighter days for United Ireland.

Nor is it race nor language that marks the division of the political pale, for the races are amalgamated, and the English tongue is everywhere in use. Rich and poor, landowner and labourer, do not form the two sides, though to one belongs the larger part of the humbler class. But in America, and in England, and wherever Irish are found, the same duality appears, whether among Catholic or Protestant, rich or poor. The Irish, or National, party is the name by which those outside the pale like to call themselves. Of the elements that form this spirit of nationality, something may be derived from old traditions of the laws and usages of their Cymric ancestors, which have not been wholly lost till within a few generations back. Between the Norman invasion and the reign of Elizabeth, the English settlers adopted the native customs and laws, in spite of such warnings as the Kilkenny Statute, which declared Brehon law to be no law, but only an evil custom. In that reign and the succeeding reign of James I. were established English legal institutions, courts and circuits and other copies of English judicial arrangements; but there could not be eradicated from the popular mind the influence of the ancient tribal and patriarchal system. The two systems lived together. From the middle of the seventeenth century, when the religious feuds broke out, the separation of the English and the National party was intensified, and it survives the abolition of the penal laws, and the restoration of equal civil and political rights to all Irishmen.

In nothing does this "national" spirit show itself so intensely and unmistakably as in hatred to England. There was good cause for it down to our own times. The oppression of the poor Irish, both by the Imperial Government and by the English possessors of the island, was as sore as was ever borne by any conquered country. In their adversity they found in the Roman Catholic priests their nearest advisers and comforters, and it is not surprising that the faith of Romanism has thus become associated with the national spirit. The rulers of the Romish Church are clever in taking advantage of this feeling, and our rulers in the State are led to suppose that Romanism is the one essential element in the "national" policy. But some of the chief leaders of the Irish National party have been Protestants.

The hatred to England shows itself by occasional outbreaks, as of Fenianism, but more constantly by a chronic discontent and disaffection, ready to manifest itself as opportunity offers. The Home Rule movement is of course popular with the National party. The disestablishment of the Irish Church, and the Tenant Right movement, they regard as steps in the right direction. Anything to weaken the power of the territorial aristocracy by whom their fathers were oppressed is sure to gain their sympathy. The possibilities of striking a blow at the imperial power, during some foreign war, are always contemplated. "England's extremity is Ireland's opportunity," they say. It was curious to note the interest with which the Irish watched the negotiations in the Alabama controversy; and again, how they canvassed the rival claims of Grant and of Greeley for president, the chance of war with England being always the uppermost element in the calculation. When the hope of using force is remote, there are always civil and political ways of showing animosities. Home Rule candidates are chosen members of Parliament, and abject followers of the Pope, and even convicts like O'Donovan Rossa. Anything will do to hurt or to spite England. Nevertheless, apart from the cunning priestly influence which keeps up some of the bad feeling, there is a spirit of patriotism at the root of this National party, which may yet rise to nobler ambition and use. The history of Scotland encourages us to this hope. It is not much more than a century since over a large part of Scotland the ancient national spirit was strong, and the hatred of England was as intense as even among the descendants of the Irish Septs. Yet the Jacobite spirit of last century is now utterly merged in one common Scottish patriotism and nationality. It may be the same in Ireland, if the mistake is not made by the Government of dealing with the Romish Church as the sole representative of the National party.

As Home Rule is the present project of this party, it may be well, instead of meeting it with abuse and ridicule, to examine what is said in its favour, and see how far the demand can be considered, for the advantage of Ireland, and without detriment to imperial interests.

CHAPTER VIII.

HOME RULE.

Right Limits of Home Rule—Earl Russell's Proposal—Lord Chancellor O'Hagan's Opinion—Grand Juries and County Boards—Presentment Sessions and Cess-payers—The Shannon Improvement.

HOME RULE may be a good thing or a bad thing, according to what is understood by the term. If it means independent and separate legislation by a Parliament sitting in College Green, it would throw Ireland back into a state of wild confusion and conflict; but if it means only an enlargement of local and national government, increase of Home Rule would be a boon to Ireland, as it would be a relief to the already overburdened imperial Government. It was in this sense, and in connection with the pressure of parliamentary business at Westminster, that Earl Russell made the proposal which caused so much discussion last summer. "It appears to me," said the veteran statesman, "that if Ireland were to be allowed to elect a representative assembly for each of its four provinces of Leinster, Ulster, Munster, and Connaught, and if Scotland in a similar manner were to be divided into Lowlands and Highlands, having for each province a representative assembly, the local wants of Ireland and Scotland might be better provided for than they are at present. The Imperial Parliament might still retain its hold over this legislation, and refuse, if it so chose, to give a third reading to any bill assented to on its first and second readings, and on the report by the local assembly." It was a crude and hasty proposal, and the idea of giving Ireland four Parliaments for its four provinces, and dividing Scotland into Highland and Lowland, met with fair ridicule. "Repeal the Union? Restore the Heptarchy!" as Canning said. But there was a sound principle at the root of the idea, and the time must soon come when the Imperial Parliament will be unable to overtake the mass of business which comes up year by year for consideration. The time and labour given to private bill legislation have steadily increased, and threaten to overwhelm the most patient and industrious of legislators. Most of this business could far better be attended to in the parts of the empire concerned. Enormous costs are needlessly incurred, from which parliamentary agents and lawyers reap undue harvests. At first sight, it might seem that local jobbery and influence must be counteracted by carrying such business to Westminster, but the truth is that there is less hope of impartial decision in Parliament, owing to the large powers held by certain classes—the railway interest, the banking or brewing interest, or the landed interest, for instance,—who readily combine upon non-political questions brought before the House. A local or provincial Parliament would have no such predominance of moneyed and class interests, but would be likely to decide upon grounds affecting the well-being of the district.

In fact, this legislation would be analogous to the States' legislation in America, sufficient in all matters not interfering with the interest of the Union. It would be a miserable thing if every measure affecting the welfare of the several States had to be settled at Washington, even down to water supply or sewage schemes. Boston or Chicago, San Francisco or New Orleans, could not tolerate such centralization. Yet this is what is done in England. With some check such as Earl Russell proposes, in requiring the third reading to be by the Imperial Parliament, or assent to be otherwise registered, the discussion and maturing of local and provincial matters might well be provided for under some system of "Home Rule."

This seems to have been mainly the kind of business indicated in Earl Russell's proposal, for on being asked for an explanation, by the London correspondent of an American paper, he wrote thus: "In Sir Robert Kane's 'Industrial Resources of Ireland' you will find an enlightened review of the material wants and necessary remedies for the welfare of Ireland. I wish to see these wants and these remedies fairly examined, and means employed to promote Irish improvement and bring about Irish prosperity. But I fear if an Irish "Parliament" is set up in Ireland all her energies will be wasted in political contention. I therefore wish to divert the forces which might give heat and comfort, instead of concentrating them in a manner to produce a conflagration. This is the more necessary, as the Irish nature is so very inflammable that it prefers a bonfire to the warmth of a moderate fire. I fear, however, that wisdom will be wanting both in England and Ireland."

Earl Russell rightly fears that Irish representatives, whether in a provincial Parliament, or in our national Parliament, would waste their energies in political or in religious contention. But there are subjects on which men of all creeds and parties could unite for the good of the commonwealth. There are subjects on which they now work harmoniously together. In many commercial and financial undertakings of great magnitude, witness the insurance companies and mining companies and railway companies, the boards of direction are composed of Whigs and Tories, Protestants and Catholics, Orangemen and Home Rulers alike. They know no party in matters affecting their own interests and their country's welfare. There are questions also on which they could decide better than the Imperial Parliament. I give one instance. When Sir Wilfred Lawson's Permissive Bill was under discussion, and the whole question of licensing public-houses, public opinion in Ireland was far in advance of public opinion in England. Even under existing licensing laws, Ireland possessed safeguards and restrictions not adopted in England. The advantage of having legislative support in the cause of sobriety is far more recognized in Ireland than with us, and we do not hear from Irishmen the stupid remark, that "you cannot make men sober by Act of Parliament." Law cannot make men temperate, but it can lessen temptations and inducements to intemperance. While every year a considerable majority of English votes are given against Sir Wilfred Lawson's Bill, the Irish vote in its favour has been very nearly two to one, the Irish majority being made up of men of the most diverse political and religious opinions. This demonstrates that Irishmen can combine on matters that they think pertain to the welfare of their country. Let them have larger power in such direction, and they would not abuse it.

But it must be confessed that "Home Rule" has been adopted as a watchword and war-cry by political agitators. It has been seized by the people, ever ready to catch at any phantom which promises relief from present trouble, or gives hope of prosperity without individual effort and self-denial. Several elections have been carried by Home Rule candidates; sometimes, as in Mr. Blennerhasset's case in Kerry, against the combined influence of both priests and landlords. It is a power at present in the country, and must be dealt with. What Sir John Coleridge said of it lately in his speech at Liverpool is worthy of being noted. "Home Rule is a very different thing from Fenianism. Fenianism murdered innocent policemen in the face of day while doing their duty. Fenianism tried to slaughter unoffending citizens by blowing up the walls of prisons in crowded streets. Fenianism was a mere system of sheer physical brutal terror. Home Rule is nothing of the sort. Home Rule aims at an end which I think absurd, impracticable, and untenable, but an end which they have a perfect right to aim at, if they can get it. Home Rule professes to respect the monarchy, and to move to its ends by means which they have a perfect right to use, and which are perfectly legitimate. Home Rule has for its head a Queen's counsel, an able and accomplished lawyer, and not a Fenian Centre. These are great advances.

It is a great thing to have your enemy face to face with you in daylight, when you can grapple with him. It is a great thing to have a controversy converted from one of force and violence into one of reason and argument."

Sir John Coleridge refers to Home Rule under the idea that its only form must be an independent and separate legislation, as that of Scotland was from the accession of James I. till the Union; or that of Norway, with its political independence, after its transfer, by the peace of Kiel in 1814, from Denmark to Sweden. This may be "absurd and impracticable" in the case of Ireland in relation to England, but the extension of Home Rule in the sense of allowing fuller discussion of Irish questions, and adoption of measures conducive to Irish progress, is not absurd or impracticable. Irish patriotism is worthy of being trusted, and Irish loyalty also.

But there is a disturbing element which hinders the fair consideration of the question. A large and influential body in Ireland is neither patriotic nor loyal. The Vatican is their country and the Pope their ruler. All their best sympathies are abroad, not at home. While this disturbing and disloyal element retains its influence, the question cannot be entertained. In the existing state of Ireland, Home Rule simply means Rome Rule.

The crafty attempt of the Ultramontanes to identify themselves with the National party ought to be resisted by true Irish patriots, as much as the Ultramontane claim to be above the civil courts of law should be resisted by Government.

On a recent occasion, when the Government issued an order on the Education question, establishing a new rule of the National School Board as to the relation of managers and masters, a meeting of the Roman Catholic prelates was convened in Marlborough-street Cathedral. Why should a meeting like this be treated with respect, and its resolutions received by the Government with deferential courtesy, while a meeting of the National party would be dogged by detectives and watched by police spies? The deliberations of the Romish prelates are far more mischievous, and more avowedly hostile to the Queen's Government, than any discussions of the Home Rule party. The real peril to the British Government, and the chief hindrances to the peace of the country, are to be found not in the Irish, but in the Italian conspirators against the laws and constitution of England.

There is an old law, 33rd George III., c. 29, known as the Convention Act, still unrepealed on the Statute Book, by which any conference in Ireland on national affairs may be forbidden, and those who take part in it punished. This law has not for some time been enforced against political assemblies, as I understand, but it is maintained *in terrorem*, to prevent the Irish people from assembling by representatives or delegates, to consult on affairs that they think might advance the national interest. The Irish members can meet at Westminster, as the Scotch members do, to agree as to any course of action in the House during the session of Parliament, but a conference in Dublin, however peaceable or orderly, is at present illegal. The discussion of Irish questions is thus left to the press, and the newspapers being mostly strong party organs, there is little progress made towards agreement for the common welfare. The repeal of the Convention Act could do no real harm. It is not as if a mock Parliament were desired in College Green; but an Irish representative body, agreeing to petition the Legislature on any given object, would bring out healthy public opinion, and would also test the practicability of Home Rule.

It is now exactly thirty years since the Lord Chancellor of Ireland, then Thomas O'Hagan, Esq., barrister-at-law, thus declared his opinion as to Home Rule, and Union with England. It was at a meeting of the Loyal National Repeal Association, in the days of O'Connell: "I believe that the system of centralization, as it is developed in these islands, has been partial in its action, and mischievous in its results, and that local legislature, for local purposes, conducted by men of the country, who know its people, understand their wants, respect their opinions, sympathise with their feelings, and are identified with their interests, would be of great practical utility to Ireland. I believe that such a legislature, developing our resources, and applying them with intelligence and faithfulness to our own local improvement, may fairly and hopefully be sought, and that, by the peaceful attainment of such a legislature, our material prosperity and our intellectual progress would be materially advanced. But I believe also that, for imperial purposes, not touching her internal economy, Ireland should not abandon such influences as she may fairly claim to the general legislation of an empire which has been so enriched by Irish treasure, so glorified by Irish bravery, and so cemented by Irish blood. And thus distinguishing between the proper objects of local and imperial legislature, and securing to our country proper guards, sanctions, and guarantees for her honour and her rights, in a federal connection with Great Britain, I am satisfied that the aims of reasonable men would be accomplished, all danger of separation effectually obviated, the real welfare of Ireland promoted, and the integrity of the empire consolidated and secured."

An important practical step in the direction of efficient Home Rule would be gained by a clearer definition and enlargement of the functions of the Grand Juries. To an English mind the name is misleading. The duties of the Grand Jury in England are merely accessory to the administration of justice. In Ireland the Grand Jury not only exercises a function analogous to that of the English Grand Jury in criminal matters, but has large administrative and financial power. It is, in fact, the governing body in all local county matters, excepting such as are provided for by stipendiary magistrates, and by Government officials, under special Acts of Parliament. With the educational or poor-law departments, for instance, the Grand Jury has no connection. But in regard to most county matters, such as making and repairing roads, building and repairing prisons, prison and police expenses, appointing and paying all county officers, management of public charities, repayment of Government advances, and many miscellaneous affairs, the Grand Juries have large power. The necessary funds are raised by rates, "the Grand Jury cess," imposed on the occupiers of land. The cess used to be paid by the tenant only, but under the new Land Act, in the case of tenancies created after the passing of that Act, one-half of the cess is payable by the landlord. These various duties represent a large financial control; in fact, above a million yearly is expended by the Grand Juries. The only control as to the amount of the cess, and its application, is that the going Judge of assize has to signify his sanction to any proposed work, and that the work has been previously assented to by the Presentment Sessions of the barony, if the work affects that barony only. In works for the benefit of the whole county, as prisons or police, the *fiat* of the assize Judge, generally a mere formal assent, is sufficient.

The functions of the Grand Juries thus are similar to those of County Assemblies in Prussia, or Conseils Généraux in France. An improvement of the Constitution and enlargement of the power of the Irish Grand Juries, so as to make them more really local Parliaments, legislative as well as executive, seems to be a desirable extension of Home Rule, and much more practical than Earl Russell's proposal to have a Parliament for each of the four provinces. But in order to do this the mode of constitution would need to be amended,

At present, the members of the Grand Jury are appointed by the Sheriff or Under-Sheriff, himself a nominee of the Crown. The choice almost invariably is made of landlords to the exclusion of tenants. Nominally a fifty-pound freehold is a necessary qualification, but this is disregarded in the frequent nomination of the paid agent or steward of non-resident or resident landlords. Peers are not eligible as Grand Jurors, and the consequence is that their agents are usually selected as their representatives. That the cess-payers have no voice in the election of those by whom they are taxed and governed is not in accordance with free representative institutions.

Similar objection exists to the constitution of the inferior local court, the Presentment Sessions. The members of these Sessions are county magistrates, appointed by the Crown, and a certain number of cess-payers (not to exceed twelve), the number in each barony fixed by the Grand Jury. These assessors or colleagues of the magistrates, styled "Associated Cess-payers," are not elected by their fellow cess-payers. The Grand Jury nominate double the number ordered to attend the Court, and then decide by lot who are to be the associate cess-payers. The whole arrangement is one of enforced inferiority for the cess-payers, who ought to have more direct voice in the taxation and management of the county.

The existing system is partly the result of the old penal code, the majority of the rulers being Protestant, and the majority of the ruled being Catholic. The political rule of landlord over tenant has also been in this way perpetuated.

A sensible suggestion was lately made in a letter in the *Times*, signed F. N., in which the writer proposed that the functions of the Grand Jury should be limited, as in England, to assisting in the administration of criminal law, and that new "County Boards" should be created, to which all financial and ruling powers should be assigned. The members of these boards should be chosen either directly by the cess-payers, or by the Presentment Sessions, if the members of these are elected by the cess-payers. The machinery for carrying out these changes already exists, as the majority of the guardians of the poor in each district are so elected. The residue of the guardians consists of the magistrates of the poor-law district. The poor-law guardians control the expenditure of over £800,000 a year, for which they have power of enforcing rates. It might be advisable, both for economy and efficiency, to amalgamate the two bodies comprising the Presentment Sessions and the Guardians of the Poor. The anomaly of peers being debarred from the Grand Juries might be removed, if they were eligible for seats in these county boards or councils. I believe that these local parliaments could, with due provision for appeal to higher Courts, whether legal or parliamentary, be entrusted with all the affairs which it is reasonable to include in any system of Home Rule. Matters of religion and education might for a time be excluded from local legislation or administration, but in every other department of life Irishmen could well manage their local affairs for their own benefit and the improvement of their country. The power of appeal to a higher Court, and the presence of Her Majesty's Judges on circuit, would be enough to maintain the association of local with central government, of Imperial with Home Rule.

If the functions of the Grand Juries remain as at present, one change ought certainly to be made. It would be better for the magistrates to elect them, than that the selection should be at the sole pleasure of the under-sherriff. The best constitution I think would be, half the Grand Jury elected by the magistrates and the other half by the cess-payers, the choice being limited by certain qualifications. There is a great advantage in having, as at present, two distinct authorities to consider every question. The local Presentment Board discusses matters affecting the district, and the central Grand Jury exercises a useful control in reducing or in rejecting claims for what it may deem unnecessary or imprudent expenditure. The local cess-payers are generally disposed to look only at roads near their own farms, or from their homes to the market town, and do not enter much into improvements of wider range. It is essential to have for such questions the services of magistrates and others who are above the suspicion of jobbing or using influence for local affairs, but who will take up presentment accounts with a general regard to the requirements of a whole barony, or the county at large.

At the same time, there would be a benefit in accustoming farmers to act on public boards on equal footing with the rest of the council, and not merely as associated cess-payers. If elected by their fellow cess-payers, the men of most knowledge and public spirit would be chosen, and they would become accustomed to act with more independence for their own order. Landlords and tenants, Protestants and Catholics, equally like good roads and safe bridges, and equally object to pay too much for them. They have equal interest in having good police and well-regulated prisons and other county requirements. When accustomed to act together on such matters, these barony or county boards might gradually come to act with equal harmony on questions of wider hearing, and local school boards would be possible, for education is a matter equally of common interest, and of more importance to the rate-payers for their children than it is to the celibate clergy, who have now too much hold on the schools.

In matters affecting the interests of several counties, or larger parts of the country, there is no reason why a central board or council, representing the several county boards, should not have power to deliberate and act for the common good. Take a special case for illustration, which will explain better than any general argument the scope there is for practical Home Rule. The river Shannon, running through several counties, is subject in various parts of its course to inundations. Crops are destroyed, lands periodically flooded and injured, and vast tracts of country permanently kept in a state unfit for cultivation. On account of the condition of the main river, its tributaries spread similar ruin. On the river Suck alone there were about 80,000 acres of land lately flooded, with incalculable injury and loss. It is the same with the lesser streams, the flat districts near which are flooded for months every year. These could all be reclaimed and protected, but drainage works are rendered impossible by the state of the Shannon. Of course the owners of land in all the regions thus injured and impoverished, suffer and grumble, but are helpless. The proprietors in one county do not know the condition of other counties, and if they did, there is no way of combined action. And so large tracts of country remain unprofitable, and a vast amount of wealth is lost to the country.

That this is not only a lamentable but disgraceful state of things it is needless to say. I have only referred to the loss to agriculture caused by the inundations of the river and its tributaries. But there is a larger view of the subject, in considering the great development of the wealth of the country that would certainly result from the improvement of the navigation. The Shannon is the largest and most beautiful river in the united kingdom. Its estuary is far better than that of the Thames, and has roadsteads where a magnificent navy might ride. It has a capacious port, capable of being a busy mart of commerce. From Limerick to the sea it is a tidal river. Communication is open both by rail and canal with every part of Ireland. Through its whole course of above two hundred miles, from its rise in Lough Allen, county Leitrim, the river passes through a country rich in mineral as well as agricultural resources. Round Lough Allen there is abundant coal and the richest ironstone. The middle Shannon runs through a region containing some of the most fertile soil in Ireland, both arable and pasture land. Between Killaloe and Limerick there is a fall of about a hundred feet in a space of fifteen miles, with a volume of water capable of giving enormous mechanical power, at present almost utterly wasted. The minimum discharge of water at Killaloe, in the dryest summer, is about 100,000 cubic feet of water per minute. This is equal to 188-horse power per foot of fall. In great floods the discharge has been estimated at 1,000,000 cubic feet per minute, equal to 1,885-horse power per foot of fall. Taking the discharge at various seasons, the average power has been estimated at about 450-horse power per foot of fall. Sir Robert Kane, reviewing these estimates, says, "In order to avoid any suspicion of exaggeration, I take the average force of water available per foot of fall at 350-horse power, which for 97 feet of fall between Killaloe and Limerick gives a total of 33,950-horse power in continuous action, day and night, throughout the year."

Yet there is hardly a mill to be seen in all the distance! If for nothing else, what a place for peat-fuel factories! The portion of the river which is full of power remains valueless, while the quieter parts are only half utilized, and allowed often to spread devastation instead of fertility. It is only an instance of the manner in which natural advantages are thrown away in Ireland.

Returning to the drainage, the lakes which form a chain in the course of the river, especially the larger ones, Lough Allen, Lough Rea, and Lough Derg, are vast reservoirs, as if provided by nature for protecting the river from disastrous floods. These lakes could be easily kept at proper levels, and by receiving and retaining the flood-waters could be made to regulate the discharge throughout the whole course of the river. There are at present various navigation works of importance, but the service they render at one part is counterbalanced by the mischief they produce elsewhere. It is true that the fall between Lough Allen and Lough Derg is small for so large a river, and the fall that exists is neutralized by the monopolising weirs, generally unprovided with flood-gates. But still there is a total fall of about sixty feet in that distance, and always sufficient flow and delivery of water to render drainage improvements practicable, if the main flow of the river were attended to.

Forty years ago, Mr. Rhodes, civil engineer, member of a parliamentary commission appointed in 1831, said in his report: "Taking a view of this majestic river, its lakes and lateral branches, which receive the drainage of a considerable portion of Ireland, they appear as if formed and designed by nature as the great arteries of the kingdom, for facilitating its agricultural and commercial purposes, by marking out a splendid line of intercourse through a populous country superior to any in the empire, and only requiring a little assistance from art to render it beneficially useful to an unlimited extent. But the grand designs of nature had been hitherto in a great measure frustrated, and may not improperly be compared to 'a scaled book.' This is caused by a few natural, but the greater part are artificial obstructions, which dam up the water, and inundate the country to a formidable extent; this renders the navigation very imperfect by the great accumulation and expanse of its waters in winter, and in summer the water is too shallow at several parts for a laden vessel, even with a moderate draught, to get over them. So that, taking it altogether, it almost amounts to a prohibition of any trade being carried on with certainty, at present being very limited; which is to be regretted, as it tends greatly to retard any general or permanent improvement taking place throughout this great extent of fine country, fertile and abundant in its agricultural and mineral productions."

In 1834, after inquiry before a select committee of the House of Commons, an Act was passed for "The Improvement of the Navigation of the Shannon," and commissioners appointed to make surveys, and prepare plans and estimates, both for improving the navigation of the river and preventing the inundation of land. The lands deriving benefit were to be chargeable in a degree proportioned to the estimated benefit. On this commission, besides Mr. Rhodes, were no less personages than Sir John Burgoyne, Sir Harry Jones, R.E., Sir Richard Griffin, and Mr. William Cubitt. The plans and estimates were approved, and by another Act, passed in 1839, the recommended works were authorized, half the cost to be defrayed by a Government grant and half chargeable to the counties. For a time operations seem to have been vigorously carried on; weirs were cleared away, sluices provided, channels dredged, and at some places, as Killaloe and Meelick, more costly works undertaken. Unhappily the expectation of the Commissioners and of the Government were not realised, and the inundations continued as before. Major W. Le Poer Trench (R.E., M.P.), in a valuable report published in the *Times* of January 24, speaks of the great stone-dam at Meelick as forming "one of some very extensive navigation works which have a terrible effect upon the country."

In 1850 the works were handed over to the Commissioners of Public Works. They had no funds to alter or to complete what had been done by the parliamentary commission. Receipts from tolls do not nearly meet the cost of maintenance, and even the weeds in the river's channel can hardly be kept under control. The land continues to be injured, the landowners and farmers continue to complain, and inquiries continue from time to time to be made and plans projected. In 1862 Mr. Bateman, civil engineer, made a report, and again in 1866; Mr. Lynam, well versed in Irish drainage works, and Mr. Forsyth, the engineer to the Board of Works, also reported. An inquiry was instituted before a select committee of the House of Lords in 1865.

There are thus voluminous documents bearing on the subject. At length, in 1870, the Government took resolution to deal with the most important part of the river, and while the main cost of new operations was to be levied on the lands improved, a provision was made for the expenditure of £100,000 as a free grant. Circumstances have delayed the carrying out of this Act, and it is as well, since delay has allowed fuller consideration of the subject. The chief difficulty seems to be that works intended for improving the navigation of the river do not necessarily assist, but rather hinder, the reclamation and improvement of the land. Mr. Curley, formerly engineer under the Irish Board of Works, says that "the several governments who, from time to time, granted public moneys for carrying out the navigation works, did so with the best intentions; but the government who will cause them to be demolished will deserve the thanks of all landowners whose lands are periodically inundated." This is not a very pleasant or satisfactory statement, after all that has been given and done. But there is surely some way of harmonizing the two sets of works and making the best of both land and water. The canal and railway systems make the river navigation of less importance than once it was, and when certain obstructions are removed, the improvement of navigation ought to be a matter rather for shipbuilders than engineers. On many European rivers great traffic is carried on with boats of very little draught. If the Limerick corporation or the river commissioners would consult some boatbuilder from Pesth on the Danube, or a steam engineer from Cincinnati on the Ohio, they would soon learn how to make use of the Shannon. But at all events, the number of persons and amount of property on the banks of the Shannon and its tributaries far exceed those affected by the navigation of the waters. To this object the attention of the commissioners should be mainly directed. The injury now submitted to can hardly be calculated. It is not merely the actual loss of crops by floods, and the waste of ground now periodically or permanently under water, but the injury extends to lands above the flood levels, the produce of which is deteriorated by the cold, damp atmosphere and the early frosts thereby produced. Agricultural improvement is retarded, and I have the authority of Sir Robert Kane for the statement, that "the property lost in a single year is so great that it would, if judiciously expended, pay the entire cost of remedying the evil."

I have said thus much about the improvement of the Shannon, because it is a subject associated with the past history and future prospects of Ireland, and is likely to be again before Parliament. In old times nothing was thought of by the Government about this river, except that it was a useful barrier and defence against the hostile septs who dwelt beyond its boundary. Money was gladly spent in building and keeping in repair fortifications to guard "the passes of the Shannon." It is the happy proof of a new and better epoch, that the river is now regarded as a channel of intercourse, and as a means of developing the peaceful industry and productive resources of the country. And I have included my remarks in the chapter on Home Rule, because this seems an example of public undertakings, the designing and carrying out of which could be well delegated to native ingenuity and skill. The British Government has undertaken the postal and telegraph service of Ireland, and its police and schools, and is likely to have charge of its railways also; but it is too much to expect the overburdened British Government to attend to the rivers and roads of a country. An Irish board, or Council, or whatever it might be called, in Dublin, could manage such affairs better than a committee at Westminster, and any board of commissioners there appointed.

Shortly after I was at Limerick I heard of the celebration of an ancient custom connected with the river. A steamer, freighted with the corporation and various official personages, sailed down the tidal stream to where it joins the sea, and there a javelin was cast towards the ocean, in symbol of the sovereignty of the Mayor of the port over the magnificent river. Bombastical speeches were made, not without the usual references to Saxon oppressors, and the glories of the green isle, "first flower of the earth, and first gem of the sea." The whole scene was characteristic of Irish public life, in matters where rhetorical patriotism is alone within attainment. But if entrusted with practical power of home government, Irish enterprise and Irish capital would find in such works as the improvement of the Shannon, useful and remunerative occupation, in the prosperity resulting from which, all parties and creeds and classes would share.

Give the Lord Lieutenant a Council, representing County Boards, and consisting of men such as formed the Executive of the Industrial Exhibition, and Irish home affairs would be "ruled" in Dublin better than they can be at Westminster.

CHAPTER IX.

A CHAPTER ON IRISH HISTORY.

Celtic Records—Annals of the Four Masters—Before and after the Norman Invasion—Mr. Froude's Lectures.

MY old master, John Williams, Archdeacon of Cardigan, Rector of the Edinburgh Academy, imbued me with early respect for Celtic lore. He believed that Britain in ancient times was peopled by a race far in advance òf other northern nations, who brought from Phœnicia and the East rich stores of knowledge and art. After the Roman and Scandinavian invasions, the ancient civilization of the island declined, and the records of it only remain in Welsh Triads and Taliesin fragments. He used to affirm that the Cymry of Britain crossed over to Ireland, and civilized the savages there. The Irish tongue, he said, was only a dialect of the ancient Cymraeg, "a most primitive and vigorous offshoot of the orginal language of the Noachidæ." All which is learnedly discussed in his book, "Gomer: an Analysis of the

Language and Knowledge of the Ancient Cymry," which I had the pleasure of reviewing in 1854 in the "Literary Gazette," of which I was then one of the editors. Peace to the memory of my enthusiastic teacher and good friend, Archdeacon Williams!

Probably from this early bias I always used to look with profound respect on those who professed to be versed in ancient Irish lore. From ordinary books it was not easy to gather any clear knowledge of old Irish history. Milesians and Firbolgs and Tuathana-Danains, and the rest of them, they all had a hazy existence, not historical, scarcely legendary. But in hearing learned men referring to venerable native manuscripts, especially "The Annals of the Four Masters," I supposed there must be rich sources of wisdom, the entrance of which was shut out by ignorance of the language. The notion was dispelled on seeing the actual "Annals of the Four Masters," the great authority on the subject, and reading the translation, which the learned labours of Dr. O'Donovan brought within the reach of English students. A portion of the work, down to the year 1171, had previously been edited by Dr. O'Connor, from an ancient MS. in the library at Stowe. There are two manuscripts, more perfect, in Dublin—one in the Library at Trinity College and the other in that of the Royal Irish Academy. From these Dr. O'Donovan edited the remainder of the Annals, from 1171 to 1616. A third has lately been brought to Dublin from the Irish College at Rome.

The work turns out to be no Cymric treasure, but only a monkish chronicle, compiled by four Franciscan brethren in the early part of the seventeenth century! These patriotic scribes, in their retreat in the monastery of Donegal, spun their history out of tangled threads of song and legend, tradition and fiction, the last element being not inconsiderable. They tell us, for example, that "in the year of the world 4604, died Ugainé Mŏr (the great), monarch of Erinn, and of the whole of the west of Europe as far as the Mediterranean." Other legends, equally unsubstantial, appear; but they were as good as true for the patron of the chroniclers, Feral O'Gara, Lord of Moy O'Gara, in Sligo, and member of the Parliament held in Dublin in 1634.

The names of the four monks or "masters" were Michael O'Cleary, his brothers Cucagny or Courcy, and Conary O'Cleary, and Ferfean O'Mulconry, said to be sprung from a king of Connaught in the seventh century. It was a creditable work for Irish monks of the time (after Bacon and Shakespeare), and considering the materials out of which it was prepared. Irish antiquaries are proud, as well they may be, of "The Four Masters," and are going to erect a monolithic cross to their memory among the ruins of the ancient monastery where they resided. It is a laudable design; but I confess it is some relief, in still confessing much scepticism and ignorance, to learn that these Annals "to this day constitute the basis of Irish history."

Wearied and bewildered by dry researches in the Library of Trinity College or of Armagh Cathedral, it was a pleasant change to get away to the ruins of the Seven Churches at Glendalough, or to "the Steeple" at Antrim; and there, sitting in sight of one of the venerable and mysterious "Round Towers," to weave out of the few recorded facts an early history of Ireland, quite as satisfactory as that of the "Four Masters." Christian settlers, colonists, or it may be exiles, in the troublous times that fell upon Britain and the Continent in the decline of the Roman empire, came to remote Ierne. They spread over the island, planting in many dark places bright homes of learning and piety—centres of light, "whence savage clans and roving barbarians derived the benefits of knowledge and the blessings of religion." They were not molested; were probably looked upon with superstitious veneration by the untutored natives, many of whom were converted to Christianity. Ireland became renowned as "the island of saints." Their greatest saint was Columba or Columkill, in the sixth century. It was he who, having incurred the anger of King Dermot by his faithful rebukes, went, with seven of his disciples, to Scotland, and first settled at Iona or I-Columkill, the island of Columba. Another great saint was Patrick. After the learned discussions of Dr. Todd and other Irish scholars, it is as vain to doubt his personal existence as that of Homer; but so many events are associated with the name that I suspect there were several St. Patricks. Certainly many of these events belong to times long after the reputed age of the patron saint of Ireland, though he is said to have lived 122 years. Patricius was no uncommon name among the descendants of Roman settlers, and in the countries of their adoption.

Whoever were the chief agents in the work, the Irish nation was largely gained to profession of the Christian faith. Princes and chieftains were nursing-fathers to the Church; and the triumph of the cross under Constantine was repeated among the little Hibernian principalities. Cormac, King of Munster, combined temporal and spiritual sway over his subjects; and on the Rock of Cashel beside his palace was his cathedral chapel, and its campanile or Round Tower. There is no doubt that these structures, about which so much controversy has been raised, were built by the Christian Irish of those times. The names of the builders, and the dates of some of them, have been ascertained, and their uses are no longer matter of wild conjecture, though it would take too long here to set down the proofs.

During these ages we also glean from the history of other countries interesting notices of Irish Christians, especially missionaries, men of zeal and learning, like St. Gall, and Fridolan, and in later times, Scotus Erigena.

It was not by the native Irish, or by Celtic violence, that the Christian churches were made ruins. It was by pagan pirates, Saxons and Danes, and other northmen, that the holy places were plundered and desolated. In the times of disorder and violence that followed, the peaceful influences of Christianity diminished, and the Irish chieftains and their septs relapsed into semi-barbarism, notwithstanding the existence of their Brehon law, and other restraints. Any history of the ancient Irish conflicts would be as profitless now, as the record of the wars of savage chiefs in Africa and New Zealand in prehistoric times. There are a few authentic facts that stand out in bright relief, notably the battle of Clontarf in 1014, when the great Brian Boroimhe or Boru (the brave) fell, after defeating the Danes.

Brien Boru is the hero of Irish romance—the Alfred of their annals. Illustrious in war, he defeated the

Danes in twenty-nine pitched battles, and innumerable encounters. No less illustrious in peace, in his reign the arts flourished, learning was encouraged, property respected, law maintained, religion venerated. It was in his reign that a beautiful damsel, covered with jewels, travelled from one end of the island to the other without molestation. The popularity of such a fable to this day in Ireland, speaks well for the honour and virtue of the people. An anecdote like that would not be current in a nation of lawless violence. The praises of the great and good king, "the glory and grace of his age," are celebrated in song and legend, and even Tom Moore has his ballad, "Remember the glories of Brien the brave." Yet it must be told, that if any one in Ireland begins to talk in prose about Brien Boru or the battle of Clontarf, there is a comical smile on every face, just as there was when Lord John Russell in his speeches came to "the British Constitution," or as when Sandy M'Bore commences a harangue about Bruce and Bannockburn.

Since Brien the Brave there is no name that stirs the common patriotism of Irishmen. After his death feuds and strifes increased, and it was by invitation of an Irish chief that Strongbow and his armed followers invaded the island. It was from the Pope (Adrian IV.) that King Henry II. received his commission to annex it to the English Crown. Patriotic orators forget this, or trust to the ignorance of their hearers, when they combine Popery and Liberty in their declamation. The Pope of Rome "blessed" the sword that struck down Irish freedom, and Ireland can never be truly free till the ban of Popery is removed.

But Rome had already sent invaders, who brought upon Ireland woes more ruinous than those of the armed Normans. Papal emissaries had come, who treated the Irish Christians as if they were worse than heathens. The "rude and ignorant people" paid no respect to the Bishop of Rome as the Vicar of Christ, did not worship the Virgin nor Saints, did not venerate relics, elected bishops without lawful authority, paid no tithes or firstfruits, worshipped in irregular forms, and sent no Peter's pence to the Pope! But after St. Malachy, the Romanizing reformer, and his companions had been among these "Christians in name, Pagans in deed," St. Bernard, his biographer, records that "rudeness gave way, barbarism was allayed; the rugged race began gradually to be softened, gradually to admit correction, and submit to discipline. The barbarous rule was put away; the Roman rule was introduced; the customs of the Church were everywhere received; the contrary customs were rejected. . . . In fine, all things were so much changed for the better, that it might be said of that nation, in the words of the prophet, 'A people which before was not mine is become my people.'"

There was resistance for a time among the Irish clergy, as there was resistance among the clergy of the early British Church to the emissaries of Rome, but with the aid of the strong arm of power, the rule of Rome was firmly established. When the Norman barons came over in the time of Henry II. the ancient Church of Ireland was reduced to submission.

Modern Irish patriots sympathize with the Irish chiefs who were subdued by the ruthless invaders of the island; why do they not also sympathize with the Irish bishops who were forced into subjection to the Papacy, and compelled to receive the novelties of Romanism, instead of the faith of the early Church, and of their own St. Patrick and St. Columba? The conquest of Ireland in the twelfth century was not a conquest by England, but by Rome, and by the Norman kings and barons with the banner of Rome.

"The history of Ireland from the Conquest to the Union is the miserable history of a half-subdued dependency. Its annals are the weary annals of aggression on the one side and of rebellion on the other; of aggression sometimes more sometimes less cruel and systematic, of rebellion sometimes more sometimes less violent and extensive, but of aggression and of rebellion without end. Few are the points, few are the characters of moral interest in such a story. It is a long agony, of which the only interest lies in the prospect of its long-deferred close." Such are the words in which Professor Goldwin Smith begins his lectures on "Irish History and Character," the best book that has been written on the subject.

Mr. Froude, in his American lectures, and in his recently published volume, has re-opened many old chapters of Irish history. It is a great intellectual treat to read what he writes on the subject, but for the practical work of legislation and administration in our day, these historical retrospects are of little advantage. In fact, they do more harm than good, by stirring up angry feelings about long-forgotten strifes and divisions. Mr. Froude heard that O'Donovan Rossa, the Fenian convict, was making a tour in the United States, dilating upon English tyranny and the wrongs of Ireland. "Irish patriotism has many charges to bring against England which can be but too well substantiated. There are features, however, in the long tragical story," Mr. Froude said, "which, if they do not palliate, at least explain and make intelligible much that we could wish undone—features which naturally enough the Irish overlook, yet which should be borne in mind if an impartial judgment is to be formed of the controversy." He felt, too, how great an influence America possesses in Ireland, and so resolved to go over to give some lectures on Anglo-Irish history. It was a generous impulse, and has been well carried out. The Americans have had the historical case laid before them, and they can correct any wrong judgment they had formed. It is their business quite as much as ours, for all these events happened before the Declaration of Independence.

The truth is that the Americans know all about Ireland as well as most Englishmen do, and they have their own "Irish difficulty." There is an Irish nation in the American Republic larger than in the British Empire, and the most troublesome section it is of the commonwealth, to both governments. Mr. Froude's mission was in this respect somewhat needless, but in regard to its influence on Ireland itself, it has been already attended with evil rather than good result. Father Bourke's replies to the lectures, repeating to sympathizing audiences all the false and libellous abuse of England, have been published in the cheap Irish newspapers, and in a sixpenny pamphlet widely circulated. Mr. Froude's stately orations will not be read by many hundreds in Ireland, and can have no effect on the popular feeling towards England.

It is a mistake altogether to go back to old times for explanation of the alleged grievances and wrongs of Ireland in the present. The wildest Fenian never speaks of disturbing the former settlements of property, the most recent of which has prescriptive rights of two centuries standing. There may sometimes be poetical and rhetorical rhapsodies about Saxon robbers, but in the political arguments even of the Home Rulers, the complete fusion of all the races now inhabiting Ireland is a settled point. "There is scarcely an Irishman," says one of the ablest of the Home Rule advocates, "there is scarcely an Irishman of Celtic name, a Maguire, or an O'Donoghue, or a Sullivan, without some Saxon or Norman lineage; scarcely a Butt, or a Martin, a Smyth, a Shaw, or a Daunt, whose Saxon or Norman blood has not had a Celtic intermingling. All are in birth, in race, and in feeling, Irishmen; and to speak of them as descendants of people conquered by Great Britain betrays confusion of thought and inaccuracy of language, not to speak of its being a revival of reminiscences which had better be let die."

It is not of any practical importance, but to the disparaging way in which Mr. Froude refers to the ancient Irish laws and customs, I take exception, as a matter of history. He echoes the contemptuous remarks of the English chroniclers, who in ignorance of the language were unable to form fair judgment of the Irish social state. The Brehon law was a codification of the chief customs which regulated the social and domestic life, as well as the public relations of the chiefs or kings, and their clansmen or subjects. Many things may appear strange and even barbarous to us, but some of these arose from abuses and perversions of the ancient customs. These customs had descended from earlier times, and had been preserved by the Kymry in their migration from the east. I have no hesitation in affirming that on many points the Brehon law was far superior to the Norman and English law by which it was supplanted. It represented patriarchal instead of feudal government.

It does not seem to be known, or has been little mentioned, by writers on the ancient Irish laws and customs, that many of these were found till a far later period among the Highlanders of Scotland. Even the characteristic names of many customs were preserved. As a curious illustration I may mention that there is, or was lately, in Glenfinnan, at Fassiefern, the ancestral home of the Camerons, a house pointed out as that of "the *Tanister* of Lochiel," or the next heir to the chief. At the time of the rebellion in '45, John Cameron, of Fassiefern, brother of the "gentle Lochiel," was Tanister, and occupied the house, a drawing of which was given in a Memoir of Colonel Cameron of the 92nd, who fell at Quatre Bras. This work, by the Rev. Archibald Clark, minister of Kilmallie, printed for private circulation at the cost of Sir Duncan Cameron, Bart., of Fassiefern, contains curious details about ancient Highland customs and legends. The colonel was nursed by the wife of one of his father's tenants, whose son, Ewen M'Millan, the foster-brother, attended him in youth, followed him through the wars, and was at his side when he fell at Quatre Bras. "Kindred to twenty (degrees). fosterage to a hundred;" "Woe to the father of the foster-son unfaithful to his trust," are old Gaelic sayings in the Scottish Highlands.

The chapter of the past political history of Ireland which it is most important to keep in remembrance, is that which relates to the penal laws, partly because the shadow of that dark epoch was projected into our own times, and partly because while persecution of the Catholics continued, and civil disabilities remained, it was useless to expect any good influence to be exercised by Protestants, either in Church or State, on those by whom they were feared and hated. Is any reader in these happier and more tolerant times ignorant of the cruel enactments generically known as the Irish Penal Code? Here are some of them. No Papist could hold any office, civil or military, serve on grand juries, or vote at elections. No Papist could be at the bar, and barristers or solicitors marrying Papists were subject to penalties. No Papist could purchase land, or take

A Chapter on Irish History.

a lease of land for more than thirty-one years. If the profits of land leased by a Papist exceeded an amount settled by Parliament, the farm passed to the Protestant informer. If the son of a Papist turned Protestant, the father's estate could no longer be sold, or charged with debt or legacy. No Papist could be in a line of entail; the estate passed to the next Protestant heir, as if the Papist were dead. If a Papist died intestate, and no Protestant heir appeared, the property was equally divided among all the sons, or, if there were no sons, among all the daughters. No Papist could be legal guardian to his own son. If a child declared himself a Protestant, he was delivered to the guardianship of some Protestant relation. If the son enrolled the certificate of conversion in the Court of Chancery, the Court compelled the father on oath to state the value of his property, and to make a competent allowance for the son for maintenance. Property could not be held in trust for Papists. Papists keeping schools were chargeable with felony. If children were sent to any Papist seminary abroad, the parents were fined, and the children declared incapable of inheriting property. Surely with truth Edmund Burke said of the Penal Code, "It is a truly barbarous system, where all the parts are an outrage on the laws of humanity and the rights of nature: it is a system of elaborate contrivance as well fitted for the oppression and degradation of a people, and the debasement of human nature itself, as ever proceeded from the perverted ingenuity of man."

The law against suspected persons was one of the most grievous of all the penal enactments, as it meddled with those who sought no public notoriety, and were willing to live quiet and peaceable lives. "Two justices may summon any person whom they shall suspect to be disaffected, by writing under their hands and seals, to appear before them at a time prefixed, to take the oaths of allegiance, supremacy, and abjuration, which summons shall be served on such person, or left at his dwelling-house or usual place of abode, with one of the family there; and if such person shall neglect or refuse to appear, then, on due proof made upon oath of serving the said summons, they shall certify the same to the next sessions, to be there recorded; and if such person shall neglect or refuse to appear and take the oaths at the said sessions (his name being publicly read at the first meeting of the said sessions), he shall be taken and adjudged a Popish recusant convict. And the same shall be from thence certified by the clerk of the peace into the Chancery or King's Bench, to be there recorded." For the unfortunate recusant thus recorded as convict, there remained not disabilities only, but manifold penalties and exactions, some of them not only unjust but mean, such as payment of double land tax, horses seized for militia service, with other insults and injuries.

While these enactments were in force, the wonder is, not that Ireland was disaffected, but that the nation did not rise long before in rebellion. The most atrocious portions of the Penal Code were destroyed before the Union, but it is only in our own time that Catholics have been admitted to equal civil and political rights with their Protestant fellow-citizens.

In regard to the persecution of Catholics, and the oppression of Ireland generally, it ought to be remembered that Irishmen were its chief oppressors, and that it was not the British Government, but the Irish Parliament, which imposed the worst parts of the Penal Code. English ministers and English lord-lieutenants often interfered to shelter the helplessly subjected Catholics from the cruel tyranny of the dominant Protestant oligarchy. It was not till far on in the reign of George III. that the national and patriotic party in the Irish Parliament obtained any influence. Before 1780 the Irish Parliament never touched the penal laws, and when the relaxation of persecution began, Irishmen were the stoutest opponents of the movement. Flood is sometimes spoken of as a national patriot, but his eloquence was constantly exercised in shutting out the Catholics from political power, and maintaining the laws of the Protestant ascendancy. The crowning Relief Act of 1793 was admitted by Grattan himself to be due mainly to the liberality of the English Government.

It ought also to be remembered, especially by such anti-English orators as Father Bourke and other ecclesiastics, when they speak about the oppression of Ireland for seven hundred years, that, for four centuries out of the seven, England was Catholic, not Reformed, and the worst woes of Ireland flowed from the grant of that kingdom to Norman rulers by the Pope.

CHAPTER X.

THE QUESTION OF RACE.

Fusion of Races—Irish Nationality—The Scottish Highlanders—Welsh Nationality.

"ALIENS in blood, language, and religion!" It was an unfortunate phrase of Lord Lyndhurst, and we know what use was made of it by Sheil, and less scrupulous agitators. But what of this question of race? How far has it to do with the history, or how far is it answerable for the woes, of Ireland? Whatever influence race may have had in olden times, it certainly is a small element in the actual condition of the people. In regard to the upper classes and upper middle classes, it would be hard for any ethnologist to analyse the social blood of Irishmen. Phœnician, Spanish, Milesian, Celtic, Scandinavian, Norman, Anglo-Saxon, French, Scotch,—there never was a greater fusion and confusion of race in any land. Lord Desart made a good point in criticising Mr. Froude's attacks on Irish landlords. "In the desire to free the Irish peasant from the yoke of landlordism," says Mr. Froude, " I do not yield to the most irreconcileable Fenian." "What," retorts Lord Desart, "is this mysterious yoke? Is it the payment of rent? If so, then the yoke is worse in England, for rents in Ireland are allowed to be excessively low. If all property is robbery, and the land belongs to the tillers of the soil, a quite different line of argument is opened up, and rather a long one; but it has no particular reference to Ireland, her history, her land laws, or Fenianism. As property just at present does exist, it exists equally in Middlesex and in Leinster, though perhaps the Land Act has rather shaken people's faith in it over here. If the yoke is, that a majority of the landlords are Protestants,—but I need not discuss this, as Mr. Froude has elsewhere said that he approves the arrangement. There remains only that the landlords are not national, not thoroughly acclimatized; and although I do not believe that this has any weight with Mr. Froude, still it is so favourite a weapon of the lower class of agitators, that it is quite worth notice.

"Perhaps the majority of large landowners in the south of Ireland came over either in Elizabeth's or Cromwell's time. Of course they were English enough then, and perhaps they are English too much now; but I do not understand the principle on which they could be deprived of their landlordism for this reason, unless, indeed, there be a hard-and-fast line drawn by some eminent natural history teller, which limits the power of nationalization. If a family which has been in Ireland since 1665 is not Irish, when is it to be? When will the representative of it be allowed to claim kindred with the people? In 1972 or 2072?"

The same repudiation of nationality for the higher classes in Ireland appears in an able book by Mr. John George MacCarthy, "A Plea for the Home Government of Ireland:"—"Saxons and Normans came over here in vast numbers and incessantly for centuries. After the longest strife in history they made good their ground, and effected a compromise with the Celtic population, in which the latter got the worst of the bargain. It may be doubtful whether the Celtic races were conquered; but there is no doubt that the in-coming races were not conquered. These were the conquerors, if any conquest there were. *Their blood is in all our veins: both races have been fused long ago.*"

And again, "The Celtic, Saxon, and Norman races are in reality almost as much fused in Ireland as they are in Great Britain. They are inextricably mingled together in all social, commercial, and neighbourly relations throughout the country: nay, as we have seen, they are actually intermingled in the lineage and the blood of most Irishmen."

When the tenants or labourers in Ireland talk of "the ould stock," or of "the family," Saxon or Celt are never thought of. When they "came over," or whether they came over, or whether they bear the name of ancient Milesian chiefs and kings, it matters nothing; "the family" means the possessors of the property for two or three generations, and the attachment is the same for a Burke or a Boyle as for an O'Donoghue or O'Brien. No Highland clansman or feudal retainer could do or suffer more than the poor Irish will "for the sake of the family" of a resident landlord. In the most famous of Maria Edgeworth's Irish tales, "Castle Rackrent," Thady Quirk, "honest Thady," "old Thady," "poor Thady," was as attached to the Rackrent family as his grandfather ever had been to the O'Loughlins, from whom the property had passed. It was all "out of friendship for the family, upon whose estate, praised be Heaven! I and mine have lived time out of mind."

Hear Lord Desart again: "I do not think that the average Irish tenant looks upon his landlord as a tyrant. I have, in my very limited sphere, found nothing but kindness and good feeling among the farmers and peasantry, and I have had the luck to see and to experience gratitude for any little, perhaps worthless kindness I have been able to do, which I am sure was not occasioned, as Mr. Froude somewhat unworthingly sneers, by the fact that "they had experienced so little of it!" But perhaps if he did tell them of it they would afterwards feel it. As a rule a farmer in Ireland, when he hears all the vaporous nonsense of the Fenians, or the silly rhapsody of the Home Rulers, smiles disdainfully, seeing through their shallow sophistry. But when it is whispered in his ear, 'What we really mean is that you shall have your farm rent free,' it is a different matter. Whisper the same thing to an English or Scottish farmer, and if he believe you he will join the Patriotic Club at once."

It is true that the mass of the peasantry in the south and west are more purely Celtic. But does this necessarily mean that they are less Irish? They are not aliens in language now, thanks to the progress of education, and if they are aliens in religion, and disaffected in politics, this is not an immutable property of the race. Circumstances have made them what they are, and there are moral influences stronger than the elements of blood and race, as the history of the Celtic Welsh or Scottish Highlanders can prove.

There are some who ascribe the contrast between the north and south of Ireland to race and not to religion. The dominant race in Popish parts of Ireland they say is Celtic. The Ulster people are mainly of the same race as the Scottish Lowlanders. But what of the Scottish Highlanders? Hugh Miller says, "The Papists of Ireland and the Protestants of the Highlands (both Celtic) have this much in common, that they are poor, very poor; but the difference is, that crime, which is a prevailing condition with the first, is comparatively unknown among the second. The one are poor and criminal, the other are content to be poor. Now we ask, how does it happen that both being equally in a bad physical condition, and weighed down by the same sufferings, the Irish Catholics are flagrant violators of the laws (he was then referring to agrarian outrages), while the Protestant Highlanders are exemplary for their virtuous and peaceful conduct? The political misgovernment of Ireland, however bad it may be, is nothing compared with the terrible social and moral disorganization which reigns there, and certainly it is this last evil which leaves the least hope for the future of Ireland. Now to what is it to be ascribed if not to Protestantism that the Scottish Highlanders, in the midst of the greatest privations, have maintained their social and moral character intact, while the Irish, deprived of this preserving salt, and having instead of it a principle of disorder and debasement, have broken down into complete corruption? Can we have any more striking proof of the innate vigour and purity of true Protestantism on the one hand, and on the other of the innate depravity and ruinous tendency of Popery? We do not say that the Highlanders are faultless. They have their faults, but the crimes which have rendered Ireland so unhappily famous throughout the world are not among the Scottish Highlanders. Where do they find among them the amount of homicides and murders committed in broad day, of midnight robberies and assassinations, of crimes which pollute the soil of Ireland? Is there to be found in the history of the Highlands for a century, a landlord murdered by his own tenants upon his own threshold? Where will they find the perjured witnesses, and the juries who refuse to give a verdict, paralyzing the law and arresting the course of justice? Where are the soldiers to keep the Highlanders in awe? When the Queen goes into the north to live among these Highlanders without law and faith, how many regiments are deemed necessary to protect her person? Not a sentinel is seen near her castle."

It may be said that the Celtic character has died out in Scotland, while it is persistent in Ireland. Grant even this for argument sake. Then how is it that the Celtic race in its purest state is not able to withstand the same influence which has changed Scotland? The transformation may be witnessed in the island of Achill, at Dingle, and many places in Galway, thoroughly Celtic districts, a change from degrading superstition to elevating faith and its fruits.

In speaking of the Celtic race as opposed to the Saxon, and of the hatred of the Irish to the English, it is natural to turn to the other branches of the Celtic race in Great Britain, and see what light can be obtained from their history. The Highlanders of Scotland are as purely Celtic as the Irish, and were at no distant period in chronic rebellion against the Southerners. They are now the most loyal and orderly and exemplary of all the people under Her Majesty's dominion. Politicians may doubt or sneer, but the one great cause of the revolution in Highland feeling was the propagation of the Gospel, and the Christian training of the people by a Protestant ministry. The same revolution has taken place in North Wales, where the hatred of England was as intense as in any part of Ireland. On this point I give the testimony of a remarkable Welshman, the late Rev. William Howels, of Long Acre Chapel. His name may be known to few in the present day, but his chapel was a place of resort forty years ago for many of the most distinguished men of the time. In the Life of the Duchess of Gordon, and in the

Remains of Mr. Bowdler, interesting records are preserved of this man of genius and piety. The Earl of Roden, Viscount and Viscountess Powerscourt, and other Irish notables were members of his church. Mr. Howels used to say that the one antidote to the ills of Ireland was in the spread of scriptural truth, not by the English language only, but in the vernacular tongue of the Irish. He said, that "just as the Irish now look on the English, with hatred and disdain, so once did Welshmen regard Englishmen as their greatest enemies." And he gave an instance to show how deeply rooted that hatred was. A relative of Lord Talbot told him that riding in Wales he came to a river which he wished to cross. He asked a labouring man hard by, if he could cross in safety, speaking in English. The man said he could. However, the horse knew better, and refused to go. He then asked the same question in Welsh; the man answered, "Sir, I beg your pardon, I thought you were an Englishman. If you attempt to cross here, you will be drowned." It was at a meeting of the Hibernian Society, for spreading the Gospel among the Irish, that Mr. Howels told this anecdote, and he continued, "Nothing but the Gospel can overcome such bigoted national hatred as this. The same remedy which anglicised Wales can alone be effectual in Ireland also. Ireland must be reconquered by being brought under the Gospel yoke. Many quack doctors have been trying to heal her wounds, but all their attempts have failed. To remedy her evils is beyond the power of politicians. Let us bring her to the Physician who is able to heal every disease. The Gospel is His panacea, and it is the one thing needful for Ireland. The Gospel only can unite her to England." Then Mr. Howels told his own Welsh experience as to national feeling. "I remember about the time of the first French Revolution my mind was so impregnated with hatred towards England from reading Welsh history, that I actully harangued my fellow-scholars on the propriety of shaking off the galling yoke of the Saxons. My hatred continued till I went to Oxford, and at Oxford the Gospel first reached my heart from the lips of an Englishman. From that time forth I loved Englishmen as warmly as before I hated them. There are hundreds of thousands in Ireland who bear the same rancorous hatred towards the English, whom nothing would better please than to slake their vengeance in the blood of our sons; nothing could subdue this hatred but the Gospel. Nothing but the Gospel can identify the Irish with us, and united to us by that tie, though all Europe, though the world in arms should surround our shores, we might bid them all defiance."

CHAPTER XI.

CATHOLIC AND PROTESTANT CONTRASTS.

The Real Root of Ireland's Sorrows—Protestant and Catholic Lands Contrasted—North and South of Ireland—The Remedy for Ireland's Troubles.

IN the second volume of the Life of Charles Dickens, in the account of his residence in Switzerland, we read the following, in a letter to Mr. Forster: "I don't know whether I have mentioned before, that in the valley of the Simplon hard by here, where (at the Bridge of St. Maurice over the Rhone) this Protestant Canton (Vaud) ends and a Catholic Canton begins, you might separate two perfectly distinct and different conditions of humanity, by drawing a line with your stick in the dust on the ground. On the Protestant side, neatness, cheerfulness, industry, education, continued aspiration, at least, after better things. On the Catholic side, dirt, disease, ignorance, squalor, and misery. I have so constantly observed the like of this, since I first came abroad, that I have a sad misgiving that the religion of Ireland lies as deep at the root of all its sorrows even as English misgovernment and Tory villainy." *

"I have a sad misgiving that the religion of Ireland lies at the root of all its sorrows!" If this were said in a speech at Exeter Hall, or by a Protestant zealot, it might be set down to prejudice and bigotry. But it is the conclusion at which a man so "liberal" in religious views as Charles Dickens was led by personal observation. The idea was apparently new to him, or at least the expression of it; as it seems also to be to his biographer, who remarks that "something of the same kind appears in one of Lord Macaulay's later works." The passage to which Mr. Forster alludes is in one of Lord Macaulay's most celebrated essays, originally printed in the *Edinburgh* as a review of Ranke's "History of the Popes." He is comparing the social condition of the Catholic and Protestant nations of Europe. "The geographical frontier between the two religions has continued to run almost precisely where it ran at the close of the Thirty Years' War, nor has Protestantism given any proof of that expansive power which has been ascribed to

---

* In another letter, from Geneva, in 1846, describing the opposing parties at the time, Mr. Dickens says, "If I were a Swiss I would be as steady against the Catholic cantons and the propagation of Jesuitism as any radical among them; believing the dissemination of Catholicity to be the most horrible means of political and social degradation left in the world."

it. But the Protestant boasts, and boasts most justly, that wealth, civilization, and intelligence have increased far more on the northern than on the southern side of the boundary, and that countries so little favoured as Scotland and Prussia are now among the most flourishing and best governed portions of the world; while the marble palaces of Genoa are deserted, while banditti infest the fruitful shores of Campania, while the fertile sea-coast of the Pontifical States is abandoned to buffaloes and wild boars. It cannot be doubted that since the sixteenth century the Protestant nations have made decidedly greater progress than their neighbours. The progress made by those nations in which Protestantism, though not finally successful, yet maintained a long struggle and left permanent traces, has generally been considerable. But when we come to the Catholic land, to the part of Europe in which the first spark of reformation was trodden out as soon as it appeared, and from which proceeded the impulse which drove Protestantism back, we find at best a very slow progress, and on the whole a retrogression. Compare Denmark and Portugal. When Luther began to preach, the superiority of the Portuguese was unquestionable. At present, the superiority of the Danes is no less so. Compare Edinburgh and Florence. Edinburgh has owed less to climate, to soil, and to the fostering care of rulers, than any capital, Protestant or Catholic. In all these respects Florence has been singularly happy. Yet whoever knows what Florence and Edinburgh were in the generation preceding the Reformation, and what they are now, will acknowledge that some great cause has, during the last three centuries, operated to raise one part of the European family and to depress the other. Compare the history of England and that of Spain during the last century. In arms, arts, sciences, letters, commerce, agriculture, the contrast is most striking. The distinction is not confined to this side the Atlantic. The colonies planted by England in America have immeasurably outgrown in power those planted by Spain; yet we have no reason to believe that at the beginning of the sixteenth century the Castilian was in any respect inferior to the Englishman. Our firm belief is, that the north owes its great civilization and prosperity chiefly to the moral effect of the Protestant Reformation, and that the decay of the southern countries is to be mainly ascribed to the great Catholic revival."

The same truth has been illustrated by many writers. "It is religion," says M. de Tocqueville, "that has given form to the Anglo-Saxon communities in America. In the United States, religion is blended with the national customs, and with all those feelings that one's native land inspires; this gives it a special influence." "The Americans blend so completely in their minds the idea of Christianity with that of liberty, that it is nearly impossible to bring them to conceive the existence of the one apart from the other." "There are European populations whose infidelity is only equalled by their depravity and ignorance, whilst in America we see one of the most free and enlightened nations in the world cheerfully fulfilling all the outward duties of religion. On my arrival in the United States it was the religious aspect of the country which first attracted my attention. By degrees, as I prolonged my stay, I perceived the great political results of these facts, so new to me. Among ourselves I had seen the spirit of religion and the spirit of liberty almost always move in opposite directions. Here I found them closely connected."

I have quoted these sentences from De Tocqueville because they serve to define the points on which comparison is to be made between Catholic and Protestant lands. Some Romish writers, in attempting to meet the statements as to the influence of these opposite systems of religion, have, either ignorantly or wilfully, included under the term "Protestant," all opinions outside the Church of Rome, thus including infidelity, which is as great a source of misery and crime as is Popery. It is an old trick in Romish controversialists to put down all crimes, from the days of Luther downwards, to "the spirit of Protestantism," which culminated in the Reign of Terror during the French Revolution. M. de Tocqueville understood this, when he spoke of European populations whose infidelity is only equalled by their depravity and ignorance. In these results, popery and infidelity are much alike, as the state of many countries proves, where the religion of the Bible is unknown.

Hear M. Quinet, also speaking of the United States as contrasted with papist parts of America: "The Protestant principle is realized there with a manifest result; and it is surprising that many writers amongst us who have treated of American democracy have only seen in these institutions the vague influence of religion in general. Whereas these institutions bear the exclusive stamp of the Reformation, of the religion of the open Bible and of the Gospel."

Belgium may at first sight appear an exception to the general principle which has been tested in other countries, being industrious and prosperous, and yet a Roman Catholic state. But what is the real condition of Belgium? It has a teeming population, with vast mineral resources and manufacturing advantages. I turn to the official reports recently published in the Consular Blue Book relating to the condition of the working classes in the various countries of Europe. It is a fact that a very large proportion of the entire population of Belgium are on the lists of poor relief, and these are for the most part the lower grades of working men and their families, whose social condition is truly deplorable. Intemperance is not a national vice among the Belgians more than in England, so that this element in their degradation is not conspicuous; yet the poverty of the Belgian workmen is apparent, and pauperism abundant. Popery is the demoralizing influence. In health there are temptations in the multitude of saints' fête days and holidays, so numerous that the workmen lose a sixth and often a fourth of their whole working days. In sickness and poverty there are too many charities to which application can be made, relief being always ready at convents and in the workhouses. The growth of independence of spirit is thereby prevented, and prudent habits discouraged. This is certainly one cause of the low *morale* and wretched condition of the working classes. There is no lack of free schools, yet great ignorance prevails, and the grossest superstition as its sure concomitant. In 1867, of the recruits drawn for the militia, forty per cent. were unable to read or write. The proportion is said to have diminished in the last four years, but there is ignorance and misery enough to dispel the fancy of Belgium being an exception to the demoralizing national result of Romish influence.

This contrast between Catholic and Protestant nations has been often made.* The contrast has been also drawn between different parts of the same country. Mr. Dickens was not the first to describe the relative condition of the Catholic and Protestant cantons of Switzerland. The great inroad of foreigners upon this holiday ground of Europe, and the more serious invasion of French social and political life, have of late years made the contrast less conspicuous than it once was, but still what a difference between Lucerne and Basle, between Friburg and Berne!

One traveller, M. Raoul Rochette, says of the two last-named cantons, "Without an inspection of the heraldic insignia, the eye of the traveller will at once detect the line of demarcation between the cantons of Friburg and Berne. We cannot go fifty yards on the road without being sensible of the difference. Never, perhaps, within so short a distance, and in the same

---

* Never more remarkably than by Mons. Nadaud, in his recent able "History of English Workmen," in which he devotes a whole chapter to the statement and illustration of the historical fact, that Popery has ever been hostile to liberty and social progress, Protestantism the reverse. Nadaud was a member of the French Legislature, in exile here, during the Empire, for his republican opinions. In a work by M. Napoleon Roussell, "Catholic and Protestant Nations Compared," many historical and statistical proofs will be also found.

country, do we meet with signs so striking of the different effects of government." This testimony is the more remarkable, as the writer goes on to ascribe the difference to administration, without referring to the religion of the people. Another traveller says, "On leaving the canton of Friburg we enter the smiling, prosperous vale of the Canton de Vaud. The pleasure of the contrast detained us for hours." And a Frenchman, M. Cambry, entering the same canton from the side of France, says, "In a moment you pass from the poverty, the disorder, and the neglect of the Pays de Gex (Catholic) to the Canton de Vaud, where all is order, industry, and propriety."

One more quotation I must give, as it contains the testimony of a writer whose philosophical spirit and freedom from bigotry will not be questioned, M. Sismondi. "The Grimsel marks the division between the Catholic cantons of southern Switzerland and the Protestant cantons of the north. Again the contrast in the moral, social, and religious influence of the two forms of faith is forced upon us. That the comparison is altogether favourable to Protestantism cannot be doubted. It is admitted by the Romanists themselves. Leaving the Valais with its squalor and wretchedness, and crossing the pass into the bright, cheerful valley of Meyringen, everything seems thriving and prosperous. The partisan of Rome may endeavour to explain away the inference, but he cannot deny the fact." "We have cantons whose frontiers interlock with one another as do my fingers," said Sismondi to Mr. Shepherd, of Frome, "and you need not be told, a glance suffices to show you whether you are in a Protestant or Catholic canton." To the same traveller a Catholic priest admitted the fact, but with great *naïveté* explained it by saying, "The Bon Dieu knows that you heretics have no hope for another world, so he gives you compensation in this!" Even so zealous a Catholic as M. Raoul Rochette says, with regard to the mixed cantons of Appenzell and Glaris, "Generally the Catholics have continued to be shepherds, while the Protestants have turned their attention to trade or manufactures. The poverty of the former contrasts with the comfort of the latter, so that at first sight it would seem to be better in this world to live among the Protestants than the Catholics, but there is another world in which this inferiority is perhaps compensated!"

At the time when I am writing, a few days after Christmas, the price of the British Government consols is $91\frac{1}{2}$ per cent.; of the Spanish 3 per cent. Government loan the price is $28\frac{1}{2}$. The price of United States six per cent. Government stock is $92\frac{1}{2}$; of Mexican three per cents., $17\frac{1}{2}$. Portuguese three per cents. are 43; French Rentes, 52. Prussia has no stock on the market, having no national debt. Italian five per cents. are 48. We must be cautious in drawing any conclusions from what is a purely commercial list, as to the social or political condition of the countries whose public stocks are daily priced in the money market. Many special circumstances, both financial and historical, must be known and taken into account. The student of the list must consider, for instance, the depression of France as the consequence of the war with Prussia; and the difference between the value of Spanish and Portuguese stock as due to the less settled political state of the former kingdom. But making due allowance for all exceptional or disturbing causes, it is apparent at a glance that certain countries possess the influence and security arising from settled government and healthy political condition, and that these countries are Protestant. No temporary or exceptional causes can produce the contrast between the Government credit of Great Britain and Spain, a difference of $91\frac{1}{2}$ to $28\frac{1}{2}$; or, taking in Portugal also, $91\frac{1}{2}$ to 35. Equally striking is the contrast between the Protestant and Catholic republics in America, the Government securities being in the relative value of 46 to 17. In both these instances, in all natural advantages of climate, fertility, mineral wealth, and the elements of material prosperity, the Catholic countries have the advantage. If

Scotland and Ireland were to-day both separated from England, and both enjoyed home rule, and had a loan in the market, what would be the difference of value? and why?

The contrast between different provinces or districts of Ireland is not so marked as between countries wholly Catholic or Protestant, or as in the Swiss cantons. It is a country of mixed population; not merely mixed in the sense of partly the one and partly the other religion in different localities, but so intermingled in the same provinces as to make the contrast not at once evident. Add to this that in Protestant countries the Roman Catholic Church is so modified in its outward aspects, as to be scarcely recognizable as identical with the Church of dark ages and dark countries. In Ireland the people can no longer be kept in ignorance, for "the schoolmaster is abroad." Even Sunday-schools are becoming common among Roman Catholics,—a thing unheard of at no distant time. It must be remembered also that to Protestants the Catholics are chiefly indebted for these educational advantages, the national schools being mainly supported by a parliamentary grant. Nearly all the charitable schools also, before the national system commenced, were supported by Protestant contributions; the Kildare-street schools, the London Irish Society, and others, as well as the Irish Church Mission schools of the present day. In the face of all these educational appliances, the Catholic people cannot be kept in ignorance, as in former times, or as in countries where Protestants do not stir them to emulation. Their bishops cannot check this flow of knowledge, though their effort is to obtain the control and guidance of it.

Yet, making all due allowance for the number of Catholics in the north of Ireland, and of Protestants in the south, and for the modified character of Popery in the presence of the reformed faith, the contrast between Ulster and the other provinces is notorious. Here is the testimony of a Catholic traveller: " I left," says M. Prevost, " the industrious colonies of the north, and suddenly the scene changed, and I found again the deserts, the bogs, the hovels, in which live the miserable people." The same traveller in another part of his journal says: " Kilkenny was an important town when Belfast was only a village: it had several factories, eleven water-mills, and such a carpet factory that its English rival, to avoid the competition, demanded the repeal of the Union. In 1781 Belfast was an unimportant place, with a poor harbour, and the revenue of the port only £1,500." The statistics of population alone will suffice to show the progress of the northern borough. In 1782 it was 13,000; at the Union about 20,000; in 1821, in round numbers, 37,000; in 1831, 53,000; in 1841, 75,000; in 1851, 100,000; in 1861,

119,242; and in 1871, 174,394. Kilkenny at the last census had 15,609. As an inland town it could not be expected to increase largely, but it had the elements both of mining and manufacturing prosperity, if the people had the energy to use them. With far greater advantages, the city of Cork need not have allowed its northern and modern rival to get so far ahead. The population is about half that of Belfast.

To any one who has travelled or resided in Ireland it is waste of time to tell of the contrast between the Catholic and Protestant provinces. But a few statistical facts will be understood by strangers. Of the 25,000 troops usually stationed in Ireland scarcely 3,000 are in Ulster, and these chiefly in the border counties. Of the 13,000 constabulary less than 2,000 are in Ulster. Of committals for crime not one-sixth are in the north, though in other places the difficulty of obtaining evidence on conviction, from conspiracy and connivance, makes the proportion less than actually exists. During the famine-time, out of £10,000,000 relief money not £1,000,000 went to Ulster; and of this a large part was for the poor Catholics, who flocked thither from less prosperous parts of the country. Everywhere throughout Ireland at that sad time, the great mass of the relieved were Catholics, of the relievers Protestants. With one-third of the whole population, Ulster's share of the police, jail, and poor-law expenses is not above one-eighth. Its pauperism, its crime, its poor-rates are all less; its education, its wealth, its industry, its benevolent and religious institutions are all more, in proportion to the numbers of the people. In short, there is a condition of social and moral health, and an atmosphere of prosperity in the north, utterly diverse from the south, with its filthy cabins, swarming beggars, decaying villages, and its Catholic faith. The contrast is the more striking when we remember that in some of the northern counties the Catholic population is large, and also in some of the towns, especially Belfast and Derry, where a considerable portion of the lower labouring class is from the south; but notwithstanding this mixture of population, the contrast between Ulster and Munster is almost as marked as between the Protestant and Catholic cantons of Switzerland.

Dr. John Forbes, author of "A Physician's Holiday," in his book on Ireland, said, "One of the objects I had constantly in view in my journey being to ascertain practically, from actual examination and inquiry, the relative numbers of the adherents of the two religions among the great body of the people, I naturally took advantage of the great facilities afforded to me on this point by the schools and workhouses. The workhouses, more especially, peopled as they are exclusively by the most destitute members of the community, are calculated to supply the best possible criteria for determining this point in regard to the most numerous class of the people. Those who have taken the trouble to follow me in my visits to the individual unions cannot fail to have been struck with the great superiority of the numbers of the Catholic inmates, not merely in the more Catholic parts of Ireland, but even in the most Protestant districts of Ulster itself. In going back over the reports I have given of the individual workhouses I find the general result is as follows: In seven of the unions in the south and west of Ireland the proportion of Catholics to Protestants is about forty-two to one ; in five of the unions in Ulster, together with that of Sligo (in which the proportion of the Protestants is large), the proportion is about five Catholics to one Protestant ; taking all the unions together, the general proportion is about twenty Catholics to one Protestant." The proportion of the population of all Ireland at the time was about five Catholics to one Protestant.

Dr. Forbes' testimony as to the general result of the Catholic religion to produce inferiority in the social condition of its adherents, is the more weighty, as he is among those professed liberals who would have endowed the Catholic Church. "The easiest and simplest mode of bringing about the equalization of the Churches is that which, by merely putting an end to the present Church Establishment, would leave all the three Churches of Ireland in the same predicament of Free or Voluntary Churches, to look for support from their respective members; the revenues of the present Churches being assumed by the State, and devoted to the purposes of national education. A second mode would be for the State, after the assumption of the Church revenues, to redistribute them equally among all the ministers of the three Churches; the national education being supported as at present by Government. Of these two modes of dealing with this great matter I confess I have a strong leaning in favour of that which contemplates the paying of the clergy."

I think it of interest to recall this opinion, as it certainly represented the judgment of the majority of Englishmen up to within a few years ago. Among Dr. Forbes' Scottish countrymen there was a stronger minority against endowment, but even among the religious classes in England, and especially among Churchmen, this was the desired solution of the ecclesiastical difficulties of Ireland. The fear of the question of disestablishment being raised in England, was the chief element in the "levelling-up" principle as to Ireland. But the march of events decided otherwise, and the three Churches will now contend on equal terms, with a free field and no State favour legally shown. Some time must pass before statistics of any value can be obtained as to the social results of Protestantism under its new conditions. Judging by the past, and by the wonderful expansive power of the unendowed free churches in Scotland, we may expect, even before the year of another census comes round, to see the beginning of greater changes than have yet taken place in the relative power of the Catholic and Protestant religions, in respect to the moral and social condition of the Irish people.

In former times the clans of Scotland were as wild and lawless and uncivilized as the septs of Ireland. They remained so during the ages of Popery. It is as the light of the Gospel spread after the Reformation, in some parts in comparatively recent times, that they have become peaceable, law-abiding, and God-fearing. With change of religion there has been social and civilizing change. So poor a country cannot be made rich by religion, but the moral influence of Protestantism is conspicuous the more amidst its poverty. It is this which gives the best-grounded hope for the possibility of Ireland's regeneration. What the Gospel and Protestantism have done for the Celtic race in Wales or Scotland can be done in Ireland also. Excepting by occasional and irregular impulse no attempt has, till very recently, been made to spread the reformed faith in the Popish districts. The Presbyterian Church was chiefly confined to Ulster; the Established Church chiefly looked after its own members. Now and then a zealous minister laboured among the Roman Catholic and Irish-speaking people, but these were only exceptional cases. That so little impression has been made on Roman Catholicism during three centuries might seem strange, but for the fact that the only rational means were not employed for the work. The same necessity for using the Irish language, at least to the same extent, does not now exist, for the native tongue is less used, and among the new generation, since the extension of education, English is becoming universally understood. The experience of the past gives no ground for discouragement, and the means now used for the spread of scriptural religion by the Protestant churches will in due time assuredly be effectual.

Edmund Spenser's famous "View of the Present State of Ireland" is well known and often quoted. So little has been done (till recently) for spreading scriptural truth among Catholics, that his description is in some things applicable to our own time. Spenser knew the real source of the evils which mere politicians vainly endeavour to remove. "The fault which I have to find in religion is but one, but the same is universal throughout all that country; that is, that they are all Papists by their profession, but in the same so blindly and brutishly informed, for the most part, that not one amongst a hundred knoweth any ground of religion or any article of his faith, but can say his Pater or his Ave Maria, without any knowledge or understanding what one word thereof meaneth." And among the remedies proposed, Spenser says that "true religion is the one hope for Ireland." "Yet in planting of religion thus much is needful to be observed, that it be not sought forcibly to be impressed with terror and sharp penalties, as now is the manner; but rather delivered and intimated with mildness and gentleness, so as it may not be hated before it is understood, and its professors despised and rejected. And therefore it is expedient that some discreet ministers of their own countrymen be sent over among them, which by their meek persuasions and instructions, as also by their sober lives and conversations, may draw them first to understand, and afterwards to embrace, the doctrine of their salvation." These were wise words of Edmund Spenser, but the advice was very slightly acted on. The first book printed in Irish was a catechism or primer, in 1571. In 1603 the New Testament was first translated, the Book of Common Prayer in 1608, and the Bible not till 1685. To show how little use was made of this agency, for which the pious and learned Mr. Boyle pleaded earnestly and contributed liberally, there was no reprint of the Irish New Testament between 1681 and 1811, nor of the Irish Bible between 1685 and 1817! The counsels of Spenser and Boyle, of Bedell and Usher, to carry the Gospel to the poor Irish, were never adequately carried out. Throughout the eighteenth century a deep slumber rested on the Protestant Church, broken only at intervals by the voices and labours of a few earnest men. One of these was the Rev. Nicholas Browne, a rector in the diocese of Clogher, early in that century. Understanding the language thoroughly, he used to read prayers and preach, just when mass was ended and before the people had dispersed. Crowds gathered round him, to the annoyance of the priests, when they heard what he was preaching. One of these called out during the prayers that the Protestants had stolen them from the Church of Rome. To which an old man replied, "Truly, if so, they had stolen the best, as thieves generally do." Dr. Samuel Madden in 1738 warmly advocated the appointment of itinerant preachers to speak to the Irish in their own tongue. A little later, this was again proposed, but in vain, by good Bishop Berkeley of Cloyne.

Bishop Berkeley put the matter in the form of delicate suggestions in his little book, "The Querist," asking, "Whether there be an instance of a people's being converted, in a Christian sense, otherwise than by preaching to them and instructing them in their own language? Whether catechists in the Irish tongue may not be easily procured and subsisted? And whether this would not be the most practicable means for converting the natives? Whether it be not of great advantage to the Church of Rome, that she hath clergy suited to all ranks of men in gradual subordination, from cardinals to mendicants? Whether her numerous poor clergy are not very useful in missions, and of much influence with the people? Whether in defect of able missionaries, persons conversant in low life, and speaking the Irish tongue, if well instructed in the first principles of religion and in the Popish controversy, though, for the rest, on a level with the parish-clerks, or the schoolmasters of charity-schools, may not be fit to mix with and bring over our poor illiterate natives to the Established Church? Whether it is not to be wished that some parts of our liturgy and homilies were publicly read in the Irish language? And whether in these views, it may not be right to breed up some of the better sort of children in the charity-schools, and qualify them for missionaries, catechists, and readers?"

What has been since attempted and effected will be presently referred to; my object here is to show that the absence of sufficient teaching left the native Irish under the influence of Popery, with its demoralizing consequences, both social and spiritual.

There was a clever cartoon two or three years ago in *Fun*. "Poor Ireland," "the sick sister" of the British family, is sitting in doleful plight, surrounded by above a dozen political doctors, every one pressing his peculiar specific. Dr. Russell offers his "Whig mixture," Dr. Bright a "land cordial," Dr. John Stuart Mill insists on severe "heroic remedies," while Dr. Gladstone recommends "generous treatment." A Communist shows a dangerous knife, a Romish priest has a prescription for "complete isolation." Dr. Disraeli is feeling the patient's pulse with puzzled shake of the head, while Dr. Robert Lowe in the background holds up his hands in hopeless despair of any good being done. The only true remedy (as usual with the press), is unrecognized. Give to Ireland the same reviving and restoring power which has made all Protestant nations healthy and prosperous, and she will yet rise to new life and strength. No palliative or mere political measures will do any permanent good, though they may remove some of the troublesome and irritating symptoms. Without an open Bible, and without religious freedom, poor Ireland will still remain the sick sister of the British family.

In speaking of Protestantism, it is not merely the

system antagonistic to Popery that is meant. A negative theology or atheistic system would be worse for Ireland than the reign of priestcraft and superstition. When Queen Victoria presented a Bible to the African chief, and said that this was the secret of England's greatness, the same truth was proclaimed which we intend in saying that Protestantism will save Ireland. It is the open Bible that will bring healing and strengthening power to the national life, as it does to the individual life. With godliness will come not cleanliness only, but industry, and independence, and truthfulness, and many a manly and homely virtue which Popery crushes down among the poor Irish.

CHAPTER XII.

ROMAN CATHOLICS AND IRISH CATHOLICS.

Hindrances to Concord—Ultramontane Claims—Political Orangemen—The Catholic Laity.

IN the recently published despatches of the Duke of Wellington there are some interesting references to Irish affairs. The Duke, as Sir Arthur Wellesley, was for two years—1807, 1808—Chief Secretary of Ireland, under the Portland ministry. He did good service at the time, but he left with no hopeful view of the prospects of the country. He feared that no Government measure could ever make the people contented and loyal. The restoration of the soil to the descendants of its ancient owners was the idea underlying all the agitation of those times. This feeling was shared by the priests, generally themselves springing from the peasant class. Though they could not proclaim their disaffection, they dared not oppose the people, on whom they depended for subsistence. It was this dependence which led Sir Arthur Wellesley, like many men of all political parties, to advocate the payment of the Roman Catholic clergy by the State. The *Edinburgh Review* on this point agreed with the *Quarterly Review*, in the articles through forty years on Ireland. It was a policy of expediency, which would have had no good result, and which we have happily outlived. But the clear sagacity of the man appeared in his views on national education, which were far in advance of the time. "The great object of our policy in Ireland should be to obliterate, as far as the law will allow us, the distinction between Protestant and Catholic, and avoid anything that can induce either sect to recollect or believe that its interests are separate or distinct from those of the other. I would apply this principle to education."

"To obliterate the distinction between Protestant and Catholic" is the policy which has been carried out since the passing of the Catholic Emancipation Act, the establishment of the national system of education, and the foundation of the Queen's colleges. The disestablishment of the Irish Church was a painful sacrifice to the same demand of equality, and the opening of Trinity College more largely to all Irishmen will be also a step in the same direction. But to consent to any scheme of separate education, would be a sad retrogression, and would perpetuate the remembrance and influence of times when the interests of Protestant and Catholic were distinct and hostile. There never could be the possibility of common patriotism, far less of a common faith, if the two creeds were to be thus stereotyped in separation and antagonism. Let the churches remain separate, if they will, till happier times of Christian unity arrive, but let the nation be one, and its education Irish, not Romish.

Every passing year confirms the wisdom of the policy which unites Catholics and Protestants, under common laws and co-equal civil rights. They meet together at school and college, in business and the intercourse of daily life, in the professions, on juries, at the bar, on the bench. There are no subjects in the empire more peaceable and law-abiding, more patriotic and loyal, than are many of the Catholics of Ireland. Some worthy Protestant people express regret that Catholic emancipation was ever granted, and some, no doubt, are sorry that the penal laws were ever relaxed. Rome, they say, can never be satisfied by concessions, but will plot and agitate for supremacy. They do not distinguish between Irish Catholics and the Ultramontane party—the emissaries of the Vatican, who are the real fomentors of discord, and the worst enemies of Ireland as well as of England. It is the restless aggression of this faction which keeps in activity the opposing power of the Orange confederacy. The ignorant people on both sides do not see that these are two hostile extremes of opinion, the collision of which hinders the union and peace of the nation.

There never can be tranquillity in Ireland while these religious feuds are kept up. Within a month of the Lord-Lieutenant's "progress" through Ulster, when he congratulated the nation on the peace, prosperity, and progress everywhere manifest, the startling announcement came that "civil war raged in Belfast." The most peaceful and prosperous town in Ireland was under a reign of terror. The place was divided into two hostile camps, and a state of siege was proclaimed. For several days the conflict continued, and daily returns were made of the killed, maimed, and wounded. Strong forces of police and of troops failed to overawe the combatants, and when repressed in one part of the town the battle broke out in another. Shops were shut and business suspended. By order of the mayor all public-houses were closed, but the mob broke into them, and were maddened to fresh violence. Houses were wrecked, and Protestants and Catholics who had been peaceful neighbours became active enemies. Up to the day of the outbreak the two were living and working side by side, making their profits out of the same trades, enjoying the protection of the same laws. There was no parliamentary or municipal contest in progress;

there was nothing to fight for, nothing to win or lose. There was not even the excuse of resisting an illegal demonstration. The "Party Processions Act" had been repealed. The Protestants, it was thought, might shout "God save the Queen!" and "No surrender!" one day, until their loyalty was satisfied or exhausted; and the Roman Catholics might plant disloyal emblems and sing Fenian songs another day, until they too had let off their steam. But neither party is contented with license for itself unless it can refuse it to the other.

"The Protestants are the more intolerant of the two," said the *Times*, in commenting on this deplorable outbreak. I happened to be in the society of some zealous Orangemen a few days before the 15th of August, and was amazed and pained by the intolerant spirit manifested. I spoke of the forbearance and good conduct of the Catholics on the 12th of July, and pleaded for a similar forbearance towards the opposite party. Even the apprentice boys of Derry were capable of recognizing the right of the Catholics to make a public demonstration on their day. After the 12th of July, the *Nation* newspaper could fairly point to the conduct of the Catholics, as worthy of generous imitation by their opponents. "The bloody Twelfth is past, and no red burials have attended the influence of Orange teachings or the fervour of Orange enthusiasm. The *dies iræ* has passed over Ulster; the day so long devoted to insult and tumult, to drunken orgies and murderous violence, has dawned and set, but the peace has remained unbroken. "So quiet a Twelfth has not been known in Ireland," say the reports, "for the last quarter of a century. There were no schools sacked, no convents wrecked, no churches desecrated. There were no riots, no stone-throwing, no head-breaking. To the lively reverer of the Immortal Memory, who remembers the stirring events of the past, the proceedings of the last anniversary must have appeared insufferably tame. The spirit of Dolly's Brae and the Battle of the Diamond seemed to have died out, and belligerent Orangemen shook their heads mournfully, as they wended their way homeward without having had the satisfaction of seeing a single Papist maltreated. The Green and the Orange had not once come into collision. The Orangemen behaved not less offensively than of yore, but the wearers of the Green were insensible to provocation, and a peaceful Twelfth was the consequence."

"If it might be permitted to us," continued the writer in the *Nation*, "to reason with the Lodgemen of Ulster, we should point out to them that forbearance so trying and so great deserves something besides revilings in return. We would remind them that, even in the districts disgraced by their commemoration of civil war, they form the minority, and depend for immunity in their practices on the forbearance of the Catholics around them. We would remind them that through the exercise of that forbearance, they have been enabled to carry out their miserable programme unfettered and uninterfered with, and have been enabled to obtain the repeal of the only statute which stood as a check upon their irritating displays. In actions like this there surely might be some reciprocity. Let us hope that after the celebrations which have given some of our contemporaries so much satisfaction, the outcries raised against every popular demonstration elsewhere may have no revival, and the example set by the Catholics of Ulster find some reflex, however faint, in the conduct of their political opponents."

To this appeal even the apprentice boys of Derry, as has been said, were not insensible, and the Catholic demonstration of the 15th of August, though in some ways peculiarly offensive to loyal susceptibilities, was not interfered with. Green processions, with music and banners, went round the historic "walls" without being interfered with, though a crownless harp and a French tricolour were among the emblems. All passed off quietly. Not so at Belfast, where the Lady-day procession ended in violence and bloodshed.

At the risk of giving offence to bigots on either side, I must give the impression made by what I saw of the extreme parties of the two creeds.

The two most "dangerous classes" in Ireland are the Ultramontane Papists and the extreme Orangemen, or the mere political Protestants. There are among the Orangemen some of the noblest and best of Irishmen, but they are little aware of the evils that are done under the shelter of their name. The true Protestants know that the weapons of their warfare are not carnal but spiritual, and that more ground will be gained by spreading the truth in a loving spirit, than by party demonstrations. The organizers of party processions are the people who keep Ireland in strife and disturbance, far more than Fenian plotters or Home Rule agitators.

The present aim of the Ultramontanes is to get into their hands the education of the Roman Catholic population, both in school and university, and so to keep the nation in subjection to the Vatican. By offering political support to the Liberal party they are trying what can be done, but they would transfer this support to any political party that would subserve their policy. In opposing this policy the extreme Orangemen are at present in alliance with the Conservative party. This is not the result of political choice, so much as of desire of protection from Papist aggression. In Scotland, the Protestant strength is as much on the Liberal side, as in Ireland it is on the Conservative side. This state of parties will continue as long as the existing Irish difficulty remains unsettled. A Liberal Government cannot at once satisfy the Ultramontanes of Ireland, and retain the confidence of the Protestants of Great Britain. A Conservative Government cannot satisfy the extreme Orange party, and at the same time retain Catholic Ireland in peace. But a constitutional Government, disregarding the extreme on both sides, would maintain a strong hold on public opinion in Ireland, for there is a large body of independent Catholics, both clergy and laity, who would unite with Protestants in resisting the Ultramontane claims, which have influence chiefly through the connivance of Government for party purposes.

Where is this independent Catholic party? it may be asked. The Romish hierarchy seems to be united in its demands. Few protests or remonstrances have been heard. In a valuable little work, "Catholicism and the Vatican," by an Irish barrister,* the new relation of the Irish Catholic Church to Rome is clearly explained. He implores his Catholic fellow-countrymen not to shut their eyes to the designs of the

---

* "Catholicism and the Vatican," by J. Lowry Whittle, A.M., Trinity College, Dublin. Henry S. King and Co.

Ultramontane party, which are endangering Catholic truth as well as national independence.

"The decree promulgated by the Pope in the last session of the Vatican Council is referred to under various designations; sometimes as the *Constitutio de Ecclesia*, again as the decree of July 18, 1870, or as the Bull *Pastor Eternus*. It consists of four chapters, the first two containing a history of the primacy as instituted in the person of St. Peter and continued in the Roman pontiffs; the third declaring the Pope to be universal bishop; and the fourth declaring him to be the infallible teacher. These two latter are the important chapters enacting the controverted dogmas. The concluding paragraphs of each contain the explicit statement of these dogmas. First, on the universal episcate, "If any one shall have averred that the Roman Pontiff has only the office of inspection or direction, but not the full and supreme power of jurisdiction over the universal church, not only in matters relating to faith and morals, but also in those relating to discipline and the government of the church, in every region of the earth, or that he has only the higher kinds, but not the whole extent of this supreme power, or that this power of his is not ordinary and immediate, or not over all and every church, or over all and every pastor and believer, let him be anathema."

Secondly, as to the infallibility. "Therefore we, faithfully adhering to the traditions handed down from the origin of the Christian religion, for the glory of God the Saviour, the exaltation of the Catholic religion, and the salvation of Christian nations, with the approval of the holy Council, teach and declare, as a divinely-revealed dogma, that when the Roman Pontiff speaks *ex-cathedrâ*, that is, when filling the office of pastor and teacher of all Christians, he, in virtue of his supreme apostolic authority, lays down for the whole Church a doctrine concerning faith or morals; he enjoys through the divine assistance promised to him in the person of St. Peter, that infallibility which the Divine Redeemer decreed that the Church should possess in laying down a doctrine concerning faith and morals; and, therefore, such definitions of the Roman Pontiff are final in themselves, and not from the consent of the Church."

The infallibility dogma has attracted most public attention. In Ireland it has been accepted by the majority of the bishops, and being assumed as true in their declarations and public acts, the ignorant people are led to suppose that it is an accepted dogma of the Church. But it is not accepted by the intelligent laity, and is also rejected by many of the clergy. It is contrary to all the past teaching of the Irish Church. The Archbishop of Tuam, in the Council, declared that the doctrine of the personal infallibility of the Roman Pontiff could not reach the people, and find acceptance in the minds of the laity. It is not taught in any catechism in Ireland, is never preached by the parish clergy; but what is always preached is the infallibility of the Church, and by the Church the people understand the bishops in agreement with the Pope. This also has been maintained in all controversies with non-Catholics. How far the influence of the Irish episcopate will carry the dogma with the clergy remains to be seen, but the educated laity cannot be expected to receive the new and strange article of faith.

Of more practical importance on the condition of Ireland is the other dogma, of "the universal episcopate of the Roman Pontiff." "It destroys at once," says Mr. Lowry Whittle, "the whole theory of the episcopacy. Each bishop becomes only the local agent of the Pope. Greatly as the Pope's authority over the bishops had grown in the latter times of the Church, the bishop still took the oath of fidelity to the Pope with the clause *salvo meo ordine*. He had distinct rights in the Church as a member of the episcopacy, claiming to represent the apostles, and his obedience to the Pope was regulated by the canon law. The *ordinaria potestas*, or power of the bishop, was the authority to which each priest or layman was immediately subject in religious matters. Now, every priest and layman is subject to the Pope directly; the Pope's power extends over every pastor and believer.

" The practical effect of this first part of the Vatican decree is greater than that of the infallibility dogma. The sweeping away, with the consent of the episcopacy, of the whole constitution of the Latin Church, is one of the most remarkable facts the modern historian can record. All the rights and privileges of separate orders in the Church are abolished. All the customs of local and national churches, the relations of the parish priest to his flock, to his bishop, of the bishops to each other, of the various national churches to the Papacy; the whole canon law which elaborately regulated all these relations;—all these institutions of the Church have only a significance so far as the Pope may permit in each particular case. According to this dogma, those who for so many centuries relied on the canon law as a limitation of the power of the Pope, as a guarantee of special rights of bishops and of priests, and of local churches, were violating the ordinances of God."

It is quite possible that this assumption of supreme power in the person of the Roman Pontiff, and the breaking of the canon law, may in the end turn out a good thing in the providence of God, as rendering more easy the overthrow of the Papal system when its oppression can be no longer borne by the nations. But meanwhile the despotism wielded through the Papal legate and his prelates on the Irish clergy, will lead to much hardship and persecution, except when, as in the case of the parish priest of Callan, the protection of British law is invoked. In no other country of Europe would the aggression of the Papal power have been allowed to go so far as it already has in Ireland since the Vatican Council of 1870.

In the conclusion of his book Mr. Lowry Whittle takes a cheerful view as to the future of Irish Catholicism. "No greater misconception exists, among the many misconceptions of Irish questions, than the opinion that the people of Ireland are Ultramontane. Ultramontanism, as held by many men in England, Irishmen know nothing of." "It is a thing alien to the spirit of the Irish people, and they have never had any cordial feeling for Ultramontanes. The great organizer of the Ultramontane party in Ireland is one of the most unpopular prelates Ireland has ever had. With regard to the laity, the same want of sympathy is discernible. * * * The bishops are at present the only body of Irishmen with Ultramontane sympathies, and their influence as a body has been gradually waning in Ireland, owing to political questions. The lower order of clergy have, for the most part, as little sympathy with Ultramontanism as the people. A

Catholic middle class is being gradually formed in Ireland, and with its growth the chance of such doctrines finding acceptance is diminishing every day."

Why do the laity, it may be asked, submit so tamely to the episcopal domination? The question will not be asked by those who know the state of Ireland. It is not easy to act with independence when life itself depends on the good-will of the priests. A professional man, or a trader, or shopkeeper, in a Catholic town, can be ruined in his worldly calling by incurring ecclesiastical displeasure. Among the great landed proprietors one might expect more independence, but the fact is that the Catholic gentry as a rule are, for their station, the least intelligent class in the community. A well-educated Roman Catholic gentleman is the exception, not the rule. When met with, it will be found that he has been to Trinity College, or that he has attended some foreign university. According to the testimony of Professor Sullivan, the lower classes of the Irish are becoming well-educated, for their station, but the middle and upper classes the reverse. The training they get in Roman Catholic schools is a miserable training, and if not followed up by a university course, they degenerate into mere rural squireens, without much liberal knowledge, or independence of character.

It is very different with the educated minority of

the gentry who have studied at Trinity or at other colleges. It is especially different with a large proportion of the Irish Catholic bar, to whom we may look hopefully for resistance to the tyranny of Rome. The bar alone has organization and independence enough to maintain the struggle for civil and religious freedom. The alliance of the bar with the clergy gained Catholic emancipation and other triumphs. If there is to be a conflict between the Italian and the Irish Catholics, the strength of the bar will be on the patriotic side, and the independence of the Irish clergy as well as the laity may yet be secured.

CHAPTER XIII.

THE O'KEEFFE CASE.

The Callan Schools—Father O'Keeffe's Law Suits with his Curates—Interference of Cardinal Cullen,—National School Board siding with Cardinal Cullen—Debate in Parliament—The Pope's Bulls overriding British Law.

THERE are few who have not heard of Father O'Keeffe, the parish priest of Callan, county Kilkenny. His case has been constantly cropping up in newspapers during the last two or three years, and had a night to itself in the British Parliament last session. There are probably few, however, in England who have given much heed to the case, most people being repelled by all Irish questions, even when of national importance, and this being apparently only a personal squabble between a Romish priest and his superiors in Church or State. Now, if my readers will give patient audience, I undertake to satisfy them that this case of Father O'Keeffe is one of the most notable events that have occurred for many a year in Irish history. If they examine it, they will have the key to the whole mystery of Irish ecclesiastical politics, and understand thoroughly the position which the English Government now occupies in relation to the Church of Rome.

To understand the public aspect of the O'Keeffe case it is not necessary to go farther back than to his collision with the National Board, on the point of his position as school manager. But a glance at his previous history, and of the beginning of his conflict with Cardinal Cullen, will afford a most instructive view of the great questions now agitating the Roman Catholic Church—questions, the solution of which will influence the future history of Ireland. In this light the case has a far higher interest than any personal or political bearing.

Passing by his early education and his training at Maynooth, we find Robert O'Keeffe parish priest of his native town of Callan, to which he was appointed in 1863. He is of irreproachable character, zealous and faithful in the discharge of all his professional duties, and generally beloved by his fellow-townspeople. He has considerable literary reputation, and for about ten years filled the office of Professor of Science and Languages at St. Kyran's College, Kilkenny. He has always been an enthusiast in education, and he was in his element as manager of the National Schools in Callan. Of these there were four when he came, and a fifth was established chiefly by his means and exertions.

His position as manager was not because officially he was parish priest, and so appointed by his bishop. In Roman Catholic districts the parish priest may be manager, but in many cases he is not, and often a Protestant landlord is the patron and his agent is the manager.

According to the rules of the Education Board, "a patron is a person who applies in the first instance to place the school in connection with the board." He provides the schoolroom, appoints the manager and teachers, and after the school has been got into working order he asks for a salary for the teachers. If, on the report of the inspector, the applicant is found to be a person of good position in society, he is recognized as the patron in connection with the board. If the attendance of the children fails, or if any of the rules of the commissioners are not complied with, the grant may be withdrawn, or even the school may be struck off the list of the National Schools; but the offices of patron and manager, not having been appointed by the board, cannot by the board be taken away. Take an example, the facts of which I know. The Earl of Bessborough has no fewer than eleven National Schools on his estate in Kilkenny county, and three in county Carlow. Of all these fourteen schools Lord Bessborough is patron, and his agent is the manager. The children are mostly Catholics, and the teachers are Catholics, except at one school at Pilltown, where there are a considerable number of Protestants, and here the master and mistress are Protestants. But in not one of these well-conducted and well-attended schools is the parish priest the manager.

It is important to note this. The late resident commissioner, Mr. (now Sir A.) McDonnell, long ago pointed out, when the question arose in discussions about the National Schools, the nature of clerical managership. If a parish priest is appointed manager, it is because, as Mr. McDonnell expressed it, "he is supposed to represent the feeling of the people in the locality." It is as representing the locality, not as recognizing the Roman Catholic Church, any more than other and minor denominations in the place, that Mr. O'Keeffe held his appointment. The bishop of the diocese, or other ecclesiastical authorities, had nothing to do with it. The correspondence with the Education Office, Dublin, was carried on by Mr. O'Keeffe, and for many years he was the sole recognized manager of the Callan schools under the National Board.

There never was any charge made against Mr.

O'Keeffe as to the management of the schools. On the contrary, the education at Callan was noted for its efficiency, much of which was due to the personal influence of the manager. He used to spend some hours daily in the schools, teaching and directing the teachers. One of the schools is in connection with the Science and Art Department, South Kensington, and of an official inspection of this school we have seen a report. The visitor was Colonel Hassart, of the Curragh camp. He was met at the school by the Rev. Mr. O'Keeffe, chairman, with Captain Knox and other members of the education committee. The classes were examined by Mr. Walter Hawe, the teacher, and much to the surprise of Colonel Hassart the first boy brought up to the black board, to prove the forty-seventh proposition of the first book of Euclid, commenced by writing out the proposition in French (each boy in the class doing the same upon his own slate), and in proving it never used a word of English. After the examination of the classes the Colonel inspected the apparatus for experiments and illustrations, and expressed his satisfaction in warm terms. Few national schools could have a more efficient manager than those of Callan. The male school had for many years a parliamentary land endowment and a money endowment from Lord Clifden, and its schoolroom was one of the largest and best filled in county Kilkenny.

Now came a disturbing element. A gentleman named Dunphy died about the year 1860, bequeathing a sum of money to the Order of Christian Brothers, sufficient for the maintenance, in perpetuity, of two brothers, and expressing a wish that a school of the Order should be established at Callan. The parish priest of that time refused to take any part in introducing the Christian Brothers into Callan. His successor, Mr. O'Keeffe, in an evil hour assented. He laid the foundation-stone of a school and residence for the Brothers, and the building was completed and the school opened in September, 1868.

Mr. O'Keeffe must have known, or could easily have ascertained, the true character and designs of this Order of Christian Brothers. They may be zealous often in the work of education, but their main object is the propagation of extreme ultramontane popery. In Ireland, as well as in America, I have seen their wily action, and an examination of their school books will satisfy any one of the dangerous tendency of their teaching. Mr. O'Keeffe has himself to blame for encouraging this Order, which sets itself in opposition to the National Schools, as well as to those where true Christian teaching is established. I say this in order to disavow any sympathy with Mr. O'Keeffe's proceedings in any other relation than in his contest against ultramontane power. His encouragement of the Christian Brothers, his introduction of a mission of Oblate Fathers from Inchicore, and his project of establishing in the Callan Lodge "A community of holy Irish women, now living in the Convent of the Sacred Heart of Mary at Beziers," are not proceedings with which any Protestant can feel interest or sympathy.

It was not Mr. O'Keeffe's expectation, however, that the new school would injure, far less supersede the old. It was his intention to continue the National male school, considering that the wants of the locality required it. The Bishop, Dr. Walsh, expressed a wish that it should be kept open, and Lord Clifden's agent was promised that it should be continued. "However, (I quote Mr. Keeffe's own statement in a letter to the Secretaries, Education office,) notwithstanding my efforts to the contrary, the children were all drawn away to the new schools; and when your inspector made a visit in December, 1868, he found only seven boys present, while there were 220 in the new schools under the instruction of only two teachers. This large number of boys included youths of every age and degree of proficiency, and many males from my infant school."

In this state of matters the teacher of the National School resigned. In order to re-establish the school, and attract to it an attendance which would secure the benefit of connection with the Education Board, another teacher of repute was obtained. The attendance increased, and the manager was able to report numbers, in March, 1871, warranting the re-appointment of the assistant master, whose salary had for a time been withheld on account of the diminished numbers. In June, 1871, the average attendance exceeded ninety, and Mr. O'Keefe appointed a second assistant, who was examined by the inspector and found qualified. The school's quarterly returns were signed and forwarded in the usual way. No payment, however, came for the teachers, although the regulations had all been complied with, and so the manager had to pay the salaries of the teachers out of his own pocket.

Why did the Education Board fail to meet the rules as to payment of teachers? Hereby hangs the tale, to understand which we must go back to the autumn of 1869. At this time the Christian Brothers were carrying all before them, and Father O'Keeffe naturally felt annoyed at the failure of his own school. Among other appeals for its restoration he told his people, from the altar, that the Bishop wished the National School to be continued. The priests at the Friary Chapel gave this statement blank denial, and, both about the schools and about the appropriation of funds for parochial purposes, called the parish priest a liar. This was "from the altar," which in Ireland seems to be a place of proclamation on all matters, and reference to all persons, civil or ecclesiastical. These priests, curates of Father O'Keeffe, stated also that the Bishop had authorized them to make the announcement.

Upon this Mr. O'Keeffe brought an action for slander against the Bishop, but was non-suited, no proof being given that the denunciation was made by the Bishop's authority or command. An action against the two priests, Father Neary and Father John Walsh, was more successful, both of them being convicted of slander, and in each case the parish priest being awarded damages.

But before this a new character had come upon the stage, as appears from the following letter:—

"The REV. R. O'KEEFFE.

"REV. SIR,—In punishment for the action-at-law taken by you against the Rt. Rev. E. Walsh, R. C. Bishop of Ossory, I, vested with the requisite powers, do hereby suspend you from your office.

"Your humble servant, R. M'DONALD, V.G.
"St. Kyran's College, Kilkenny."

To this Mr. O'Keeffe replied in very proper spirit

"Callan, Oct. 12th, '70.

"The VERY REV. E. M'DONALD.

"VERY REV. SIR,—I have been handed a letter of yours without date, in which you say you have been vested with the requisite powers to suspend me for having taken an action-at-law against Dr. Walsh. You must be very silly indeed to think I could take your word for such an absurd statement; or you must suppose me to be as ignorant as you appear to be yourself, of the course of proceeding to be followed in the infliction of censures. After having been publicly denounced as a liar, on the altar, by authority alleged to have been given by Dr. Walsh, I wrote his lordship a letter of complaint on the 20th of August last year; and I have never since heard a word from him on the subject. I sent a copy of this letter same day to Cardinal Cullen, and finally I proposed to Cardinal Barnabo (the Common Superior of the Vicar-General and the P. P.), to bring my cause of complaint against the Bishop before a Roman court. I could get no redress for the grievous wrong inflicted upon me in any ecclesiastical court, and I have consequently been compelled to seek it before a lay tribunal. My proceeding is at variance with no law human or divine, and I shall treat as it deserves any attempt at punishment.—Your obedient servant,

"ROBERT O'KEEFFE."

Thereon followed a correspondence, the Vicar-General re-asserting his authority, and the parish priest denying it. So the matter stood till the action was brought against Father John Walsh, when the Vicar-General wrote again as follows :—

"St. Kyran's College, Kilkenny, Dec. 10th, 1870.
"The REV. R. O'KEEFFE.

"REV. SIR,—From a subpœna served on me, and in other ways, I have become aware of your action-at-law against the Rev. John Walsh, to be tried before the Court of Queen's Bench in Dublin. It is my duty to tell you that your proceeding is a grave offence against the sacred canons. Of course I do not find fault with the eminent and impartial judges who preside in the court referred to; but, in common with every Catholic, I feel that respect for the discipline of your own Church should keep you from bringing a brother priest before any lay tribunal. Some communications already received from you, leave me no grounds to hope that you will desist from your present proceeding, by reason of any mere remonstrance of mine. At the same time, it is my duty to employ the powers which I possess, to stop it, if I can. Therefore, I hereby command you to withdraw the case of the Rev. Robert O'Keeffe against the Rev. John Walsh from the Court of Queen's Bench, under pain of suspension *ab officio et beneficio* to be *ipso facto* incurred, the moment your counsel begins to state the case to the court and jury.

     "Your obedient servant,
         "E. M'DONALD."

At this time it is evident that the Court of Queen's Bench took no account of the alleged offence of an ecclesiastic seeking redress for wrong from another ecclesiastic in a court of law, for it awarded damages of £100, as it did in the subsequent trial of Father Neary for slander. Upon this the old Bishop of Ossory sent another "suspension" to the contumacious P. P., dated Jan. 11th, 1871. Mr. O'Keeffe disregarded it, and continued to exercise his parochial functions, refusing to acknowledge an arbitrary sentence, without trial or conviction.

At this stage of the proceedings Cardinal Cullen first interposed.

     "Dublin, July 16th, 1871.
"The REV. R. O'KEEFFE, P.P., Callan.

"REV. DEAR SIR,—The accounts which have reached me of dissensions and disputes in Callan have afflicted me very much.

"Being now in a position to attempt to restore peace in that locality, I am determined to make every effort to attain so desirable a result.

"Before I take any step in the matter I would be glad to have an interview with you, in regard to the present state of things.—Your faithful servant,

"✠ PAUL CARD. CULLEN."

Mr. O'Keeffe replied in a long letter, giving his own version of the whole case, telling his grievances, and describing his course of life as parish priest and school manager.

"I have now (July, 1871) one hundred boys in my National School; about twenty-five are reading Latin, and about forty, French. I have made, to a great extent, French the language of the school, and no boy pays fees. Many of the boys are the sons of small farmers in other parishes, who have come to live in town to qualify under me for a profession. I swore in the Queen's Bench that, as a general rule, I spend three and a half hours every day in reading and writing, in addition to the time I spend in the school, and that the time I give in the school does not, in any way, interfere with my parochial duties. Send, for instance, the Rev. Michael Cody, of Phibsborough, a native of this parish, to spend a week with me, and I promise your Eminence he will report to you that he is not acquainted with any other P.P. who does his duty with more regularity and exactness than I do."

A long correspondence ensued, which I have before me, but it is only necessary to quote some brief extracts which explain Cardinal Cullen's position in Ireland as the Delegate of the Vatican, and the extraordinary claims of ecclesiastical supremacy which he sets up. The Cardinal stated that he acted under the bulls *In cœnâ Domini* and *Apostolicæ Sedis*. "The present Pope, whilst limiting and abrogating other censures, confirmed all penalties of the canon law against those who drag ecclesiastics, and especially bishops, before lay tribunals, and there charge them with canonical offences. The Pope's bull regarding censures was handed to every bishop in the Vatican Œcumenical Council last December twelvemonths (1869), and is known over the whole world." (Letter to Mr. O'Keeffe, July 22nd, 1871.)

The *Bulla Cœnæ* is so called from its having been read in former times at Rome, every year on the day of the Lord's Supper. It is a bull of fearful denunciations and excommunications against all heretics, and opponents of the jurisdiction of the Holy See. It used to be an imposing scene, when the Pope, at the conclusion of the reading of the bull by a cardinal, threw down into the public place a flaming torch, to denote the consuming power of his anathema. The publication of this bull was suspended in 1773 by Clement XIV., and Pius IX. annulled it in 1869, substituting a new constitution, which was published in the *Bulla Apostolicæ Sedis*. This bull confirms the worst points of the *Bulla Cœnæ*, and renews anathemas against those who dare, directly or indirectly, to compel ecclesiastics to appear before Civil Courts. Now, the *Bulla Cœnæ* was resisted in almost every country in Europe. In France it was declared to be "a direct infraction of the temporal and civil rights of all sovereigns." It was equally opposed in Germany, in Spain, in Venice, and Sicily. Even from priest-ridden Naples it was excluded. "It was abhorred and execrated, as it was rejected and expelled from the dominions of all Catholic princes."

In 1825 and 1826, before committees of both Houses of Parliament, Roman Catholic bishops were examined on various topics, and among others on this bull. Dr. Doyle, then the representative man of the Irish Catholics, said that "if this bull were in force, scarcely anything would be at rest among all the Catholic states of Europe." "The collision which would result from the reception of that bull with the established authorities of the country, was an insurmountable obstacle to its publication. It excommunicates the sovereign and all the powers of Protestant governments, and establishes the temporal power of the Pope directly over every Roman Catholic." The late Dr. O'Hanlon, of Maynooth, stated before Lord

Harrowby's Commission at Dublin Castle in 1854, that "if the *Bulla Cœnæ* were in force in Ireland, any person printing, reading, or possessing books written by a heretic on the subject of religion or any other subject, if they should contain heresy, would incur an excommunication reserved to the Pope. A similar excommunication would be incurred by all secular magistrates and judges for trying or punishing ecclesiastics for criminal offences, except in the cases allowed by the canon law." Every judge who, without leave from the Pope, dares to sit in judgment on the Romish clergy, incurs excommunication *ipso facto*, a fact to be considered by the judges who had to sit in judgment on the Galway priests.

Such is the nature and history of the *Bulla Cœnæ*. The bull *Apostolicæ Sedis* of October 12th, 1869, goes farther than the *Bulla Cœnæ* did, in claiming for the clergy immunity from the jurisdiction of civil courts, and in its denunciations against ecclesiastics for seeking to maintain civil rights in such courts. And this is the bull which Cardinal Cullen cites as the authority for his action against Father O'Keeffe.

Having obtained in the Cardinal's own handwriting the ground of the action taken against him, Mr. O'Keeffe, after consulting able canonists, sent his defence, in which he said:—

"The constitution *Apostolicæ Sedis* has not been received in this country any more than the bull *In cænâ Domini*. The *Bulla Cænæ* was never received in France and some other countries of Europe; and we have the testimony of our ablest Irish divines that it was never received in this country. Our most distinguished prelates and other theologians stated this before royal and parliamentary commissions. When the great Dr. Doyle was asked before a parliamentary committee, on the 16th of March, 1825, 'Whether the Catholic clergy insist that all bulls are entitled to obedience,' his answer was, 'By no means: the Pope we consider as the executive authority in the Catholic Church, and when he issues a bull enforcing a discipline already settled by a general council, such bull is entitled to respect; but he may issue bulls which would regard local discipline, and other matters not already defined; and in these cases the bull would be treated by us in such manner as might seem good to us. Did we find that it was unreasonable, we would refuse to accept it.' The other divines that were examined gave similar testimony; and no Irish divine, that I am aware of, ever publicly maintained that the *Bulla Cænæ* was ever received in this country. Surely all these distinguished men would on the same principles hold the same opinion regarding the binding force in this country of the new constitution *Apostolicæ Sedis*.

"Assuming for argument sake that the *Apostolicæ Sedis* was in force here, the proceeding against me did not commence with a citation to a trial: a preliminary which all canonists look upon as essentially necessary to every judicial proceeding. There was no trial or any offence proved. There was no denunciation of me in any canonical form; although nothing is plainer than the words of the bull of Martin the 5th in the Council of Constance, forbidding the people to withdraw themselves, or to decline ministrations, in the absence of a formal denunciation by the judge who had passed the sentence of censure, or some one acting with authority from him."

The Cardinal was too wise to attempt to reply to this document, but continued his appeals to put an end to the unseemly strife which was raising scandal in the Church. Father O'Keeffe reciprocated the Cardinal's pacific aspirations, but did not see why all the exercise of charity should be on one side. "Some time ago," wrote Dr. Cullen, "I read in the life of M. Francis de Sales that some one charged him with committing a serious offence; and that the saint, rather than undertake an angry discussion, and occasion divisions among the clergy, bore patiently the calumny, until it pleased God to supply, without any effort on his part, proofs of his innocence."

A very pretty bait, certainly! but Mr. O'Keeffe was

too old to be caught by it. "I admire your eminence's charity," he said in his reply, "and the Christian spirit with which you preach it, but let me beg of you not to allow the zeal of your charity, though queen of virtues, to eat up your sense of the cardinal virtue, justice. Your Eminence's letter would be very appropriate coming from a preacher of the Word; but in the matter of restoring peace to this disturbed parish, I must look on you as a judge."

In one of his letters Mr. O'Keeffe referred to the heavy expenses he had incurred in defending his rights. The Cardinal in replying gave a new rendering of a Scripture text, well worthy of being quoted. "As for money matters, I would advise you to follow the counsel of our Lord, 'Quærite primum regnum Dei et justitiam ejus, et hæc omnia adjicientur vobis.' '*Settle first the spiritual matters, submit to the bishop, and God will settle everything else.*' 'Seek ye first the kingdom of God and His righteousness,' is the ordinary rendering, implying the vast magnitude of spiritual and eternal, as compared with temporal, concerns. "Submit to the bishop" is Cardinal Cullen's racy reading of the Divine commandment.

In the early letters the Cardinal addresses his correspondent as "My dear Father O'Keeffe;" the address tapers down to "Dear Father O'Keeffe," and "Rev. dear sir," till at length the Cardinal ended the correspondence by pronouncing the sentence of suspension, in November, 1871.

Poor Father O'Keeffe! he was now thrice suspended. First, by Mr. McDonald, Vicar-General; second, by Bishop Walsh; and third, by Cardinal Cullen.

Now comes the appearance of the case before the Education Board. In the middle of March, 1872, the Bishop of Ossory brought to the notice of the Commissioners of National Education the suspension of Mr. O'Keeffe, and requested that he might be pronounced incapable of discharging any functions in connection with the parish schools of Callan. He also informed the Commissioners that another gentleman, Mr. Martin, had been appointed parish priest in Mr. O'Keeffe's place. By a letter of the same date, Mr. Martin requested of the Commissioners that he might be substituted for the Rev. Mr. O'Keeffe in the management of the schools. On the 9th of March, which appeared to have been the first day of meeting after the receipt of the letters from the Bishop and Mr. Martin, the Commissioners considered the application. A proposal was made by one of the Commissioners that the proceedings should be adjourned for a fortnight, to which an amendment was moved that a copy of Mr. Martin's letter should be sent to Mr. O'Keeffe, who up to that time was manager. The amendment was lost by a majority of one, and the original motion was carried. On the 23rd of April, accordingly, the Commissioners again met, and it was then proposed by Mr. Justice Fitzgerald, and seconded by the Lord Chancellor of Ireland, that the certificate of the Roman Catholic Coadjutor Bishop of Ossory (that the Rev. Mr. O'Keeffe had been suspended) be received and acted upon by the Board, until the suspension therein contained should have been removed or declared invalid by a competent tribunal. An amendment was moved by Mr. Justice Morris and seconded by Mr. Waldron, "that before any action should be taken on the letter of the Rev. Mr. Martin to the Board, or on the letter of Dr. Moram, Coadjutor Bishop of Ossory, to the Resident Commissioner, the Rev. Mr. O'Keeffe get the opportunity of knowing the nature of the application made, and of offering an explanation." Upon that there was a division. The amendment was put first, when there voted for it eight, viz., Mr. Justice Morris, Mr. Waldron, Chief Justice Monahan, Mr. Jellett, Mr. Morell, the Lord Primate, Judge Lawson, and Mr. Murland. Against it were Mr. Gibson, Judge Longfield, Lord O'Hagan, Chief Baron Pigot, Mr. Lentaigne, Mr. O'Hagan, Mr. Justice Fitzgerald, Viscount Monk, and Mr. Keeman. The amendment was therefore lost by a majority of one. The consequence was that Mr. O'Keeffe never had communicated to him in any manner or form the intention of the Commissioners to consider his dismissal. The first intimation he received was the letter dismissing him from his functions as manager.

Bearing in mind that Mr. O'Keeffe's position as manager was in virtue of his local standing in Callan, irrespective of any ecclesiastical relations to his Bishop or to the Cardinal, the Commissioners had no ground for altering their attitude to the manager of their schools. Suppose Mr. O'Keeffe had been a medical man, a fellow of the College of Surgeons of Dublin, and the medical authorities had suspended him from his medical status for adopting homœopathy or any other medical heresy, this would in no way affect his position as recognized manager; or if he had been a freemason, and supended by the Grand Master, this would have had as little concern with his present office. The National Board has to do with localities and with Irishmen, not with churches or members of denominations as such. At all events, till his ecclesiastical suspension had been decided by a court of law, the Commissioners of Education had no right to assume the validity of his suspension. This was the ground taken by Mr. O'Keeffe, and on which his case was at length brought before the British Parliament.

This was done on the 5th August by Mr. Bouverie, in the Committee of Supply, on the vote for National

Education (Ireland). A petition had previously been presented from Mr. O'Keeffe, in which he stated his grievances. Here is the result of the debate as given in the *Times* summary: "Mr. Bouverie called attention to the case of the Rev. Robert O'Keeffe, the Roman Catholic parish priest of Callan. This gentleman having been censured by his Bishop and Cardinal Cullen, and dismissed from his post for bringing an action against a fellow-priest, was also removed from the office of Manager of all the parish schools by the Education Commissioners, without their giving him the opportunity of defending himself. This proceeding Mr. Bouverie strongly condemned as contrary to the elementary principles of justice, declaring that the Commissioners had thereby combined with Cardinal Cullen in a system of priestly intimidation, and to carry out the claims of the Roman Catholic hierarchy to be independent of the lay tribunals. To mark his sense of their conduct, Mr. Bouverie moved a reduction of the vote (Irish education) by £1,000. The Marquis of Hartington, in defending the Board, urged that they had acted in accordance with precedents and practice, and mentioned several cases in which clergymen had been removed, when they had been suspended by the recognized heads of the religious community to which they belonged. As the question of Cardinal Cullen's power to dismiss was about to be raised by Mr. O'Keeffe in a court of law, perhaps it would have been better had the Commissioners waited for the decision of that point. The Government, however, was not prepared to censure the Commissioners, nor to ask them to retrace their steps, but without committing themselves to any agreement with this act of theirs, had decided to await the decision of the courts of law.

"Dr. Ball blamed the Commissioners for not giving Father O'Keeffe an opportunity of being heard in his own defence. Mr. Agar Ellis (member for Kilkenny) also thought that Father O'Keeffe had been badly treated; and Mr. Henley expressed his surprise that any public body should have displayed such painful subserviency to priestly power.

"Mr. Serjeant Sherlock, on the other hand, was of opinion that the Commissioners could not have inquired into the circumstances without inquiring into the legality of the authority by which Mr. O'Keeffe was appointed and removed, but which they had already admitted by accepting him as the parish priest.

"Mr. Newdegate supported the motion, and Mr. Gladstone appealed to the House not to censure a Board which had conferred such services on Ireland for a first error in judgment. Mr. W. Williams declared that the Board had acted with flagrant illegality, which the Attorney-General for Ireland denied.

"On a division, Mr. Bouverie's amendment was negatived by 57 to 49."

Such was the brief summary of the debate in the *Times*. There was no leading article, but on another day the subject was taken up. It may be useful to quote this leading article, because the *Times* spoke in the name of public opinion, and when the case comes up again may need to be the protector of Mr. O'Keeffe against his powerful foes.

"In the autumn of 1870 Mr. O'Keeffe was suspended from his ecclesiastical office by Cardinal Cullen. Into the facts of which this suspension was the result it is unnecessary to enter; it is sufficient to refer to the immediate reason of this extreme measure. Mr. O'Keeffe had been denounced as a 'liar' from the altar of his own parish church, by his curate, at the instance, as was alleged, of the Bishop of his Diocese. At this point Mr. O'Keeffe thought it advisable to bring an action against the Bishop, a proceeding which drew upon him a decree of suspension from the Vicar-General. The action against the Bishop failed through insufficiency of evidence, and Mr. O'Keeffe instituted thereupon a suit against the Curate for slander, which the Vicar-General attempted to stop by a 'command' to withdraw from the case under pain of suspension. Mr. O'Keeffe, disregarding this admonition, was 'suspended' in due form, a resolution of his ecclesiastical superiors to which he showed little intention of yielding. He continued to act as parish priest at Callan in defiance of the Vicar-General; but soon a higher authority was brought to bear upon him. Cardinal Cullen, pointing out the censures, confirmed by the present Pope, 'against those who drag ecclesiastics, and especially bishops, before lay tribunals and there charge them with canonical offences,' finally denounced and suspended Mr. O'Keeffe. Some months after the publication of the Cardinal's decree, the suspension was brought before the Commissioners of National Education by the Roman Catholic Bishop, who requested that the incriminated priest should be superseded in the management of the five parish schools previously under his charge, and that these should be handed over to the control of the successor appointed by the Bishop in Mr. O'Keeffe's place. It was proposed at a meeting of the Commissioners, that before proceeding to dismiss Mr. O'Keeffe, he should be asked for an explanation, but the ecclesiastical element on the Board, consisting principally of the pronounced Catholics who have lately claimed a predominance in Irish educational policy, rejected this appeal. Mr. O'Keeffe was

The O'Keeffe Case.

dismissed and evicted, without a chance of redress or a word of vindication, from the management of schools upon the foundation of which it is admitted he had bestowed a great part of his personal exertions and of his private means.

"It is not surprising that Mr. Gladstone manifested some embarrassment in dealing with the case, that Lord Hartington sheltered himself behind the narrowest technical view of the question involved, or that the House of Commons, even at this advanced period of the session, when the supporters of the Ministry vastly outnumber the independent or opposition members who have the patience to sit out 'Supply,' rejected Mr. Bouverie's Amendment for reducing the Irish Education vote to the amount of £1,000 by a bare majority of eight in a House of 106 members. Of course Mr. Bouverie did not wish to cut down the vote, nor could the Government assent to such a course; but the judgment of the House, plainly enough expressed, may be regarded as equivalent to the old verdict of a sensible though illogical jury, 'Not guilty, but don't do it again.'

"It is hardly necessary to follow Lord Hartington into his elaborate analysis not only of Mr. O'Keeffe's case, but of all the cases arising since the National Education Board was established in Ireland which seemed to be analogous to his. He does not produce a single instance in which the Commissioners have deposed a minister of religion from his educational authority, merely on the ground of his deposition by an ecclesiastical superior. But the principle upon which he founds his approval, qualified though it be, of the course taken by the National Board, certainly appears to require some consideration. Is a Roman Catholic priest, as a consequence of his clerical function, deprived of the ordinary right of resort to the tribunals of his country for the redress of ordinary wrongs? Mr. O'Keeffe had done nothing more than attempt to protect himself against what he considered a wrong, by an action for slander, and this course is punished formally, not only by a suspension from his ecclesiastical functions decreed by his superiors, which it is not the business of the State to criticize, but by deprivation, without appeal or inquiry, of control over the schools within his parish, to which a public body like the National Board should never have lent its sanction.

"Lord Hartington quoted with a little hesitation the opinion of the Rev. Dr. Henry, an eminent Presbyterian divine, a member of the Board, who urged upon the Commissioners the duty of removing any ecclesiastic from his educational authority, on its being certified by his superiors that they have suspended him from his ecclesiastical office. We are glad to recognize the fact, that though Lord Hartington made this singular principle of educational policy a prominent feature in his defence of the Commissioners, Mr. Gladstone, noticing the dangerous use which Mr. Serjeant Sherlock made of it, distinctly declined to accept it. The acceptance of such a principle by a Liberal Government would, indeed, be strange, but its novelty would be less remarkable than its mischief. The position of the National Board in Ireland is not so secure that it can afford to convict itself of being an instrument in the hands of Cardinal Cullen to enforce secular penalties for ecclesiastical offences. The effect of such a policy would be suicidal; for, though Parliament has little sympathy with Mr. Newdegate's feverish suspicions of Roman aggression, it would not be difficult to arouse a jealousy of attempts to use national organizations for sectarian purposes. It is inconsistent with the spirit of fair play we pride ourselves on introducing into all our institutions, that a man should be condemned without being heard, and judged on the fiat of a priest, who regards an appeal to the Common Law of the country as an inexpiable offence."

Accepting this "summary" and "leader" as an accurate report, so far, of the parliamentary discussion, let us now read a little between the lines. The allegation that the Board was justified in deposing the manager merely on the ground of suspension by his ecclesiastical superiors broke down in the debate. The cases cited by the Marquis of Hartington were not in point. Dr. Henry's dictum seems to have influenced the vote of the Commissioners, but his opinion can surely never be accepted by the Ulster Presbyterians. When some of the ministers of the Church of Scotland were served with interdicts, which they considered *ultra vires*, and consequently disregarded, did the General Assembly treat these ministers as guilty, before the validity of the interference was decided by the law courts? Mr. Serjeant Sherlock said that no Court in this realm could deal with questions relating to the internal organization of the Roman Catholic Church. This was an assertion of spiritual independence which Mr. Gladstone took care to question. If any of the arrangements of the Roman Catholic Church interfere with the civil rights of a British subject, the Civil Courts will protect him. They did so when it was proved that the Church of Scotland had interfered with civil rights, and they have interfered with non-established as well as established churches. The supremacy of law must be maintained in all matters affecting civil rights, as in the case of Father O'Keeffe. The sense of the House was so strongly expressed as to his having been unjustly treated, that Mr. Gladstone did not defend the action of the Commissioners. He made an appeal to the pity of the House, not to pass what would be a vote of censure. He said that the Board had for forty years performed most arduous duties. It was a body without which we could hardly ever have established national education in Ireland. When the system was founded it was extremely difficult to give to it anything like solidity or permanence. It was met by determined and angry hostility from various quarters, and much of character, much of ability, much of prudence and policy were required in order to obtain for that system anything like fair play. For that purpose, the best and wisest men that could be found in Ireland were selected by successive Governments; they had undertaken this most important, difficult, and invidious labour, and by that labour, which seemed almost hopelessly exerted for a long series of years, they brought the system to such a state that, instead of a condition of things in which the supporters of the National Board were continually threatened by their opponents (and it was hard to say which way the balance would incline), now, on the contrary, there was a competition between all parties of politicians in this country, each declaring that they were the most zealous advocates of the National system. This, too, was an unpaid Board—that was a point which ought to be mentioned; but the main point to which he wished to direct attention was the arduous nature of its labours, the difficulties it had had to encounter, and the success which had attended its patriotic efforts. He would therefore ask his right hon. friend whether he would call upon the House to pass a vote of censure on such a body.

The effect of this apologetic and somewhat humiliating appeal was that Mr. Bouverie's motion was negatived. The majority was only 8 in a House of 106, the officials of the Treasury, with "the Pope's brass band," forming a large section of the majority.

The number of Irish members who took part in the division was 26, of whom 19 voted against, and 7 for, Mr. Bouverie's motion. The number of Irish members absent was 77!

The result of the parliamentary vote was naturally discouraging to Father O'Keeffe. He published a letter complaining of the conduct of the Government, and especially of the action of Mr. Gladstone. In this letter he quotes the statements of a number of Roman Catholic prelates to show that, before Cardinal Cullen, Irish bishops never assumed the power to interfere in civil matters. "If I am given an opportunity in any way of proving that Cardinal Cullen is endeavouring to propagate in Ireland Ultramontane opinions, I am prepared with my proofs.

I have his own handwriting to produce, both in reference to the *Bulla Cœnæ* and the bull of October the 12th, 1869. I laughed at Cardinal Cullen's attempts to degrade me before I committed a fault; but when the Prime Minister of England allows a public board to degrade me after being informed I had got no trial, I submit to my fate, and content myself with praying that Almighty God may open the eyes of the blind. Lynch law has failed to strike me down when my assailant was a minister of the Church; but when a minister of the State inflicts the blow, I 'readily bite the dust.' Other tyrants I can fight and conquer; but if a Prime Minister of England will use might against right, I succumb."

To complete the materials for understanding the present politics of the case, two or three other points must be mentioned. Following the Commissioners of Education, the Poor Law Commissioners removed Mr. O'Keeffe from the chaplaincy of the union workhouse. If the Irish law courts decide the validity or invalidity of the suspension, the restoration to the chaplaincy as well as to the school managership will follow. What the law courts may do is uncertain, when we see a man like Lord O'Hagan, the Chancellor, in his new position in the House of Lords, justify the conduct of the Education Board. The suspension of Mr. O'Keeffe was declared without his being charged with any crime or cited to any court. It is as well established in the canon law as the civil law that no condemnation can occur, or produce any effect whatever, without a trial, or at least a citation to one; yet every one of the censures pronounced against Mr. O'Keeffe was written behind his back, and without a formal intimation, and without any cause assigned, except that he went to law with an ecclesiastic. And public boards, not ecclesiastical, but civil and national, endorse these illegal proceedings, and deal with Mr. O'Keeffe as if he were condemned after trial! Conceive such a thing in England! Why, it costs a bishop endless trouble and no small expense to secure the suspension of a clergyman even for notorious immorality. But in Ireland this sentence against Mr. O'Keeffe is pronounced by mere arbitrary will, without trial; and the civil power, represented by the Education and Poor Law Boards, obsequiously carries out the irregular ecclesiastical sentence. Surely the courts of law cannot sanction and make a precedent of such a case, and so admit, not ecclesiastical law, nor canon law, but the will of the Vatican and its emissaries, to override the laws of the United Kingdom.

An action was brought before the Recorder of Dublin by the Callan National School teachers against the Education Commissioners for the amount of their salary. The Judge decided that the Commissioners are not liable in regard to the payment of salaries of teachers in non-vested schools. The contract of the teachers is with the manager. The manager, Father O'Keeffe, with whom the contract was made, having been removed, the Board is not liable for the payments. This decision will be carried on appeal to a higher Court, but in the meantime the Commissioners have placed themselves in submission to the ecclesiastical power, against which Father O'Keeffe is struggling. The National Board holds its authority from the State, and is a civil and not an ecclesiastical department. The aid given by them to the Callan schools was withdrawn, not because of any violation of the rules laid down, or failure to meet any appointed requirements, but solely because of the interference of an external and unauthorized influence. The teachers were examined by the district inspector, and all the regulations of the Board were attended to in the appointments. At the close of each quarter the schedule returns were filled up and signed in the usual way. The manager paid the salaries, the teachers agreeing to repay what was allowed to them by the Education Office. By the refusal to pay these teachers, Father O'Keeffe has been deprived of the money, and, when unable longer to pay, he assisted the teachers to emigrate to America.

Another ecclesiastic, Bishop Moran, in the course of events appears upon the scene. He is the Bishop Coadjutor (cowjootherer, as the Irish call it) to the aged Dr. Walsh, prelate of the diocese. At a confirmation held at Callan he gives his account of the position of Father O'Keeffe. After some general observations on the duty of submission to superiors and the sin of dissension, and after hearty abuse of the Dublin *Mail* and *Express*, and the London *Times* and *Standard*—" the defaming *Times*, and most stupid of British prints, the *Standard*"—the Bishop proceeds: " The Vicar of Christ, the divinely-constituted centre of Catholic union, the fountain of all jurisdiction in the Church, has suspended the late pastor of Callan from all sacerdotal functions. Opposition is not now merely to the Bishop or any delegated authority, it is to the Vicar of Jesus Christ, to the supreme Pastor on earth of your souls. Designing men have been working hard to make it appear that these lamentable disturbances are the result of a private quarrel between the late pastor and me; but I never had a private quarrel with him. The question is now narrowed to this—is the authoritative sentence of the Vicar of Christ to be obeyed by a priest or defied? Are we to see a conventicle, a synagogue of Satan, set up in your midst? Whosoever now shall willingly and knowingly attend mass in the house now darkened by the shadow of the interdict commits a grievous sin, is witness to an appalling sacrilege, and as far as in him lies, acts once more the part of those who witnessed with mockery the sacrifice of Christ on the cross. He who knowingly and willingly accepts the ministrations of this suspended priest at his dying hour, receives not the strengthening grace to die in peace with God, receives not God's strengthening assurance, but the seal of his own eternal perdition. Whoever knowingly and willingly approaches the tribunal of penance where this intruder, struck by the censures of the living Peter, fears not to sit, his sins are not forgiven to his soul. The beauty of grace is not imparted; he perpetrates a horrid crime. I trust you are now so fully aware of the nature of the position in which your late pastor has placed himself, as no longer to be deceived into opposition to the Vicar of Christ."

One would have expected the sentence of excommunication to follow, but the Bishop contented himself with causing it to be intimated from the Friary chapel that, unless "the late parish priest" and his supporters at once submit to the Vicar of Christ, he would excommunicate them with bell, book, and candle, and cut them off as rotten branches. I may add that this Bishop Moran, who spoke with such insolence, is nephew to Cardinal Cullen, who seems to get any one appointed to Irish Catholic sees at his own nomination.

Nothing daunted by this denunciation, Father O'Keeffe on the following Sunday charged his Bishop with being afraid to carry out the threat of actual excommunication. It would be futile, he said, even if he ventured; whereas his excommunication of the Bishop would be a real exercise of power, under one of the canons of the Fourth Lateran Council. He would continue the struggle, and would serve a writ upon the Bishop.

The condition of the town of Callan during all these proceedings has been deplorable, as may well be supposed. From rival altars denunciations were hurled, and the partisans of the two sides lived in constant strife. Not only the people of the town, but the paupers in the workhouse, were dragged into the conflict. Sometimes mass was said in the chapel, sometimes the inmates were allowed to go to the parish priest's church. On one occasion one of the curates threatened to go to Mr. O'Keeffe's church and strip his vestments off him. The clerk heard of the threat, and prevented violence by locking the outer gates. "There were more than 3,000 persons in and around my church," says Mr. O'Keeffe, "and I firmly believe, if he assaulted me in their presence, he would never leave the church alive. He paraded the streets very late at night, escorted by a gang of the very worst characters of the town, abusing me everywhere in the most violent manner. The leader of the party was a notorious Fenian, Heffernan Dunne, the former mock candidate for the county, and a ruffian who was convicted three times of violent assaults at the single sessions held here in July, 1871." In the September sessions there were above seventy cases of assault and battery by the adherents of the rival factions. The four justices who formed the court had their hands full. About twenty men and women were sent to jail, and nearly fifty fined or locked up for short periods.

All through the autumn months of last year the town continued in ferment. The people were divided, the great majority siding with their parish priest. A large and violent body, however, took the part of the "mission" priests. Not in Belfast nor in Derry itself could there be more bitter hostility between Orange and Green, than there was in this Kilkenny town between the two Catholic parties. Sunday after Sunday vehement harangues were addressed to the excited congregations, the preachers on both sides launching threats and defiances against their opponents. Week after week the people were stirred. At length, one October Sunday evening, after service was concluded in his own chapel, Father O'Keeffe, having given previous notice of his intention, drove down to the Friary chapel to challenge the Commissioners to repeat before his face the calumnies which they had long been uttering. Nearly three thousand people followed him along the streets, cheering vociferously. Some of them, no doubt, were neutral, and wished "a plague on both your houses," but the Irish love of a skrimmage or fight made them swell the hubbub. In vain Father O'Keeffe waved his hand and called for silence. "Down with Cullen," "Three cheers for O'Keeffe," "Who sold Ireland for Peter's pence?" and other tumultuous shouts, drowned his voice. On reaching the chapel gates the mob was confronted by several magistrates and a strong body of constabulary. On a rush being made to force the gates, the police had to keep the people back by showing cold steel and firm front. Father O'Keeffe did his best to restrain his followers, and the police having sheathed their weapons, he obtained silence sufficient for a brief address. Telling the people that he was a minister of peace, but that the priests in the mission-house were emissaries of strife and contention, he besought them to disperse quietly, and give no handle to their enemies by any riotous conduct. He was determined to maintain the independence of the Catholic Church and their rights as Irishmen, with more to the same effect, responded to by cheers for himself and groans for his opponents. The firmness of the authorities on this occasion prevented what might have been a serious outbreak, and a strong permanent reinforcement of police afterwards kept order in the town, but this scene will give an idea of the excitement that prevailed. No wonder that it was spoken of as "the civil war of Callan."

The Fenian Dunne and Father Neary, a recently appointed curate, seemed the chief fomentors of dispeace, the majority of the respectable people of Callan siding with their parish priest. The estimation in which he is held will appear from the following circular, asking aid for the law expenses:—

"Callan, Nov. 15, '72.

"SIR,—Our respected parish priest has been now struggling for more than two years against an unheard-of oppression. The battle he is fighting in defence of his own position is one of liberty, civil and religious, for all classes of the community, and we therefore appeal to the public at large to aid us in keeping him in the position which he has held for the last ten years, with credit to himself as a zealous priest and a loving pastor, and with the gratitude and love of the generality of his flock, notwithstanding all the efforts made by merciless men in Church and State to degrade him before his people.

"We are, Sir, your obedient Servants,

"PATRICK TORPY, *Treasurer.*

"EDWARD A. O'DWYER, Clk., } *Honorary*
"PATRICK KEEFFE, } *Secretaries.*"

There are other reasons besides the peace of Callan or of the Roman Catholic Church, or even the question of civil power being overborne by ecclesiastical assumption, why this O'Keeffe case must be settled. Since the alleged suspension, endorsed by the act of the Board in dismissing him from the school managership and the workhouse chaplaincy, Father O'Keeffe has not ceased to solemnize marriages, and exercise other spiritual functions. None of these rites are recorded in State registries. Will the State forbid this clergyman to solemnize marriages, since by accepting the notice of suspension it has, through the National Board, declared he has no legal spiritual position, and is not the recognized district registrar? Father O'Keeffe declines to deliver the certificates of marriage to other officials. Legal questions may hereafter arise in family arrangements affected by these celebrations, and even questions of validity of marriage and of legitimacy.

These difficulties will multiply if the decision of the case is postponed. It may be very troublesome to the Government to give offence to Cardinal Cullen by resisting the unconstitutional aggression of Rome, but the sooner the supremacy of British over Roman law is declared the better, for the sake of civil as well as ecclesiastical peace and order.

Whatever may be the decision of the Irish courts of law, it is clear that the question will be again a prominent one in England. If the decision is against Mr. O'Keeffe, there will probably be an appeal to the House of Lords. The Marquis of Hartington made the extraordinary statement, that "Cardinal Cullen did not shrink from the inquiry, and would maintain he was invested with the necessary authority for what he did. He did not mean to say that Cardinal Cullen would feel himself bound by the decision of the court, but the Cardinal did not shrink from arguing the question." This is not the chief question with which the English public have to do. The question is as to the action of the National Board, not that of the ecclesiastical authorities. The educational grant is for national, not denominational purposes, and the matter will have to be brought again before Parliament to have this point clearly settled.

If fresh difficulties should arise in the working of the existing Educational Commissioners, it will be better to have a new National Board, under the Minister of Education, with rules more explicit than now exist. If the Roman Catholic bishops object, they have the remedy in their own hands; let them either support their own denominational schools, or join in seeking from Ireland itself a rate for national education. While there is a parliamentary grant, the will of Parliament must be supreme as to the rules of its application.

Until the action against Cardinal Cullen commenced, the latest public incident in the O'Keeffe case was an action in the Irish Court of Queen's Bench, brought against the Rev. John Walsh for slander. The defendant did not appear. The defence was that the words were not slanderous, and that they were spoken on a privileged occasion. This means, I suppose, that they were spoken at the altar, which to an English mind aggravates rather than extenuates the offence. The case had already been tried, and a mixed jury, half Protestants and half Roman Catholics, gave a verdict for the plaintiff, with £100 damages, but on a technical point a new trial was appointed. Mr. Coffey, Q.C., in stating the plaintiff's case, denounced the conduct of the defendant in neither making appearance nor giving assent to judgment, and so putting the plaintiff to the trouble and expense of carrying out the new trial. The jury found a verdict for the plaintiff, with £250 damages. The Lord Chief Justice, in his charge to the jury, said that "the plaintiff occupied the very influential position of a parish priest, and had very onerous duties to discharge, and the defendant was his curate, and whether churchwarden or layman, bishop, priest, or parson, all were equal in point of law when their cases came to be submitted to a court of justice. Every subject of the Queen was in her courts entitled to the benefit of the same law, and to the same measure of justice, neither more nor less. No rule, no regulation, no canon, could deprive a subject of the right to complain of and to seek redress for a temporal wrong, and the courts of justice were open to all equally."

Noble words from the Lord Chief Justice; and it is only to be hoped that the same assertion of the supremacy of the laws of England will be made when Mr. O'Keeffe brings another fellow-subject of the Queen before the Court, though he bears the foreign title of "Cardinal" Cullen. If there is any tampering with justice in that case, it will be disastrous to the future of Ireland. The Cardinal was in Rome last year, probably for consultation with his friends, the General of the Jesuit order, and other chiefs of the Ultramontane party. It was rumoured that he was staying in Italy so as to divest himself of his British citizenship, but this seems to have been overruled, and when the trial comes on, as is expected, in the course of this year, the people of Ireland will then be taught that "the courts of justice are open to all equally."

Mr. O'Keeffe is fighting the battle of every parish priest in Ireland, and of the Irish Catholic Church, against the tyranny of Rome. The prelates of that Church have been gradually brought into complete subjection, every appointment for many years having been an arbitrary one from the Vatican, the nomination of the Irish Church being a thing of the past. Formerly three names were sent to Rome, as we have already stated, and from these the selection was made, preference being usually given to the name indicated on the list. But this old usage has been contemptuously disregarded, all recent bishops having been appointed in the interests of Rome, not of Ireland. They are mere satellites of Cardinal Cullen, and he is the delegate and agent of Rome. The Irish priests are being brought wholly under subjection to these Ultramontane bishops, and the rights of the laity are utterly disregarded. If Mr. O'Keeffe is successful in his conflict, it will be a national protest against the tyranny of the Ultramontane party.

But whatever may be the issue of the O'Keeffe case, a wider question has been raised, which the English nation will not suffer to remain unsettled.

Are the laws of England or of Rome to have the supremacy in the British dominions? A foreign power, unrecognized by the law or the constitution, dares to interfere with the British courts, and to limit the rights of British citizens. The papal legate proclaims that every Catholic priest is debarred from bringing before the lay tribunals a brother ecclesiastic. The exigencies of party politics have brought the British Government into such relations with the Ultramontanes and their leader that these monstrous claims are not repudiated with indignation, as they would be by other European Governments. The press, the ordinary exponent of public opinion, has too much been influenced by the same reserve, imposed by party politics. But there is an appeal even from the press to a wider public opinion, and the Prime Minister, whichever party is in office, must make his choice between the support of the Ultramontane faction and that of the great body of the people, whether Protestant or Catholic, who wish to maintain the laws and constitution of England.

I refrain from saying anything about the case of *O'Keeffe* v. *Cullen*, because while I write the case is being pleaded before the Irish Court of Queen's Bench. *Adhuc sub judice lis est.* Some explanation is desired of the ugly fact that the Commissioners of National Education announced the withdrawal of the grant to the Callan schools on the very day that the pleadings commenced in the law courts. The announcement of this step at such a time was calculated, if not intended, to prejudice Mr. O'Keeffe's case in the action against Cardinal Cullen.

CHAPTER XIV.

THE KEOGH JUDGMENT.

The Galway Election—Priestly Terrorism—Judge Keogh's Speech - The Troubles of the Franchise.

I WAS moving about in Ireland during the storm of angry indignation excited by the Galway Election Judgment. A shell pitched into a room full of stealthy conspirators could not have caused more commotion. It was not so much the judicial decision, as the language in which it was delivered, that made the impression. The stern denunciation of priestly terrorism was unexpected from such a quarter. "A peal of thunder from a cloudless sky could not have caused greater astonishment, than this fulmination from the serene atmosphere of the judicial bench. The audacity of the Catholic equals the energy of the judge. If this judgment had come from a Protestant chief justice, or from a committee of the House of Commons, which Protestant prejudices might be assumed to ˙sway, it might have been borne with equanimity. The language would have been set down to partisan zeal, and the unseating the priestly nominee would have been merely a single turn in the fortune of war. But Mr. Justice Keogh is himself a Roman Catholic. Twenty years ago he was himself one of the champions of that Church in the House of Commons. At the election of 1852 he was returned to Parliament pledged to obtain the repeal of the "Ecclesiastical Titles Bill," then newly added to the statute-book; and when he joined Lord Aberdeen's administration as one of the Irish law officers of the Crown, it was in company with politicians who were generally well-disposed to the Catholics and their claims.

"How comes it," says the *Times*, in thus commenting on the outburst of priestly clamour, "how comes it that such a man should now, when the vivacity of youth is past, and the rhetoric of the Bar and of Parliament is but a fading reminiscence, declaim with fervid eloquence against the tyranny of bishops, and the violence, dishonesty, and equivocation of priests? There can be but one answer—that something has been developed of late years in the character of the Romish Church in Ireland, and in the demeanour of the priesthood, which is intolerable to the educated layman, good Catholic though he be, and accustomed to suppress his emotions and measure his language." That this is the true answer, we are assured by Mr. Justice Keogh himself in the closing of his speech in delivering the judgment. After referring to the gratitude due from Catholics to Edmund Burke, and Plunkett, and Grattan, and Canning, and other Protestants who helped to secure emancipation, and equality of civil and political rights, Judge Keogh said: "In the year 1869, sitting in this very place, I expressed, as I express now, the belief that if an attempt was made to set up a Roman Catholic ascendancy in the place of that which Parliament was then engaged in abolishing, the intelligence, the spirit, and the independence of the lay Catholics of this country would prevent its establishment. I shall never forget the way in which that statement was received in a court crowded, as the present court is, by all classes, rich and poor; whilst the Roman Catholic Bishop of Galway sat under this bench, looking at the whole of the crowded audience which filled every point to hear the decision of the then Galway election petition. I say I shall never forget the way in which that sentiment, uttered by a Roman Catholic, born in this Roman Catholic town, of Roman Catholic parents, with scarcely a relative in the world who was not a Roman Catholic, was received by a densely-crowded court. The sentiment which I uttered did not grate upon the feelings of any one then present. That attempt, I am bound to say, though three years only have expired since I uttered these words, has since been made. It has been met and defeated by the spirit, the independence, and the intelligence of the Roman Catholic gentry of this great country; and I cannot say that I feel otherwise than proud of my countrymen, at having had the spirit, the courage, and the independence, rich and poor, the peer and the peasant, the gentle lady and the stalwart yeoman, to come to this court and give their evidence, as they have done, with the most perfect frankness, fearlessness, and truth. I now, in closing this case, entertain a well-founded belief that the lesson to be learned from the whole of these transactions will not be thrown away. I, at all events, sincerely pray, that when the agitation caused by this petition has subsided, all parties and classes will recur to the maxims of our great Teacher, whose every word was a parable of love:

> ' By whom we learn our hopes and fears to guide;
> To bear with envy, to contend with pride;
> When grieved, to pray; when injured, to forgive;
> And with the world in charity to live.' "

Then followed the decision, that "the seat of this county must be declared void, and Captain Nolan must pay to his antagonist (Captain Trench) the expenses of this petition."

Of the justice of the decision, upon the evidence given, not a shadow of doubt has been raised. The proofs of undue influence and priestly intimidation were clear. Denunciations from the altar, threats of excommunication, defamation of character, and even incitements to assassination, were among the charges proved. The latter charge was denied, the priest who used the expression, "the death-knell of Sir Thomas Burke," saying he only meant "political death-knell." "I would like to see," said Judge Keogh, "the Tipperary man with a blunderbuss in his hand at night, who would draw the nice distinction between a physical death-knell and a political death-knell." Another priest said from the altar, that "any renegade Catholic who would not vote for Captain Nolan would be a disgrace to his God, his religion, and his country, and would go to hell! There are black sheep, not many, thank God! Any one who would vote for Captain Trench he would not attend,"—meaning that he would be cut off from the offices of religion. Another priest said, that "any who would vote for Trench would go down to their graves with the brand of Cain on them and their children after them." This same priest cursed from the altar the wife of a landlord who was expected to vote for Captain Trench, and used such indecent and violent language about her, that "the people were beating their breasts and looking at each other; and after they went out they conferred all about the chapel, and disapproved of his conduct; and some of them said it was a shame to speak of a good lady in that way." Another priest said to his congregation, "If the agents of Trench come among you, hunt them from you like devils. Better for those who have horses that the horses should have their legs cut from under them than that they should hire them for Trench;" which means, "Don't hough or hamstring the horses!" "don't nail his ears to the pump!"

These are but specimens of the influence used by the clergy. The bishops were more guarded in their utterances, but several of them were proved to have incited the priests to use their official terrorism.

With such things declared in evidence upon oath, can we wonder at the vehement indignation of a high-minded man like Judge Keogh? We may disapprove the language of his speech, but we understand the spirit by which it was prompted. "Sir Thomas Burke," said the Judge, "has been maligned, has been slandered through the papers in every way that the vocabulary of the foulest literature can at all suggest, because he used the words 'priestly dictation.' I, from this bench, having examined the whole of the evidence in this case, I solemnly believe with more care than I ever did anything before in the whole-course of my life, on a full review of the whole of the evidence, proclaim it to have been not 'priestly dictation,' but *the most astounding attempt at ecclesiastical tyranny which the whole history of priestly intolerance presents.*"

This condemnation was not passed without duly guarding himself against being supposed to deny the legitimate influence of the clergy, even in political matters. "I declared in the Galway town case the legitimate influence of the clergy was desirable; and I declare now that the legitimate influence of the clergy is desirable, and that the priests have a right to exercise their legitimate privileges, in the same way as landlords or other classes; but if influence is unduly exercised by any one of them, the higher the person who used it, the more fearlessly he ought to be dealt with." And again: "Any man has a right to counsel every one of his fellows to do certain things; and more, to urge them not to do certain things; but not to hold out 'spiritual terror,' in the words of Sir Samuel Romilly, 'on hopes of future happiness, or to threaten them with eternal misery.'"

But it is unnecessary to say more about the justice of the decision, or the proofs of the guilty charges which led to its being pronounced. The real offence against Judge Keogh is, the outspoken language in which the conduct of the priests was exposed and censured, as in the words above which I have italicized. He was immediately attacked, to use his own words just quoted in regard to Sir Thomas Burke, and "maligned in every way that the vocabulary of the foulest literature can at all suggest." The *Irishman* newspaper drew a parallel between him and Judge Jeffreys. "Fish-wife Keogh's last outrage" was the heading of an article in the *Weekly News*. The *Nation*, once a patriotic paper, but now too much under priestly control, abused him both in prose and verse, in a strain which two stanzas will suffice to show :—

> A blight on his caste—a reproach to his land,
> Castlereagh disinterred—with the knife in his hand ;
> Of no creed the guardian—of all faiths the foe—
> Behold, O my people, so help me God Keogh.
>
> The system that bred him, from step unto step,
> From the guilt in his heart to the lie on his lip,
> May shout in its devilish triumph to know
> Perfection was reached in so help me God Keogh.

By pencil as well as pen he was attacked with like ferocity, and caricatures, both threatening and contemptuous, were everywhere displayed. As the result of these attacks of the press, and the unreported but equally violent harangues of the clergy, no wonder that the Judge was burned in effigy at many places, and at the next assizes he had to be accompanied on circuit by an armed escort. To this abuse of the power of the press, in stirring up ignorant mobs to violence, several of the Judges made allusion in their charges on circuit. Baron Deasy at Tralee, in addressing the Grand Jury of Kerry, said, " I trust I am not exceeding the limits of my duty when I express the hope, the confidence, and the belief, that all right-minded persons on one side and the other, whether they approve or disapprove of that judgment; all interested in the character of our common country, all who wish to see the peace and order of the country maintained, will condemn with me those attempted demonstrations of personal hostility, and those inflammatory, I may say incendiary appeals to an ignorant and excited people. I believe such scenes do not exist in any other civilized country. It is the first occasion upon which this effigy-burning has been brought judicially before any of her Majesty's judges. . . . I make these observations not with the view or hope that my words can have any influence over these people, for I know they have none; but if they can induce any of those who can speak words of power, to use them to prevent the repetition elsewhere of these disgraceful, demoralizing proceedings, my words will not have been entirely in vain." Baron

Deasy may have been speaking with courteous irony, but he might know that an appeal of this kind would have more weight with the rudest populace than with the priestly writers or prompters of these incendiary articles. They deserve the severe punishments awarded to the rioters and effigy-burners at several places during the autumn assizes, including Galway, where I heard a poor fellow sentenced to a year's imprisonment, a punishment of which the priests who caused all the mischief are more richly deserving.

The resolution adopted by the Grand Jury of Leitrim expresses the general feeling of the better classes in Ireland as to the popular clamour. "We, the Grand Jury of the county of Leitrim, having heard with regret and indignation the manner in which Mr. Justice Keogh's judgment in the Galway Election Petition case had been commented upon by certain portions of the press, and by persons opposed to the proper vindication of the laws of the land, hereby desire to express our sincere approval of the cool and effectual exposure contained in that judgment, of the organized system of intimidation by which the constitutional rights of the electors of Galway were defeated at the last election for that county. We also desire to express our hope that the executive government will, without any further delay, take the necessary steps to vindicate the dignity and independence of the judicial bench, so grossly assailed in Mr. Justice Keogh's person, and thus evince their determination to uphold the due administration of the law."

If the Government make the prosecution of the bishops and priests reported by Judge Keogh a sham prosecution,* if they allow so clear and flagrant a violation of law to pass unpunished, they will shake the confidence of the independent Catholic laity, and of all the respectable Catholic clergy, without receiving any permanent gratitude from the Italian faction, who are the disturbers of the peace of Ireland. Many of the Catholic landlords in Galway are now living in peril, and some have been obliged to leave the county. In describing the condition of the county, Judge Keogh gave many instances of the terrorism that prevailed. Lord Kelvin, the son of Lord Westmeath, had to absent himself from church, and was afraid to allow his children outside his demesne. Sir Arthur Guinness, in going to vote, was severely cut in the head, and several of the men accompanying him were badly wounded. Worse than this would happen if a warning is not given to those who defy the

---

* The trials have taken place in Dublin while I write. Although convictions have not been obtained in any of the cases, a useful lesson has been given as to the limits of priestly interference in political affairs.

authority of law. Meekness in so flagrant a case will undo all that has been done in recent years for establishing the supremacy of the laws of England. There will be bluster and abuse again from a part of the so-called "national" press, but it is only the Ultramontane faction that keep up the agitation. Unhappily to this faction belong Archbishop Manning, and Sir George Bowyer, and all the English perverts, whose influence is brought to bear on the Government. But a firm administration will gain the respect of the Irish Catholic laity. "What the Catholic gentlemen of Galway endured in the last contest," says the *Times*, "has been endured more or less by their class for many years, and there are signs that their lot will become every year more forlorn. The lesson should not be lost upon the Queen's Government. One administration after another has been in fault in this matter, and Mr. Gladstone's is not the least weak and undignified. Englishmen live in blessed ignorance of many things which pass on the other side of St. George's Channel. But no one acquainted with Ireland doubts that Cardinal Cullen is the most powerful man in the country. The chief of the Romish hierarchy rules Ireland in all but name. . . . The judgment in the Galway Election case proclaims to us in vivid language what sort of men our rulers have laboured to conciliate, and, we may almost say, stooped to obey. The past is irrevocable; but if this abominable business teaches a more courageous and manly administration of Ireland, one sought for equally by the educated and enlightened of both religions, its scandals will not have been in vain."

One thing suggested by this case is that the disfranchisement of Galway, and of any other constituency exposed to such conflicts of opinion, would be the best boon that could be conferred on the people. The relation of landlord and tenant would be peacefully maintained but for the disturbance caused at election times. The priests are unable to lead the independent Catholic gentry at their will, but they have uncontrolled power over the small tenant farmer and the labouring classes.

Often it is by the female side of the house that the evil spirit of disaffection enters, but sometimes the native good sense of the women asserts itself, as is illustrated in an amusing scene in one of Miss Walshe's capital Irish tales, "The Foster Brothers of Doon." I must quote it as a relief to the political tension of this and the preceding chapter. Barney Brallaghan had been at a meeting where he had heard a speech from Counsellor O'Regan, a member of Parliament, like Mr. Butt, Q.C., of our time, a Protestant by profession, but fraternizing with "the ancient faith." The Counsellor had exhorted his excited audience to stand by their country against "the old hereditary enemy." Most of them thought that the enemy must be their landlord, Colonel Butler, whereas Mr. O'Regan probably meant to impersonate "the Saxon." "Barney arrived at his cabin in a high state of indignation at the wrongs of Ireland, and, flinging his remnant of a hat into one corner, he sat himself down beside the table, striking it with his fist, after certain mutterings, and a tragic stare into the turf fire."

"'Arrah, Barney, avick,' says his wife, picking up the battered caubeen, 'Barney, what's gone wrong wid ye? An' the hat, the crathur, throth an' it has got awful thratement intirely somewhere; one 'ud think the parish danced on it,' observed Mrs. Barney, holding the article regretfully, with due appreciation of how long it would be ere her lord could get another.

"'Tut, woman, to be thinkin' ov an ould caubeen, when we ought all to be cryin' over the miseries of our counthry, an' the wrongs ov our posterity an' our ancesthors! 'Twould melt a heart of stone to hear how his honour the Counsellor expounded all about the way the Parlyment trates us, an' the Lord-liftenant, an' the——'

"'Why, thin, Barney Brallaghan, is it yer ancesthors that's throublin' ye this way? Aisy known, there isn't much on yer mind else, honest man, an' 'tisn't to dig up that patch o' flax ye would this evenin'; only goin' off to listen to speeches, just as if the Counsellor had any other business in life but to be talkin' like a house a-fire. An' look here, av he talked till he was black in the face you'll have to vote for the Captin all the same, an' you *know* you will. What's anybody's wrongs to us, or all the wrongs in the world, compared with the wrong of not havin' a cabin to put our head into?'

"This unanswerable logic seemed rather to pose poor Barney, who merely looked into the fire with a very wise face, and shook his head slightly a few times. One glance at his wife had showed him that lady in an attitude not to be trifled with—a hand on each hip, and a belligerent countenance gazed straight at him. The girl of the Malonys had asserted herself before now, and governed Barney for his good; and so, in the present instance, when she ordered him to bed, remarking that he would never be in time 'to overtak' mass in the mornin' av he didn't go at wonst,' his remonstrance was very feeble.

"'They're the ganders for men, they are,' was her uncomplimentary soliloquy as she 'raked' the fire— which process means the preserving of some turf in a smouldering state under a heap of dry ashes, to act as kindling next morning. 'They b'lieves every single word that's said to them, an' would sooner be takin' care of their ancesthors than their own little haggarts (potato patch); just as if their ancesthors would ever be worth the value of a pratie to 'em. What do I care av they were killin' one another from morning to night long ago? They're welcome, as long as nobody comes to kill ourselves; an' the long an' the short of it is, Barney must vote for the Captin that owns the roof over him, if all our ancesthors was to die on the spot.'

"Next morning the worthy couple went to 'get mass,' which was to do them some imaginary good, like a charm, for the week to come. From the wonderful sermon of Father Pat Costello, here are a few sentences:—'Now, boys, ye'll be wantin' to know somethin' about this election that's comin' on Friday. I'm fond of a whole skin meself, an' a roof over me head, an' indeed I don't see rightly how both of them is to be had together on this occasion. I'm afeard ye must take yer choice agin, boys—or let the wives take it for ye. There's a dale o' sinse in the women's heads, boys, an' a dale o' sinse outside 'em too. Somehow I think the Counsellor has put his comedher on a good many o' them, an' they'll coax their husbands to give him one vote, anyhow. I'm not sayin' they're rong or right, remember. I christened a dale o' ye, an' 'twould be the sorra day I got ye into any trouble through advice of mine. Talkin' o' christenings, why then, Misthren Ryan, is it yerself I see standin' over under the window? Yer welcome to mass agin, ma'am, an' so is the little stranger that ye has in yer cloak; an' that was a dacent christenin' ye gave him, an' didn't forget yer priests nayther, signs by he'll have all sorts of prosperity.' And so he went rattling through a discursive 'sermon' on all sorts of domestic and personal as well as political topics.

"'Troth an' it would puzzle a conjuror to tell out o' that sermon who 'twould be plazin' to his riverence we'd vote for,' said thick-headed Barney, rubbing his brows. 'But somehow it don't seem as if he meant the Captin; sorra bit o' me but wishes they never came for elections, to be botherin' a poor man's little han'full of brains this way.' The latter sentiment he had gathered from the lips of his better half, and dutifully repeated without owning the authorship; and Mrs. Barney, like all true wives, was well pleased to minister an idea in secret to her liege lord, and merge her own wisdom in his.

"'Well, you got mighty meek-spirited since you got married,' observed a bachelor companion with whom he walked, 'you that used to have the best shillelah at every fair and hurlin' match, an' thought the greater ruction the bigger fun.' 'Wait till yer married yerself, Shamus, an' ye'll find it's not pleasant to be sittin' by the fire wid yer head in two halves, an' yer eyes like blackberries.'   *   *   *

"'As to my Pat,' said another wife, 'he's most out of his mind already, listening to speechin' from mornin' to night; and he roars out in his sleep, rousin' up all the childer like a clap of thunder, an' flourishin' his arms as if they was windmills. An' sure we wouldn't care if he was to get any good by it; but he won't; only comin' home to me wid' his bones in smithereens, maybe.'

The women were recognizing, in their own homely way, the great fact that an overweening attention to political agitation was a domestic and social bane in Ireland.

CHAPTER XV.

IRISH AGRICULTURE.

Soil and Resources—Agricultural Statistics—Tillage and Pasture—Hindrances to Progress.

IRELAND is, to a greater extent than England or Scotland, an agricultural country, manufactures or trade forming a far less proportion in the employment or resources of the people.

There was a return obtained last session of the total number of electors, parliamentary and municipal, in England and Wales, in Scotland, and in Ireland. To the political use made of these statistics, as by Mr. Butt in a series of letters in the *Times* on redistribution of Irish constituencies, I do not here refer, but the figures are interesting as showing the comparative distribution of population and wealth in town and country. The total number of voters on the parliamentary register for cities and boroughs in England and Wales is 1,250,019; in Scotland, 171,912; in Ireland, only 49,025. The total number of county voters in England and Wales is 801,109; in Scotland, 78,919; in Ireland, 175,439.

It is quite possible that in some cases the boundaries of borough and county may have been arranged with political cleverness, as was done in the English Reform bills. But taking these figures on the whole, it is evident that Ireland is emphatically an agricultural country, and that the proprietors and cultivators of the soil are the true representatives of public opinion. Dublin has a population of about 245,000, Belfast 175,000, Cork under 80,000, Limerick 40,000, Londonderry 25,000, Waterford 23,000. These six towns are absolutely all that have a population above 20,000. The towns with population above 10,000 are only three more: Drogheda with 14,400, Galway with 13,000, Kilkenny with 12,600. Out of nearly 50,000 electors, nominally entitled to be borough voters, more than half are in Dublin and Belfast, and about 35,000 are in the towns of Dublin, Belfast, Cork, Limerick, and Waterford. All the remaining borough constituencies of Ireland have little more than 13,000 electors among them, about the size of the constituency of one average English borough of the second class, as Norwich, for instance, or Oldham. Several of the Irish boroughs have less than 300 electors. All this shows the paucity and poverty of the population of boroughs as compared with the rural population.

Agriculture is therefore the most important element in the material wealth and prosperity of the nation.

The extreme richness of the meadow and pasture land of Ireland has long been celebrated. A century ago Arthur Young said that the grazing counties were "some of the finest pastures in the world." Speaking specially of parts of Limerick and Tipperary he said, "it is the richest soil I ever saw." Sixty years ago Mr. Wakefield, in his "Statistical Account of Ireland" (1812) says, "Some places (throughout Meath in particular) exhibit the richest loam I ever saw turned up by a plough. Where such soil occurs its fertility is so conspicuous that it appears as if nature had determined to counteract the bad effects produced by the clumsy system of its cultivation." And the late Mr. M'Culloch, in his "Statistics of the British Empire," confirms these statements: "The luxuriance of the pastures, and the heavy crops of oats that are everywhere raised, even with the most wretched cultivation, attest its extraordinary fertility."

"Rich soil, poor agriculture," is the sum of these statements. But they refer to bygone times, perhaps. There are certainly great improvements on many properties, and in some places as good farming as in England. But taking the country at large, here is the report of a recent visitor well competent to give testimony. Mr. Peter Maclagan, M.P. for Linlithgowshire, in his "Land Culture and Land Tenure in Ireland" (1869) says, "The tillage lands of the south, though not so rich as the pasture land in Tipperary, Limerick, and the Meaths, are also of great fertility. I join heartily in the eulogium pronounced by Arthur Young and other judges of the richness of the soils of Ireland, though they have been sadly deteriorated by bad farming. The overcropping to which the small holdings have been subjected, amounting often to nine or ten crops of oats in succession, is enough to reduce any soil to sterility. The average rent of the tillage lands is about 15s. per statute acre. In Ulster the farming is better, and the rents are about 9s. higher than those paid for land of the same quality in the south."

Another Scottish member of Parliament, Mr. McCombie, M.P. for Aberdeenshire, says, "In the elements of natural fertility only the richer parts of England and very exceptional parts of Scotland approach it." Mr. H. S. Thompson, late President of the Royal Agricultural Society of England, who visited Ireland in 1839 and in 1869, says that "in the last thirty years wealth has increased, the condition of the labouring classes has materially improved, and the progress of agriculture, without an exception, has been highly satisfactory." In quoting this and other statements, the compiler of the Statistics of Ireland in Thom's Directory for 1873 says, that "this increase of prosperity is very much of foreign origin, and has arisen mainly from the diminished population, and from the largely improved value of stock caused by the unlimited demand in the markets of Great Britain, and the facilities for reaching these markets." The increase has not been appreciably the result of better culture; and it is added, "Notwithstanding the great fertility of the soil, political, social, and moral forces, the strength of which cannot be known for some time after they have ceased to be in action, have heretofore kept the land in a very imperfect state of cultivation." Meeting in one of the Dublin Company's steamers from Holyhead to North Wall with some English cattle-dealers and salesmen, I understood fully the influences of the new markets on Irish supply and prices. One of these dealers told me he goes over every week, and buys at better prices, cheaper for him, he meant, than at any English sales. It pays butchers in Liverpool, Chester, Manchester, and the great north-western towns, and I suppose it is the same with Glasgow and Bristol or other places with direct steam lines, to get regular supply from across the Channel. The decks of the boats are all arranged for the freights of cattle on the homeward trips. While this great English market is busy, the value if not the number of live stock must increase, and accordingly we find the estimated value, in round numbers, rising in the last three decennial periods of the census, in 1851, £27,700,000; in 1861, £33,434,000; and in 1871, £37,500,000. The real values are higher, but this is the proportional rise, the calculation being taken at the rates fixed as average by the Census Commissioners of 1841, when the prices, at average, were for horses £8, cattle £6 10s., sheep £1 2s., pigs £1 5s.

The average value had, on the low rate of estimate of 1841, risen in 1871 to at least the following,—cattle £8 10s., sheep £1. 17s., pigs £2 17s. At Ballinasloe great October fair the actual prices of horned cattle, of which altogether 14,166 were sold, ranged, for oxen, first class, £24 10s.; second, £19; third, £13 10s.; fourth, £7 10s. Heifers, first class, £25; second, £20; third, £13; fourth, £7 10s. Of sheep, at the same fair, were sold 63,500 at the following prices,—wedders, first class, £4; second, £3 6s.; third, £2 7s. 6d.; fourth, £1 17s. 6d. Ewes, first class, £4 10s.; second, £4; third, £3 7s.; fourth, £2. From these figures, compared with the general average, it will be seen that the proportion of first-class stock was not large, but the prices on the whole show great improvement since the opening of markets by increased facilities of communication.*

---

* In Thom's Directory will be found tables of the live stock in each province and county for various years.

The total number of cattle, sheep, and pigs exported from Ireland to Great Britain in 1871 is given as follows: cattle, 483,925; sheep and lambs, 684,708; swine, 528,244.

The number and value of horses, cattle, sheep, and pigs in Ireland, taking the average of seven years, from 1865 to 1871, are given thus: horses, 532,859, worth £4,942,260; cattle, 3,738,581, worth £33,055,432; sheep, 4,419,256, worth £8,179,100; pigs, 1,260,735, worth £3,652,541; total value, £44,887,063. In computing these values, the average value of horses under one year old is taken at £4; under two years, £7; two and upwards, £10 each. Cattle under one year, £4; under two years, £7; two and upwards, £11 each. Pigs under one year, £2 10s.; one year and upwards, £5. Excepting for pigs, these values are certainly now considerably under the average mark. At the valuation prices adopted in 1841 the total value would not have been above £37,000,000, the difference between this sum and nearly £45,000,000 showing the rise in value of live stock in thirty years.

A corresponding rise has not taken place in the value of agricultural produce in the same period. In fact, the value of the principal crops has been nearly stationary during the last decennial period. In 1863 the total estimated value was £29,474,583; and in

1871 nearly the same, £29,165,153. The chief produce is as follows: wheat, oats, barley, bere, and rye; beans and peas; potatoes, turnips, mangolds, flax, and hay. There has been increase in the acreage and in the value of the crops connected with pasturage and live stock, decrease in the acreage under tillage. The value of hay, roots, and green crops shows a much higher total in the last ten years, especially hay, turnips, and mangolds. The estimated value of these crops in 1871 was above £10,000,000, of which the hay crop was valued at about £7,500,000. In 1865 these three crops were under £8,000,000. Oats and barley showed increase in acreage, in price, and in total value; wheat, a decrease in produce and value.

In 1852 the acreage under cereal crops was 2,976,606; under green crops, 1,354,887; meadow and clover, 1,270,713 acres. In 1872 the average stood thus: cereal crops, 2,090,673; green crops, 1,473,916; meadow and clover, 1,799,930: showing increase of green crops and of pasture to the extent of 648,246 acres, and a decrease of cereals of no less than 885,933 acres. The total under this culture in 1852 was 5,602,206 acres; in 1872, 5,364,519 acres, a decrease of 237,687 acres. The climate is, taking all Ireland, against the cultivation of wheat. Even improved farming cannot remedy this, and there is decrease in the produce per acre as well as in the total value during the last few years.

Of flax, which at one time was represented as the special agricultural industry and the hope of Ireland, the produce fell from 819,825 cwts. in 1866, to 615,500 cwts. in 1870. The produce in 1871 was only 258,588, and the value only £727,481, against £2,049,562 in 1866; but as this was an exceptionally bad flax year, the comparison is given between 1866 and 1870. The produce per acre was the same in these two years, while in 1871 it was little more than half; 3·1 cwts. in 1870, 1·7 cwts. in 1871. The high return in 1866 was partly due to the impetus given by Government grants and other aid, in that and the two preceding years. In 1864 instructions were sent round to introduce flax-growing in new districts, under the superintendence of the Royal Dublin Society and the Royal Agricultural Society of Ireland. Grants of money were also voted for several years. It is discouraging to find that the fall in the years since 1866 has been as great as was the rise in this industry during the same number of years preceding. It is time for Irish agriculture to be independent of all Government subventions.

Of oats and potatoes, the crops on which most dependence lies for the support of the peasant population, the increase has been on the whole steady, but with the variation and uncertainty caused by the seasons. It is to be feared that the potato crop of this year will be so diminished as to cause increase of price and distress to the labouring classes. In fact, there is increase in the price of all articles of common consumption, which will more than counterbalance the rise in wages which emigration and diminished population had effected. The average wage of day-labourers, which was thirty years ago barely above 10d., is now 1s. 4d. to 1s. 6d. per day. The price of provisions has risen quite as much in proportion, a result partly due to the opening of communication by railroads. For want of markets the price of farm produce used to be low, especially poultry, eggs, butter, and bacon. The increased facilities for sale have benefited the proprietors of land and the large tenants, but make the struggle for life more severe to the small holder and the labourer.

In the parts of Ireland which were most affected by the famine I found, from inquiries in different places, that the rise in the average value of land since that time has not been more than five per cent. The value of land is relatively greater in the North than in the South. When I was in Londonderry, the tenants of the Marquis of Waterford had offered twenty-five years' purchase for the estates there, and on refusal were prepared to offer thirty years' purchase. The result I do not know; but some properties in southern counties have since been sold at twenty-four years' purchase, and less. Near towns or markets the price is larger. Near Waterford city some land required as addition to the district lunatic asylum, about twelve acres, was sold last autumn at thirty-five years' purchase, advanced by Government, to be repaid by the county and city ratepayers.

The increase in land value ought to have been much more, judging by ordinary estimate, from the lessened population and the progress of agriculture, but moral and political elements interfere with the usual calculations of political economy, especially in the south of Ireland. The advance in value is in few places above this average of five per cent. However, the reduction of taxes in proportion to rents and income, especially poor-rates,* and the great rise in the price of live stock, ought to have produced a good share of prosperity to the agricultural proprietors,

---

* The total annual expenditure in poor relief in 1871 was £685,668. It was nearly the same in 1855. The highest year of those intervening was 1868, when the expenditure was £707,556; the lowest 1858, £413,712. The numbers in 1871 were 226,076 in-door, and 56,416 out-door. In 1868, 289,471 in-door, 50,257 out-door. In 1858, 177,205 in, 5,851 out. The proportion paid for out-door relief has steadily risen from £10,000 in 1861 to £70,000 in 1871. About £72,000 additional to the rates is expended from Government grant for medical and educational purposes.

although the tenant farmers and the poor peasantry have not had their proportion of the benefit.

I cannot speak with authority, like the practical agriculturists whose opinions I have quoted, but as a geologist I know what the land of Ireland ought to be, and as a botanist I could see the nature and capability of the soils from the wild plants that most abound. In the Dublin Exhibition and at the Royal Agricultural Show at Belfast I saw that the material and mechanical appliances of agriculture are the same as our own. There are no external hindrances to the improvement of agriculture, and the fertility of the soil ought to admit of vast development of this department of national wealth and prosperity. Hitherto it has only been shown in the increased value of live stock. There is room for even greater increase in produce, from better cultivation of the land. A large expenditure of capital is no doubt required, but the return would be great and certain. Some have gone the length of asserting that, with cultivation equal to that of the best farming districts of Scotland and England, the produce could be doubled. At all events, the wealth of Ireland could be vastly increased from improved agriculture.

The most superficial observer must be astonished at the neglect and waste of natural resources. Even in the pasture lands, in which Ireland most excels, the spontaneous liberality of the soil seems to induce the greater indolence and carelessness. The aid of art has been little used in laying down land to grass, for it is only recently that the trade in grass seeds has assumed any dimensions. Even haymaking, as generally conducted, is a slovenly operation, though labour has been so abundant. Cut too late, I saw the grass often left in small cocks, to be drenched by the autumn rains. A good sweet haystack is the exception, not the rule, on an Irish farm.

I never saw such a country for weeds. I saw two men in a field with scythes mowing down ragwort! Had I been travelling afoot or in a car, and not in a railway carriage, I would have sought an explanation of so strange a sight. Had the ragwort been sown as a crop it could hardly have been closer, so as actually to be mown with scythes. Is it used as fodder for any Irish animal? I suspect it was only an extreme illustration of the miserable state of the agriculture too common in Ireland. The amount of weeds is a national disgrace. It is not uncommon to see a ton of weeds in a dozen tons of hay. Many a field has more weeds than a whole parish in England. Small tenants keep land without laying it down with grass seeds, and it becomes the receptacle for all the floating weeds of the district, and then spreads them far and wide. Even for green crops the land is seldom sufficiently cleaned. Smoking heaps of twitch and weeds are rarely seen. If the farmer would give a small reward to boys for heaps of weeds, as they used to do for heads of vermin, they could keep this nuisance under. Ragwort, for instance, can easily be pulled up by the roots in wet weather, and the boys from the workhouse school would gladly attack a field for a trifling reward, and enjoy the fun of the bonfire that the heaps would make. But fields and roadsides are alike neglected, and weeds help to keep Ireland green but poor. I am sure it is no exaggeration to say that the direct loss to Ireland from weeds is above a million-and-a-half sterling. I have heard the loss estimated at nearly double that amount.

On the drainage of land, vast sums have been expended, and under good management with wonderful results. But even in land that has been drained, there is too general carelessness in scouring ditches and keeping the outlets of drains clear. It is better to have no drains than drains choked. In many cases advances have been obtained by landlords for draining, but the neglect of the small tenants has made them regret the cost and trouble. In fact, draining is seldom of service except when the land is in the owner's hand or under efficient management. In this matter, as in the curse of weeds, the careless, indolent habits of the people make agricultural progress uphill work.

Bad fences are also everywhere evident. The direct losses from the destruction of produce through this cause are enormous, and it is a constant source of litigation and ill will.

Want of industry and want of sense account for all the backwardness of Irish husbandry. The words of the wise king have here ample illustration: "I went by the field of the slothful, and by the vineyard of the man void of understanding, and lo, it was all grown over with thorns, and nettles had covered the face thereof, and the stone wall thereof was broken down." Poor Paddy can dig, but he will not, and to beg he is not ashamed!

Of what can be done for the improvement of the most unpromising land, an instructive instance is given by Mr. Trench in his "Realities of Irish Life," in regard to part of Lord Digby's property, lying between Glashill and Tullamore:—" The tenants who had previously held these lands had, many of them, paid no rent for a long period. The lands were of the worst description of wet moor, lying on a barren and retentive subsoil. The fields had been so cut up and subdivided that it became necessary to lay out all the lands anew, to level the old fences, square and enlarge the fields, and sink a deep drain, almost amounting to a canal, to carry off the water from this extensive district. All this was done with much care and accuracy; but the lands were naturally of so unfertile a quality that it became necessary to till them thoroughly to bring them to an even texture, and lay them down with grass seeds of first-rate quality. This was done at considerable cost; and turnips, potatoes, wheat, and oats were all grown most successfully, by means of a large application of Peruvian guano, generally seven to eight cwt. to the Irish acre. The crops were enormously large, and well repaid the cost of their production. The land was then thoroughly cleaned by repeated ploughings, harrowings, and pickings, and when fully pulverized and in proper order for the sowing of grass seeds it was laid down with rape, the grasses and clovers being sown along with the rape, and the whole afterwards fed off by sheep. The land was thus left in good heart, and in a high state of productiveness.

"Land treated in this manner, which had previously been difficult to let at 4s. per Irish acre, now readily brings from 25s. to 30s. per acre; whilst the whole face of the country, changed from sterility and waste to rich and abundant pastures, well fenced, and divided into fields of sufficient size, and sheltered by belts of plantations, presents a most improved and gratifying appearance. These and similar works, such as main or arterial drainage, being carried on simultaneously over various districts of the estate, have prevented any pauperism whatever; and since Lord Digby came into possession of the property there have been no unemployed labourers upon it. So great, in fact, has been the stimulus to industry, that the only difficulty is to now procure a sufficiency of hands both for the drainage and farmers' work.

"Whilst extensive works of drainage have been and are being carried into effect, the dwellings of the farmers and labourers are by no means neglected. The houses of both were in general very bad—most of them composed exclusively of mud and thatch. Many of these have been replaced with well-built stone and mortar houses, roofed with slates and timber; whilst the existing houses and cottages have been much improved, and numerous smaller dwellings for the day-labourers have been erected all over the estate.

"In addition to these works, Lord Digby has procured the best and most improved threshing-machines to work upon his estate, as well as mowing and reaping-machines, all of which are let out at reasonable rates for the use and convenience of the tenantry. Three times his lordship has gained the gold medal offered by the Royal Agricultural Society of Ireland for the best labourers' cottages in the province of

Leinster; he held for three successive years the Duke of Leinster's challenge cup for the best-built labourers' cottages in all Ireland; and he now holds the Hall challenge cup for the most extensive and best drainage in all Ireland.

"When I recollect the miserable condition of this estate not quite ten years ago—the tenants disaffected, industry paralysed, Ribbonism rampant, and conspiracies to murder those who were most anxious for their welfare filling the minds of many of the peasantry—it is some consolation to find that steady and persevering determination, combined with kind and liberal treatment, will ever, in much-abused Ireland, produce the most satisfactory results. And Lord Digby, and those who have worked under him, can look back with pleasure at having obtained a moral victory over what, at one time, appeared as dangerous and unpromising a subject as any Irish landlord or agent could possibly undertake to manage. Were this system more generally adopted on their estates by wealthy proprietors, it would be found *to pay well*, and Ireland would soon become a very different country from what it is."

Agricultural training forms a promising department of the Irish system of National Education, but the results have not been commensurate with the plans of the projectors of the scheme. Many of the best pupils have emigrated, and too many have succumbed to the depressing circumstances of the country, but there is fresh hope now that the tide has turned, and more prosperous days seem to be dawning.

There are district agricultural training schools at Belfast, Kilkenny, Limerick, and Cork. The course of instruction embraces all the branches of a sound English education, as well as the science and practice of improved agriculture. Some of the pupils are admitted free, and the fee for paying pupils is only £3 a quarter, the Education Commissioners contributing the additional payment required for board, education, books, and apparatus. The head-quarters of this agricultural department is at Albert Farm, Glasnevin, the superintendent of which, or the secretaries of the Marlborough Street Education Board, will give every information to those interested in the matter.

CHAPTER XVI.

LAND TENURE AND THE NEW LAND ACT.

Leases—Tenant Right—Working of the Land Act—Rights of Landlords—Claims of Tenants.

INSECURITY of tenure, or, as the Irish would call it, "want of tenure," is sufficient to account for the backward state of Irish agriculture. Division and subdivision of small properties, till starvation point was reached, accounts for part of the miserable condition of *the people*. But the absence of right relations between landlord and tenant have kept *the country* poor and uncultivated. Bad laws and bad customs perpetuated bad husbandry. In most parts of the country leases were not given by the landlords, sometimes from a desire to keep their tenants in political dependence, sometimes from inability to grant them. When they were granted, they were for lives rather than for terms. Tenants for lives had the franchise, tenants with leases were excluded, until the Reform Bill of 1832. Not till 1850 was the principle admitted of enfranchisement on the value instead of the nature of the holding. It was the custom, and too generally the necessity, in Ireland, for the bare land to be let, the landlord doing nothing for buildings or repairs or improvements. The passion for land caused competition for farms among tenants as poor, if not so encumbered, as the nominal owners. The landlords, too generally absentees, pressed the agents or middlemen for money, and when they pressed the tenants, agrarian outrages were the result. There was no inducement to a farmer to spend money in better culture or in any improvements, with nothing in prospect but raised rent or eviction.

Disturbances about tenant right have not been confined to Catholic parts of Ireland. One of the most dangerous insurrections of last century, in 1772, was in Antrim. An estate belonging to the absentee Marquis of Donegal was proposed, on the expiring of the leases, to be let only to those who could pay large fines, or to new tenants. Most of the old tenants, neither able to pay the fines nor the advanced rents, were ejected. They maimed the cattle of those who occupied the farms, and committed many outrages, banding together under the name of Hearts of Steel. One of their number being confined in Belfast, under a charge of felony, was forcibly rescued, the officers of the military guard being persuaded to give up the prisoner to prevent a serious fight. The association of the Steelmen spread into the neighbouring counties, and gained formidable strength by the accession of the peasantry, who sided with the tenants. Some prisoners, tried at Carrickfergus, were acquitted by the partiality of the witnesses and jury. An Act of Parliament was passed, ordering the trials to take place in counties different from those where the offences were committed. Some were taken to Dublin, but were there acquitted, public opinion resisting an Act which was declared to be unconstitutional. The Act was repealed, and further outrages occurring, several were tried in their own counties, condemned, and executed. The insurrection was suppressed, but the discontent was so deep that at that time many thousands of Protestants emigrated to America, and took a prominent part in the war which separated the colonies from the British empire.

The arrangements as to land tenure and compensation for improvements, familiarly known under the name of "Ulster tenant-right," had their origin in no statute laws, but gradually came into force through custom. A less disreputable class of landlords on the whole, and a more independent class of farmers than in other parts of Ireland, found it mutually advantageous to adopt some principle of equitable arrangement, both in the holding and the transfer of farms.

The custom varied in different parts of the country, and on different properties, but to its existence in any form may be attributed such superiority as Ulster could boast over other parts of Ireland as to agriculture. The poverty of the soil and the smallness of holdings prevented this superiority being very marked. Even where there was not the legal security of a lease, binding on the heirs of the lessor, there was the security of a farmer obtaining repayment from his successor of all that had been spent in improvements. Disputes as to rent still remained, and other difficulties, which rendered a new landlord and tenant law desirable for Ulster, as well as for the rest of Ireland. By the new Act, which came into force on the 1st of August, 1870, provision is made for legal as well as equitable adjustment of claims, by regular land sessions, with appeal to a higher land court.

I made inquiries, whenever I had opportunity, as to the working of the Land Act, and, with the exceptions to be presently noticed, I heard general expression of satisfaction. It is thought, on the whole, to be an equitable compromise as to the rights of landlords and the claims of tenants. There is also general confidence in the administration of the new law, whether in the land sessions or in the courts of appeal. There is already a feeling of security in the relations of landlord and tenant previously unknown. The rental of the landlord is better secured, and the fee-simple of his property is worth more than when the tenant was in an unsettled state, and vague disquietude prevailed. In many counties, notices of ejection have scarcely been heard of since the passing of the Act, and evictions unknown except for non-payment of rent. Agrarian outrages have nearly ceased, most of the cases classed under such crimes being not disputes between landlord and tenant, but between tenant and labourer, about cutting turf, or right of way, or trespass, and such like offences. The amount of litigation under the Act has also been far less than was anticipated, many having prophesied that every court in the county would be overwhelmed with land cases. The decisions that have already been given in the "Court for Land Cases Reserved," have provided precedents for the chief classes of doubtful cases that can arise.

I have not at hand the most recent statistics, but there were in the last quarter of 1870, and the year 1871, 526 cases of land sessions, giving an average for all Ireland of one case in every thousand holdings subject to the Act. There were, against 292 decrees and dismisses at the previous sessions, only 52 appeals lodged; of these only 33 were heard. In four cases the appeals were reversed, in thirteen they were

Land Tenure and the New Land Act. 273

varied, in thirteen affirmed, and in three cases judgments have been held over. The total sum adjudged by decrees was £13,644, and deducting money allowed for default of tenants, etc., the net sum adjudged was £11,450. Allowing the same proportion for claims disposed of out of court, the direct protection to tenants in all the cases may be estimated at £26,500. The gross average amount decreed, without deducting allowances for setting off to landlord for dilapidation, rent, etc., gives an average for Ireland of £69 in each case. In Ulster it reaches £81; in Munster, £64; in Leinster, £49; and in Connaught, £33. It appears from these figures that, except a rare case of a claim to register improvements, the holdings in respect of which cases have been decided at land sessions, are a very small class. Of the gross amount adjudged in that period at land sessions (£13,644), £5,621, or 41 per cent., was for loss on quitting holding and improvements together; £4,558, or 33 per cent., for Ulster tenant-right; £1,908, or 14 per cent., was for loss on quitting holding alone; and £1,577, or 12 per cent., for improvement alone.

An attempt was made last session to obtain an inquiry into the operation of the Act, the motion being in the interests of the landlords. The Government refused the inquiry, and resolved to abide for the present to the principles of the new system. It may, however, become necessary to have a Declaratory Act, on account of difficulties that have arisen, but no clamour on either side should induce any serious departure from a system which has worked well as far it has gone.

The points objected to in the Land Act by landlords are these: that all improvements are presumed to belong to the tenant in the absence of any record of their being made by the landlord; and that tenants, though having made no improvements, are entitled to compensation merely for being required to give up the holding to the proprietor. The latter enactment is a perfectly new arrangement in the laws of property. That "a man can do what he likes with his own" has been an axiom in the relation of landlord and tenant in English law hitherto, the right, in the absence of contract, being restrained only by public opinion. But public opinion goes for little in questions where personal or, still more, political feeling runs high. A notable case occurred recently in Scotland, where one of the first agriculturists of the time, a man highly respected for his character and his public spirit, was ejected for his political opinions from the farm which his family had held for several generations. Compensation for such a moral though not legal wrong was not dreamed of, and the landlord enjoyed his triumph over the helpless, if not uncomplaining tenant. In Ireland the perpetrator of such a wrong might have had a bullet sent through his head by some devoted retainer of an ejected holder. For the protection of Irish landlords as well as Irish tenants, a compulsory payment is now secured to the tenant, for giving up, as some say, what does not legally belong to him. If this is equitable in Ireland, it ought to be equitable in England and Scotland; and if not equitable, the provision is one of expediency only, and not of principle.

There is in Ireland, however, this essential difference from England, that Irish landlords in very rare cases build or keep in repair tenements or farmsteads, or expend any money on permanent improvements. All this is done by the tenants; whereas in England the landlord almost invariably is at the outlay for improvements. The position of the tenant in Ireland was therefore far more precarious before the passing of the Land Act than that of the average English tenant. The Act not only ensures compensation to all tenants under £50 annual rent, but to tenants of larger holdings, if their leases are for a shorter period than thirty-one years. They cannot contract themselves out of the right to compensation for improvements, duly registered, with their cost and date of execution. The difference between the position of small and large holders only applies to questions of ejectment and disturbance, large holders being supposed to be able to protect themselves by having leases or other legal securities.

The unreasonableness of those landlords who still denounce the whole Act as an invasion of the rights of property, will appear by considering the analogous case of house property. A landlord lets a house unfurnished, without a lease. The tenant furnishes the house, a large part of the value of the furniture being in the shape of immoveable furniture and fixtures. He has no sooner done this, than the landlord claims increased rent, as for a furnished house, with the alternative of ejectment. The tenant cannot carry off his fixtures, and has to submit to the exaction of the increased rent, or the wrong of loss by eviction. This is exactly the case of the Irish landlord, who, as we have seen, does not make the improvements on his property. The tenant-farmer cannot carry off the farm buildings nor the property sunk in the soil, which are analogous to the immoveable furniture and fixtures of the house. In point of fact, the property which the landlord claims as his own, while it is his as to geographical boundaries and the bare soil, has become mixed up with property to which the tenant has as much right as the owner has to the uncultivated land. It is for the law to discriminate the property, and to secure the rights of both parties. In Ulster, the unwritten code of tenant-right gave protection against palpable injustice. It was no uniform or defined usage, but in various districts and on different properties the tenants had established such tenant-right custom as they could obtain. In other parts of Ireland the tenants were utterly at the mercy of the landlords. Sometimes they were dealt with equitably, or even generously; in other cases with as much harsh injustice as in the supposed case of the landlord of the unfurnished house. Too often the property was in the hands of middlemen or pitiless mortgagees, and the exactions and evictions drove the tenants to a resistance which under the circumstances was almost justifiable. This is the real secret of agrarian combinations, and the real origin of that Land Act which has put an end to such combinations, and which some landlords are foolish enough to declare confiscation of their property.

But, on the other hand, there are tenants who seek to push farther than what is reasonable and just, the protection which the Land Act has secured for them. They have got security against ejection without full compensation for improvements. Even if they have made no improvements, and expended no money, they are entitled to a money compensation, if required to give up the holding. This is "*security* of tenure" far beyond what was known before in Ireland, and beyond what is enjoyed in England. But many tenants are not satisfied with this, and demand "*fixity* of tenure." This is what agitators are now proposing, and what Mr. Froude has unwisely given the sanction of his name to. A few sentences of his last American lecture will express clearly the nature of the new tenant-right claim. "In Ireland," says Mr. Froude, "the law is not yet what it ought to be. The tenant must be compensated when he is evicted, but he may still be evicted. The landlord must now pay the tenant five years' rent if he wishes to be rid of him, but I have known of Irish peasants who so loved their homes that they would not leave them for a hundred years' rent. I would have no evictions." Test this rhetoric by the analogous case of house property, and see what an extravagant proposition it is. The tenant of a house might have the same sentimental attachment to the place where his family ties were formed, but if he is only a tenant, he must quit on the expiring of his lease, if the landlord requires the house. To give a money payment for him to go out, would be a strange boon conferred by law, and this is what Irish tenants have got by the Land Act. If the occupier of either land or house wishes to indulge the sentimental "love of home," it must be by possessing a freehold property of his own. Make the purchase of land more easy in Ireland if you will, but do not encourage the tenant to indulge his tastes at the cost of the lawful owner of that property of which he is only a temporary occupier.

Another unreasonable part of the new tenant-right agitation is the desire to escape from the binding power of contracts in leases. The landlord has a right to make what regulations or terms he thinks good for his property, and the tenant is free to accept or refuse the conditions. The landlord may forbid sub-leasing or sub-division, or may require certain methods of cultivation, or make what covenants he thinks fit, all which the tenant has to consider before signing the agreement.' This is the usage of all civilized nations, and the covenants in leases of land are far more minute and strict in England and Scotland, and even in America, than they ever have been in Ireland. Yet there was lately an ignorant clamour against the good old Duke of Leinster, the most liberal and generous of landlords, for requiring new leases since the passing of the Land Act. It was an unreasonable clamour. The Knight of Kerry, in referring to the agitation against the Leinster leases, quoted a yearly lease of a property in New York State, of which the following are some of the conditions: Besides rent in money, it reserves a certain produce rent of wheat, to be delivered at any place within fifteen miles of the lands selected by the landlord. It strictly reserves all right to mines, minerals, etc., and forbids the removal of hay, straw, or manure from the premises. Article 3 stipulates, in the most elaborate and stringent way, for proper cultivation, and binds the tenant " to pay $12\frac{1}{2}$ cents as liquidated damage for each and every Canada thistle or burdock that is suffered to go to seed on the premises." Article 4 binds the tenant to preserve all timber growing on the lands, and to pay for any cut or removed " the full value as estimated by the lessor's agent." Article 10 conditions for the most ample right of re-entry, not only in case of failure to pay rent, but for breach of any of these most minute covenants, and stipulates especially that no receiving of rent subsequent to a breach of covenant shall act as a waiver to the landlord's rights. Article 11 binds the tenant to a most precise course of cropping, described in an endorsement of the lease, for each field separately, and the tenant conditions, in case of failure in the minutest particle in respect of any one field, "to pay such damages as the lessor or his agent shall deem proper;" and I am further assured by the gentleman who gave me this lease, that if the tenant "fails to perform his side of the contract one month is sufficient to recover the land."

The tenant-right agitators' reply to this was that

"two blacks do not make a white," and that leases with covenants are bad anywhere. In short, tenants may do what they like with what is *not* their own, as the remedy for the landlord doing what he likes with his own. The proper and only proceeding is for such tenants to become landlords, and so be independent, which they can do easily in America, if not in Ireland.

It is not necessary to go into details about the Leinster lease discussions, or other disputed cases which have been before the public, either in the newspapers or in the land courts. Few cases have yet occurred which were beyond the power of legal decision, or of that less formal arrangement which can always be attained when there is a desire to do what is just and right. Lord Lisgar, late Governor-General of Canada, made a most sensible and reasonable speech last autumn, at an agricultural dinner given by the Marquis of Headfort to his Cavan tenantry. He said, "He believed if the law was accepted in the spirit in which it was passed, it would be found that the landlords lost little on the one hand, for no landlord would be debarred of any right before claimed, which just men would have enforced in times past; and that though tenants have greater security, they will not on their part claim more than they have been accustomed to in times past. If both parties stood on their own ground, firmly and fairly, without encroachment, all would be right."

As a contrast to Lord Lisgar's speech, listen to the words of a Roman Catholic priest at a meeting in Athy, who, after coarse abuse of the Duke of Leinster, said, "The whole transaction was a violation of the laws of the country, and of the commandment which prohibited men from taking their neighbour's goods." Another priest used more violent language, denouncing the Land Act as "a nullity, a humbug, and a sham. He trusted the tenants, with the help of God, would use the power which they now possessed, and that a conflagration would be caused in every county which would never be extinguished while there was a remnant of feudalism in the country. They would return tenant-farmers to Parliament, men who had ten times as much brains as were possessed by their big landlords, and they would create a fund to support these members. The landlords of Ireland were playing a dangerous game, for the people were beginning to know their rights, and were inquiring how the tenants of other countries rid themselves of such tyranny." The meeting resolved "to present a memorial to Government to repeal the clauses of the Land Act which enabled the tenants to contract themselves out of their rights, and that Ulster tenant-right should be extended all over Ireland." This last proposal shows the ignorance that prevails as to Ulster tenant-right, which the speaker, who wished its extension to all Ireland, described as being "well-defined, and into which neither legal chicanery nor unmeaning verbiage could be introduced."

It is quite possible that the action of the Land Act will accelerate the consolidation of properties into larger farms, as many landlords will seek to be freed from the unusual bonds which the law puts them under in regard to small holders. But this is a change for other reasons desirable, and which was going on before the passing of the Landlord and Tenant Act. Small tenancies, and subdivision of holdings, have been the bane of Irish agriculture. But the same objections do not apply to small freeholds, and the increase of such holdings, if they are not too small to involve a struggle, will be the best political defence of the country. There will be no fear of the over-multiplying of such properties, as in the days before the famine. The Irish have found the way across the Atlantic, and the young and able will go there, where they know they can better their condition, and not stay, as before, to starve on the potato patches into which the properties used to be subdivided.

In the Registrar-General's returns there is a table of the number of landowners, classified according to the extent of land held,* and the entire extent of land under each class divided thus:—

	No. of holdings in each class.	Area occupied by each class.	Proportion per cent. in each class.
Not exceeding 1 acre	44,448	25,334	8·2
Above 1, not exceeding 5 acres	74,809	266,665	12·6
,, 5 ,, 15 ,,	171,383	1,798,178	28·9
,, 15 ,, 30 ,,	138,647	3,090,114	23·4
,, 30 ,, 50 ,,	72,787	2,938,351	12·3
,, 50 ,, 100 ,,	55,062	4,048,984	9·3
,, 100 ,, 200 ,,	21,696	3,259,759	3·6
,, 200 ,, 500 ,,	8,190	2,800,603	1·4
,, 500 ,, ,, ,,	1,568	2,070,147	0·3

Between 1861 and 1871 the farms under fifteen acres decreased in number 12,548, and in the same period farms above thirty acres increased in number 1,470. Between 1841 and 1861, holdings under fifteen acres declined 55 per cent. in number. It will be interesting to watch the effect of the Land Act in decreasing the number of holdings under fifty acres.

* The total area of holdings in 1866 was 20,190,197 acres; of which there were 5,520,568 in tillage, 10,004,244 in pasture. Plantation has much increased. More than an eighth of the land is still bog. The whole area of Ireland is 20,815,460 acres. There are 625,263 acres occupied by towns, villages, railways, canals, and water. About the same area is waste and uncultivated land. Between 1851 and 1861 the area under towns had increased 3,646 acres, showing that the diminished population was more rural than urban.

CHAPTER XVII.

IRISH FISHERIES.

Government Loans—Statistics of Coast and Deep Sea Fisheries—Salmon Fisheries.

EVERY now and then we hear about Government loans to help the Irish fisheries. Mr. Lowe made reference to the subject in his famous Glasgow speech, in a way which provoked the wrath of the Irish press. Loans have been granted to a considerable amount, but the refusal to grant them on a larger scale, and for the mere asking, has become one of the stock grievances of the national agitators, and the matter deserves some consideration.

The Government "Inspectors of Irish Fisheries," in their First Report in 1869, stated that "no great improvement can be looked for in the sea fisheries until loans are advanced to a portion of the fishermen for the repair and purchase of boats and gear." In the Reports for 1870 and 1871 they say, "If much longer time is allowed to pass without our suggestion being carried out, fishing industry will nearly expire on half the coast. Ten or twenty thousand pounds judiciously expended now, not as a gift, but as a loan, would do more good than a million given away half a dozen years hence." They say that "loans could be easily and inexpensively administered, and little or no loss would be likely to be incurred."

If these statements of the Inspectors are to be accepted as well grounded, the refusal or delay about the loans would be highly culpable. There is quite as much reason for advancing public money for this industry as for draining, or any agricultural improvement. In fact, the public importance of the fisheries makes a preferable claim, on the plea of keeping up a valuable nursery for the royal navy and mercantile marine. But the outcry about loans has been taken up hastily, and by those not best acquainted with the subject. It is easy for officials in Dublin to make the suggestion, which has probably been forced upon them by the landowners and priests, speaking in favour of the fishermen. But will these good neighbours give the necessary security for the repayment of the loan? To bestow money without security would relieve for a short time the appeals of the fishermen, but would perpetuate their indolent, improvident habits. Even in the Appendix to the

Official Reports, the Inspectors print documents which are opposed to the suggestion. The coastguard officers, and the officers of her Majesty's revenue and other ships, know far more about the coast fisheries than the Inspectors do, and their testimony is not in favour of public loans. One says, that "not many fishermen would be benefited by loans, but a few might." Another in county Sligo says, "Fishermen would not be ultimately benefited by loans, or the fisheries advanced by the same. Fishing ought to be self-supporting; adequate means exist for the capture of such fish as appear in quantity." In Waterford, the local witness states that he does "not think the fishermen in this locality would accept loans, or be able to find security." And so on all round the coast, the report of those best able to judge is, that loans might do good to a few, but that they would not be beneficial generally, even if security could be found.

The real hindrances to the prosperity of Irish fisheries I take to be these: 1. The indolence and thriftlessness of the fishermen themselves. 2. The want of encouragement to greater industry, in the absence of regular markets for their produce. Even where means of transit are all that could be wished, there is no constant demand, and few curing establishments, or other ways of utilizing the supply. I had long conversations with the fishermen, including the famous men of the Claddagh at Galway, and this was the burden of their complaint, What is the use of a good catch when we cannot sell? This was when the papers had reported a wonderful supply of pilchard on the south and west coast. Of the rich harvest of the seas that might be gathered all round the coast, there can be no doubt. Capital is wanted to cultivate this industry, and to secure the produce, and capital is not ready to risk itself in such a country. It is estimated that the coast fisheries could bring nearly half a million sterling, apart from the oyster and salmon fisheries, which are worth nearly half-a-million now. But the spirit is wanting. The salmon fisheries are productive because they belong to a few rich owners, who employ paid labour to cultivate the industry. The other fisheries as yet are chiefly dependent on the exertion of the poor fishermen, who have not the physical energy or mental independence to make a successful enterprise. At the mackerel fishery of 1871 there were about 200 English or Manx boats, 50 French, and only 70 Irish. In the herring fishery on the east coast the Irish held their place better, the Howth boats and men showing a good return; but even here the English, Scotch, and Manx boats were about three times the number of the Irish.

The number of boats and men employed in the

deep sea and coast fisheries has shown a steady and sad decline ever since the famine time. In 1846, there were 19,883 Irish vessels and boats of all sizes, with 113,073 men and boys, engaged in the fisheries. In 1848, 19,652 boats, but only 81,717 men and boys. In 1852, the numbers were 11,789 and 58,789. In 1862, 11,590 and 50,220; and in 1871, 8,999 boats, and 38,629 men and boys. This table is given in the Reports, and in Thom's Irish Directory for 1873; yet the same page states that "the Irish Sea Fisheries were never in a more promising condition, and only require extensive development." This opposition of facts and assertions is an example of the difficulty attending all Irish inquiries.

About the salmon fisheries there is less to say. These have long been private property, bringing in large revenues to the possessors, as similar fisheries do in Scotland and England. I think that as Government has asserted its power in regulating the rights of property in so far as land is concerned, there is also some call for interfering in behalf of the poorer class in regard to fisheries. There used to be free fishing all round the coast by the common law; now every river-mouth and tideway is monopolized by proprietors who alone have legal, if not equitable, right to the whole salmon fishery round the coast. The fisheries are leased to agents at high rents, and a very small percentage of the produce is of any direct benefit to Irish fishermen or anglers. To Billingsgate market alone there were sent from Ireland last year nearly 7,500 boxes, besides the great supply to Liverpool and to central England. It was interesting to see the salmon breeding and salmon preserves, and other wonders of this industry, but I confess that the sight of the stake nets and fixed engines, on so many parts of the coast, raised feelings akin to that caused on seeing the enclosing of the commons and open places, for the benefit of the rich at the expense of the poor. Political economy may prove that these enclosures and monopolies, whether by sea or land, are for the greater good of the community, but in regard to Ireland there is some excuse for the scanty industry of the poor coast-fishermen, when they are tabooed from the most productive department of their calling. Some more liberal arrangement might at least be made for rod-fishing at certain times, and the proprietors might be required to allow fish to be sold in the neighbourhood, at a price which would lessen the discontent now felt on seeing so much wealth sent away, without benefit to the dwellers on the banks of the salmon rivers.

CHAPTER XVIII.

THE ROYAL IRISH CONSTABULARY.

Organization and Duties of the Force—Special Services—Grievances.

NO stranger can be many days in Ireland without observing and admiring the Royal Irish Constabulary. On the roads, in the streets, at the railway stations, everywhere in town or country, we see them on duty. Smart, intelligent, good-looking men most of them are, and a more orderly, well-conducted and loyal body does not exist in her Majesty's service. They have military dress and discipline, but the chief part of their duty is that of an ordinary police force. Their barracks are everywhere dotted about the country, some of them large and strong buildings, but generally small stations for only a serjeant's guard. Part of the force is mounted, but the greater part is not. I saw considerable numbers together during the assizes at different towns, perhaps more than usual on such occasions, as there was a good deal of excitement about the Keogh judgment. Later in the season I saw masses concentrated, at points where the disturbances were going on which culminated in the Belfast riot. The more I saw of the force the more was I impressed with its efficiency, and its peculiar adaptation to the requirements of the country. It was instituted by Sir Robert Peel, when Secretary for Ireland, and though he incurred some unpopularity at the time, as he did also for the institution of the London Metropolitan police, every one now may be grateful for the firm and far-seeing home policy of one of the best of our statesmen.

The number of the force varies with the exigency of the time, as does also its distribution throughout the country. In some parts the numbers are small, and the stations few and far between. The districts which are often unsettled have large bodies of constabulary quartered on them. One-half of the expense is paid by the Government, the other by county rates. This explains the resolutions and requests at county meetings to have the number of constables reduced. Tipperary, once a county of chronic disturbance, made such a request lately, and has a smaller proportion of police to its population than some of the northern counties. In all parts of the island, while the regular troops, "the red coats," are disliked, and are best kept out of sight, as representing "the Saxon oppressors," the Royal Constabulary are popular. Here and there individuals get into scrapes, especially in districts where there is little duty, but, on the whole, the men are on good terms with the people where they are stationed. It is a rule, I believe, that the men serve in a different part of Ireland from their native place, on the same wise principle that the Romans adopted, in making the legions serve in countries remote from where they were formed.

There has always been some discussion as to the mingling of military with civil duties in the constabulary; but the condition of the country and the organization of the force renders the separation of duty impossible. At some times and in some districts, the service must be chiefly that of police; at other times and in other districts, military duties have been more prominent. It is the merit of the force, that its civil efficiency is as great as that of any body of police in the empire, and on emergencies it has shown military efficiency equal to that of the best regular troops. Since the Fenian troubles, when the prompt services of the constabulary were rewarded by the prefix of "Royal," some have said that the military idea has too much predominated over the civil, and it is also said that the duties of the force are now unduly directed from Dublin Castle, instead of with view to local efficiency. The charge does not seem to be well founded; at least, these complaints are made by the political organs of disaffection, not by the county magistrates, nor by the body of the people. It is only by Fenian agitators and by baffled criminals that the constabulary is represented as "part of a hostile army of occupation."

There are at present about 12,600 men in the force, and 300 officers. The number of barracks, or stations, is about 1,575. Besides the usual police barracks there are special stations, either inspection posts, or protection posts, in particular localities, or at particular times, as required. The head-quarters of counties and districts are inspected, and officers and men examined in their police, and also in detective, duties, every third year, by an officer from head-quarters in Dublin. The districts and sub-districts are inspected every alternate year; the county inspector examines the men in the different duties once every three months, and the sub-inspectors once every month. A sub-inspector may have as many as eighty men under him, and about ten stations, besides protection posts. These are when men are detailed off for special duty in watching suspected persons, or in defending persons or places who are in danger, or have been threatened. The detectives of the force are of varied and tried ability, and are allowed to use their own wits as to dress, residence, and other circumstances during the service on which they are sent. There are day and night patrols, going out at different hours, two or three or more, according to the station. When protection is expected, the locality is visited at various times every day or night. On any emergency the constabulary of the nearest post take a car and go to the nearest sub-inspector's station to report, or to get additional force. In every department of police duty, except coping with the Ribbonist and other secret societies, the constabulary prove a most efficient force.*

Since the promotion of Colonel Sir J. Stewart Wood as Inspector-General, there has been considerable change in the discipline and duties of the constabulary. He has aimed to increase their efficiency as police without lessening their military training. He has reduced the amount of red-tape reports and writing, and given more discretionary power to county inspectors and sub-inspectors. The men are encouraged to mix more with the people in the neighbourhood, and to be less in the barracks. Much time had been taken up in keeping of diaries, patrol-books, and other records, under a code of regulations needlessly minute. Colonel Wood also thinks that the

---

* Most of this efficiency is due to the former head of the constabulary, General Sir Duncan Macgregor, K.C.B., some years retired. The name of this gallant veteran is best known in connection with the loss of the *Kent* East Indiaman, of which he published a narrative. He was then Major of the 31st Regiment, afterwards Colonel of the 93rd Highlanders.

police should be relieved of various duties which take up much time and render them unpopular, such as enforcing the collection of the dog-tax, looking after stray pigs and cattle, and other "road nuisances," watching fisheries and preserves against poachers, and searching for illicit stills.* This sort of work ought to be relegated to local or parish constables, excise officers, keepers, and other officials suited for the several duties.

Efficient and popular as is the force, there is at present a good deal of discontent among the men. As a matter of fact, it must be admitted that there has been for some years a dwindling away of the strength of the force, and the difficulty has increased of keeping up its efficiency. Many of the best men have emigrated, or have sought better-remunerated employment. Those who remain feel that they have "grievances," and the complaints have obtained the tardy attention of the Government. To maintain even the numerical strength, there must be a lowering of the standard both of physical and moral qualification. Towards the close of last session of Parliament, a commission was appointed to inquire into these complaints. The Marquis of Hartington, in reply to questions, stated that it would be no part of

---

* Last year there were about 400 of the constabulary looking after distillation in Donegal, Mayo, Tyrone, and Sligo.

the duty of the commission "to establish a comprehensive inquiry, nor inquire into the grievances of those who alleged the inadequacy of their payment." The report of the commission will not be satisfactory, if the whole subject is not thoroughly investigated. From what I heard throughout the country, a full inquiry is called for, so that an equitable settlement may be made on all points that have been raised. The service ought to be made attractive to well-qualified men, and loyal men, as the R.I.C. have always proved themselves. The question of pay must be considered. The increased cost of maintenance and the diminished value of money require a reconsideration of the scale of payment. The pension regulations also call for amendment. There ought to be readier provision for retirement with pension or allowance, not only after a fixed period of service, but on men being incapacitated from infirmity or from severe duty. Good-service stripes or badges ought to be introduced, the bearers of which should have slight increase of pay. The motives of hope and emulation are always stronger than the fear of fines and reprimands. Married men not having barrack accommodation ought to have sufficient allowance for house-rent. The allowances for fuel, for travelling, for making up uniform, and other expenses ought to be also increased, as well as extra pay allowed for extraordinary duty, as during elections and other periods, when long stretches of time and unusual services are demanded.

It is also a grievance that promotions are not made more frequently from the ranks, young cadets being too often introduced over the head of well-deserving and well-qualified head-constables. If these grievances were removed, young men of good education as well as good character would again press for admission into the ranks, and the efficiency of the force be increased. It is too valuable a body to allow any paltry economy to stand in the way. An increase in their strength would save much outlay in less satisfactory ways. An increase of 1,000 in the constabulary would allow of the reduction of 5,000 troops in Ireland. And the reform ought to be made before the popularity of the force is further diminished.

The total charges for the constabulary for the year ending 31st March, 1871, was £862,282. The expense of the force charged on the Consolidated Fund in 1871 was £825,737, the remainder being made up by county rates.

The Dublin Metropolitan Police has a separate organization. It numbers in all 1,068, consisting of 1 chief commissioner, 1 assistant commissioner, 156 superintendents, inspectors, and sergeants, 44 detective-officers, and 912 constables. The annual cost is

£90,000, which includes the expense of offices, and salaries of five divisional magistrates. Of this sum upwards of £5,400 is paid by parliamentary grant, the rest by local taxes and rates.

Having referred to the grievances of the constabulary, I may add that much satisfaction was expressed on the appointment, last Parliament, of the Commission to inquire into the Irish Civil Service. A more liberal and more equitably adjusted scale of remuneration may be expected as one result of the inquiry. But other questions of importance will call for settlement. If the increase of pay throughout the civil service is to be secured only by reduction of the staff in the several departments, there ought to be some guarantee for the impartial carrying out of the reduction. Let the weeding commence with the incompetent and inefficient, and the service will not complain. The chiefs of departments are not likely to report cases of licensed inefficiency, where the relatives or dependants of men in power have been thrust into places over the heads of useful and plodding public servants. The discovery of these cases can only be made by the commission examining some other witnesses than the official chiefs of departments. There ought also to be more precise rules as to promotion. The discretionary power wielded by the chiefs often causes irritation and dissatisfaction.

It is a hard case when a man is lifted over others more competent and with better claims, because of the caprice of an official chief, or under pressure of social or political influence. That the discretionary power of promotion should exist all will admit, so that the public service may not lose the advantage of unusual ability or acquirement; but, apart from these exceptional cases, promotion ought to go according to rules laid down by authority of the Treasury.

CHAPTER XIX.

IRISH PRISONS AND PRISONERS.

Crofton Convict System—Lusk Farm Prison—The Fenian Prisoners.

AT the meetings of the Social Science Association, and at Prison Conferences of various kinds, much is always said about the Irish or "Crofton convict system," so called after Sir Walter Crofton, the head of the Irish criminal prisons. The special features of this system, the working of which is highly praised, may be new to some readers.

Both in England and Ireland, all convict prisoners—that is, prisoners sentenced to penal servitude, a sentence now never less than for five years—pass the first period of their sentence in separate or "cellular" confinement, for about eight months. They are then removed to other establishments, where large bodies, or "gangs," of prisoners work together, at quarrying, as at Portland; excavating docks, as at Chatham, and Spike Island, near Cork; or cultivating the land, as at Dartmoor. Much industry of a profitable and reformatory kind is thus enforced. But the effect of this excellent feature of the treatment is largely nullified by the demoralizing and mutually corrupting effect of the congregate labour in gangs, both on the English and Irish convict public works, the prisoners being only separated at night. Hence some grave evils result, especially as the chief portion of the convicts' terms of detention is spent at the gang establishments.

In England the convicts remain at these establishments until their discharge. But in Ireland there is a third stage—namely, the "Intermediate" Farm Prison, at Lusk, near Dublin—where the better behaved class of convicts pass the concluding portion of their terms, under a discipline intermediate between the conditions of imprisonment and freedom. Thus, at Lusk, the convicts wear no distinctive dress; they are permitted to go some distance, to the village church on Sunday, mingling with the ordinary congregation, and to have various other privileges. They are also allowed about half-a-crown a week for their labour, in order to form a fund for helping them to emigrate on their discharge. It is this concluding "intermediate" stage, together with the special facilities for emigration, which constitutes the peculiarity of the Irish system, as distinguished from the English plan.

The systematic emigration of discharged convicts is one main cause of the diminution of the convict class in Ireland. And it is encouraging to find that a similar diminution has of late years taken place in the ordinary (or county and borough, as distinguished from the State) prisons of Ireland, owing to the same cause—the desire for emigration and the facilities given for it. Discharged prisoners going out as freemen easily obtain employment, which would be difficult in their own country, and are removed from temptations to new crime among their old haunts and associates. The demand for labour at home is also increased, and the amount of poverty and crime lessened.

In both English and Irish convict prisons, the industry and good behaviour of the convicts are stimulated by a graduated system of "good marks," a plan originated by the late Captain Maconochie, whose suggestions were carried out and extended by Sir Walter Crofton. These "marks" entitle the convicts to a remission of a small portion of their sentences; and most of them, both in England and Ireland, "work off" a few months of their time, or in some cases a year or two. This arrangement has an excellent stimulating effect as to industry and good conduct.

Altogether there is not so much difference between the English and Irish systems in the main term of the sentence as is popularly supposed; but the Irish system, in the intermediate stage, provides for a less abrupt termination of the imprisonment, and opens up the way to a new start in life better than the English system. The Lusk Prison Farm is thus spoken of by Mr. William Tallack, the energetic and benevolent secretary of the Howard Association: "At Lusk, the convicts are enabled to earn enough to provide real help for beginning life again. Thus a prisoner who has been there for ten years, and who was liberated lately, had earned enough money not only to emigrate himself, but was also about to take his daughter out of a poor-house and pay her passage to America, out of his earnings, the two shillings per week paid for his hard toil from morning to night. The Lusk men really do work, and to good purpose. Their labour covers, at all events, the cost of their food and lodging. In fourteen years they have raised the rental value of the land (formerly a swampy common) from ten shillings to about five pounds per acre. The moral atmosphere of the establishment is excellent, the prisoners voluntarily repressing any tendency to disorder, bad language, or other misconduct. They tidy themselves up on coming to Lusk. Two-thirds of the Irish convicts go there. Of those whose conduct never obtains this privilege, the re-committals are seventy-seven per cent., whereas of those who pass through Lusk only twenty-three per cent. are re-convicted. Lusk is a noble monument of the ability and humanity of Sir Walter Crofton, its founder, and the chief practical organizer of those wise principles previously enunciated by Maconochie, Jebb, and others. Its continued success is, however, also to be largely ascribed to its excellent officers, especially Mr. Gunnis, Mr. Organ, and Mr. Daly. Apart from these, the best system might have failed."

Of Lusk, then, almost unqualified praise may be spoken. But other parts of the Irish convict system are very defective. This remark especially applies to Spike Island, where the convicts spend the chief portion of their time. Thus, a convict sentenced for twelve years must spend eight months at Mountjoy in separate or cellular confinement, and at least seven and a third years at Spike Island; he may then, if well-behaved, spend a year at Lusk, and be liberated, on license, after nine years' total detention. So that about three-fourths of the time of Irish servitude is spent at Spike Island. Mr. Tallack strongly condemns the long period of gang labour at Spike Island. Mr. Gibson, for ten years chaplain of the island, says, "I believe that a man living in close association for years with convicts, many of whom have been guilty of manslaughter, and some of murder, learn not to think more of their crimes than other people do of ordinary offences." One of the officials said to Mr. Tallack at Mountjoy prison, "We find that some of our men, who have borne a good character here, get corrupted at Spike Island." He recommends the abandonment of gang labour, and, in fact, the abandonment of Spike Island altogether, and the substitution of longer detention at Mountjoy, with greater attention there to reformatory and educational training, from which the transition should be direct to Lusk farm labour.

In the county and borough gaols there are some great abuses. More separation and classification of prisoners would be of advantage, and more useful and profitable industry. There is a most disproportionate number of prisons for the number of prisoners. Thus in Kilkenny gaol there were lately only thirty prisoners, with eleven salaried officials. In Galway gaol the cost of all the prisoners in one year was £634; of the officials, £1,184, or £550 less for prisoners than keepers! In all Ireland last year there were thirty-eight gaols for only 2,361 prisoners. The number and expense of officials would thus seem to be extravagant. The average cost of Irish prisoners is nearly £35 per annum each. The average annual earnings are not as many shillings—£1 3s. 8d. only yearly! Where there is good management and an efficient gaoler, as at Dundalk, under Mr. H. Webb, Mr. Tallack reports that the earnings are far larger, and the whole management better. In Cork gaol there had been for three years a debtor for a debt of £15; another man, a mason, for a debt of £5 13s. 4d., although he had offered to pay his creditors by instalments of ten shillings a week. This prisoner had a wife and seven children depending on him. So that there were thus thrown upon the rates of the town for a considerable period ten persons for a united debt of less than £24—less than the average cost of one Irish prisoner. Well may he add, "O, wise men of Cork!"

In Ireland there is a class of local inspectors not existing in England. These are appointed by the local visiting justices. Hence it is against their interest to report fearlessly and impartially in cases of abuse. All inspectors should be independent of local influence, and able to report freely on the prisons under their inspection.

The dietary of Irish prisons is also very inferior. A commission of inquiry on this point lately reported strongly in favour of improvement; but, like too many Government commissions, the report has not been acted on. Better food and more work are required to make the prison work less costly and more useful.

Having referred to convict prisons, I wish to say a few words about the Fenian prisoners, some of whom are still retained in penal servitude in England. Any account of Ireland in 1872 would be imperfect without taking notice of the strong feeling manifested as to the retention of these prisoners.

The prisoners still detained are poor humble men, the Fenian chiefs having been all released. None of them were connected with the Clerkenwell affair, and only two with the Manchester rescue, when the police-sergeant Brett was killed. For that crime three lives were required, and there may now surely be forgiveness for those who were merely engaged in the riotous meeting. The larger number of the remaining convicts are soldiers. They were youths led away by appeals to their patriotism; and though the breach of the military engagement is very heinous, some consideration may be made for the circumstances both of their taking and breaking their oath. Enlistment is often a heedless act, done in a public-house commonly, and the "Queen's shilling" is taken without serious thought of the oath associated with it. In courts of justice, when a base witness takes an oath deliberately and violates it, he may be sentenced for perjury to a term of imprisonment. But these soldiers, I believe, are sentenced for life to penal servitude, among the worst felons. The British

Government may surely be as magnanimous as the American Government, who have given amnesty to the soldiers who not only conspired, but fought against the President and Constitution of the United States.

The general feeling throughout Ireland is that these are political prisoners; and though this feeling is erroneous, it is not the less powerful in keeping up disaffection towards England. To treat political prisoners with the same severity as common felons is against the usage of civilized nations, and is regarded, in the case of these prisoners, as a wrong to Ireland. These prisoners have apparently been treated with exceptional harshness. I forbear from saying anything about the case of Reddin, who has brought an action-at-law against the prison authorities and medical officers for cruelty. He is now free, after undergoing his full sentence of five years. If he had been a common felon, he would probably have had his time shortened, and his sentence alleviated. The case of Davitt is even more painful. He is a maimed man, with one arm, and has been injured by forced labours which humanity would have spared him. His sentence of fifteen years was not so much for the heinousness of his crime, selling or purchasing arms, as "to be a warning to others," as the Chief Justice said. If the statements made by Reddin and Davitt, which have been widely circulated in Ireland, have the least foundation in truth, there has been cruel severity exercised, and the alleged treatment of these convicts by the prison officials is a scandal demanding investigation.

The feeling of indignation among the people is very deep, and there will be no peace while inquiry is refused. Meetings are held, not only in Ireland, but in the great towns of England where Irishmen can meet in large numbers. The appeals are in temperate language, and I must avow that they are in themselves just and reasonable. Why should the few followers be retained, when the more guilty leaders have been released? The petitions for amnesty have been signed by larger numbers than any petition since the time of Catholic emancipation, and magistrates, clergy, and leading gentry and merchants, have presented addresses pleading for clemency. The majesty of law has been fully vindicated in the severity of the sentences, and pardon may be extended without any danger to public peace, and without offering the least encouragement to disloyalty. Mr. Gladstone once had the matter before him, on the appeal of the late Mr. Maguire, of Cork. He referred to the Home Office, and was told that the treatment was only that to which all convicts are subject. If this is the case, there is the more need of public inquiry; for the treatment of some of these prisoners has been a disgrace to English justice and to common humanity.

CHAPTER XX.

PARTY PROCESSIONS.

Green and Orange—The Belfast Riots—Party Spirit.

THE repeal of the Party Processions Bill was moved by Mr. W. Johnston, as representative of the Orange, and seconded by The O'Donoghue, as representative of the Green. Mr. Johnston strongly condemned repressive legislation, as creating more irritation than all the party processions. The common law, he thought, was sufficient to repress all disorders, and to protect life and property. The O'Donoghue also preferred to trust to the ordinary powers of the common law, to the impartiality of the Executive, and above all to the spirit of conciliation and good feeling which he believed would spring up among all classes. At the same time, he made an earnest appeal to the Protestants to discontinue their manifestations, and to abandon their irritating claims to ascendancy, which were untenable and unjust, now that all were equal before the law. The O'Donoghue's generous and forcible appeal was well received by the House.

It was wise policy to repeal the Processions Act, because it was found impossible to enforce it. As in the case of the Ecclesiastical Titles Bill, discredit is brought on law if it remains unenforced, and can be defied or evaded with impunity. But having repealed the Act, and admitted party processions to be legal, the Government is under obligation to protect those who join them, except it resolves to leave the processionists to their own ways, and fight it out at their own peril. "If you have your procession, you must abide the consequences;" this might be said, and it would be an easy way of shirking responsibility. But no good government could submit to leave a town or district at the mercy of violent and riotous factions. It will be remembered that when the Orangemen of New York, in 1871, determined to have their procession, many lives were lost, although they were protected by a strong force of State militia and police. The procession was again held this year, with less public excitement; but the words of a leading New York paper, on the eve of the Orange anniversary, expressed well the views of sensible Americans:—"The Orangemen have a perfect right to parade if they choose, and if nothing but bayonets and bullets will protect them in it, the bayonets and bullets should be promptly forthcoming. The police and militia are ready for business, and if another interference is attempted like that of last year, more blood will be shed over 'the battle of the Boyne.' But what could be more ridiculous folly than for men to be butchering one another about something that happened generations ago?"

Before the processions of 1872 began in Ireland, an earnest appeal was made to the Orangemen to desist from party irritation. The Catholics solemnly declared that they would not interfere with any Orange demonstration, but as firmly stated that for every Protestant procession they would have a larger Catholic procession. What is to be the end of a rivalry like this? Law cannot check it, and the only hope is in an improved state of public opinion. There are not wanting signs of this improvement being seen. The ruffians who interfered with the Catholic procession of the 15th August in Belfast belonged to no recognized organization. It was stated by the prison chaplain, that among the numerous prisoners there was not one Presbyterian. The ship-carpenters, who were charged as a body with having taken large part in the riots, through the committee of their trade society, repudiated the accusation. The interference, which resulted in so much mischief, seems to have been commenced by a rabble who, if Orangemen, were a disgrace to the name and the cause.

What the Mayor of New York, though a Catholic,

did with effect, the Mayor of Belfast ought to have done. The disturbers of the procession ought to have been dealt with summarily, and a little severity at the moment would have proved mercy in the end. The *Times*, commenting on the riots, made the same reference to American precedent: " A Catholic procession in the north of Ireland, acting within the limits of the law, may claim a similar escort, and the Executive Government would be justified in sending it, whether claimed or not. If under such circumstances Orangemen attempted to stop the procession, and declined to disperse when duly warned, they should be fired upon. Less than this we cannot do without conniving at organized lawlessness calling itself Protestant Christianity ; whether we ought to do more is a matter on which we are not at present compelled to pronounce an opinion."

Whatever may be intended by this writer as to ulterior measures, it is plain that the disturbance is kept up by a comparatively small section of the people. The numbers seen at a procession are gathered from a wide extent of country, the two parties striving in emulation to make an imposing display of numbers as well as of banners and insignia. All respectable citizens, except fanatics in religion or politics, condemn these party demonstrations ; commerce and business suffer, and the payments of rates and expenses will impose no light penalty on districts and towns which have been the scenes of violence.

I cannot leave this subject without reminding the reader that this violent party spirit in Ulster is comparatively of recent growth. At one of the Orange meetings last autumn, a Presbyterian minister, the Rev. William White, told an anecdote that he had heard from one of the leading citizens of Downpatrick. At a dinner many years ago the toast was given—"The glorious, pious, and immortal memory of the good and great King William." The parish priest of Downpatrick, Bernard M'Cauley, a Catholic of the old school, well known in his day, drank the toast, and said that "King William was one of the men who knew the best, and encouraged the most, the spirit of toleration." It may surprise some readers still more to learn that in 1789, when the centenary anniversary of the Relief of Derry was celebrated, Doctor M'Devitt, the Roman Catholic Bishop of Derry, with his clergy, joined the public procession of the citizens, and was present in the cathedral when thanksgiving was offered to God the Deliverer. The Mayor and Corporation, the Bishop of Derry, and a numerous body of clergy, Episcopalian and Presbyterian, with these liberal Catholics, united in a celebration which touched the sympathy of all the inhabitants of the maiden city.

The Orange societies were no doubt at first organized for defensive purposes, the Protestants resenting the gradual encroachments, as they considered them, of the Catholics. But not going back to olden times of defiance and violence, it is worth remembering that in the year before the accession of Queen Victoria, during the session of 1836, the whole question of Orange societies was very fully discussed in the House of Commons, and after long debate the House was so satisfied of the evil results of the association, that an address was presented to the King, William IV., to which his Majesty sent the following answer: "I willingly assent to the prayer of the address of my faithful Commons, that I will be pleased to take such measures as may seem to me advisable for the effectual discouragement of Orange lodges, and generally of all political societies excluding persons of different religious faith, using secret signs and symbols, and acting by means of associated branches. It is my firm intention to discourage all such societies in my dominions, and I rely with confidence on the fidelity of my loyal subjects to support me in this determination." The consequence was that the Duke of Cumberland, as head of the Orange society, recommended the immediate dissolution of the body. How the intention of Parliament and the Crown was evaded, and how the nuisance of secret political and religious societies again grew, it is not necessary here to narrate. But the existence of these Orange lodges, accompanied as they always must be by counter-organizations of Catholics, is the chief obstacle to peace and harmony in the north of Ireland. If they were for political purposes only, their *raison-d'être* might be justified, but the union of motives has a mischievous influence, producing confusion in politics, and bringing discredit on religion. The home mission-work of the Protestant churches is the true way to meet the Catholics as a religious body. Insulting demonstrations and uncharitable hatred will not commend to the Romanists the purer creed which the Orangemen profess to hold. On religious, on social, and on political grounds the Orange organization is one of the most baleful evils of Ireland. No wonder that an Englishman, Mr. Whitworth, of Drogheda, lately said, in referring to a false rumour of an intended massacre of Protestants, that he would far sooner entrust the safety of himself and his family among the Catholics of Drogheda than among the Orangemen of the north.

Statute laws cannot with efficiency be much in advance of public opinion, and the attempt to suppress Orange lodges would be even less successful than that of putting a stop to party processions. But as the vast majority of wise and good men agree in the reprobation of such disturbances of the peace of society, let them give stronger expression to their opinions. Why should not the Synod of the Irish Church and the General Assembly of the Presbyterian Church lead the way in this work of Christian forbearance and generosity? Let them disown the sanction of such societies as in any way connected with religion and the spread of the Gospel, and let them declare the divorce of the Protestant from the political element of Orangeism. It is to be feared that politicians are merely using the religious prejudices of weaker brethren to promote their own secular and selfish ends, to the injury alike of true patriotism and true religion.

CHAPTER XXI.

THE NEWSPAPERS OF IRELAND.

Statistics of Journalism—The National Press—Political Ballads.

MR. GRANT, in his "History of the Newspaper Press," bears testimony to the great improvement which has taken place within the last few years in the external appearance of the Irish journals. "Not many years ago the Irish provincial newspapers resembled, both in typography and paper, the backwoods journals of America. Now the majority of their number look better than the majority of our provincial English papers. And in Dublin the penny press will not suffer by comparison with the penny press in London, either as regards paper or printing. Leaving the material part of Irish journalism, if one comes to speak of the mental part, we shall find that on the whole it need not shrink from a comparison with the journalism of Great Britain. In Dublin, Belfast, Cork, and other places, the ability with which the Irish papers is conducted is certainly not inferior to that which is shown in the editorial department of the journalism of this country." Whatever weight may be given to Mr. Grant in other matters, his long experience as a metropolitan editor makes his opinion of value on matters relating to journalism.

In 1846 the number of Irish newspapers was 106. There was then only one daily paper, *Saunders' News Letter*. There were no cheap newspapers; now there are 42 penny papers. There are 19 daily papers in Ireland, 6 of which are published in Dublin, 6 in Belfast, 4 in Cork, and 1 in Waterford. The statistics of Irish journalism may be thus tabulated:—

Daily, 19; tri-weekly, 6; bi-weekly, 26; weekly, 84; fortnightly, 1; monthly, 1; total, 137.

In their professed politics,—liberal, 34; liberal conservative, 6; liberal independent, 3; ultra-liberal, 2; conservative, 36; moderate conservative, 1; independent conservative, 2; Protestant conservative, 1.

These are the political descriptions given by the papers of themselves. There are besides about 45 calling themselves independent and neutral, many of which are advertising sheets chiefly, or are devoted to agricultural, commercial, shipping, and other special interests.

As to religion, there are 25 avowedly Protestant and Church of Ireland, 12 Roman Catholic, and only

1 avowedly Presbyterian. But there are many others in which Catholic and Presbyterian influence is evident, both in editing and in management.

The prices of the papers are very various : 3 at ½d., 42 at 1d., 4 at 1½d., 29 at 2d., 3 at 2½d., 30 at 3d., 5 at 3½d., 14 at 4d., 2 at 5d., and 1 at 6d. Four are gratis advertisement papers or circulars.

The oldest papers are the *Dublin Gazette*, 1711; the *Evening Post*, 1725; *Belfast News Letter*, 1737; *Saunders' News Letter*, 1746; *Waterford Chronicle*, 1760; *Londonderry Journal*, 1772; *Kerry Evening Post*, 1774; *Clare Journal*, 1776. The youngest is the *Belfast Times*, 1872.

Of the Dublin daily papers, those which have the largest circulation are the *Freeman's Journal* and the *Irish Times*, which are about equal. Next come the *Daily Express*, *Morning* and *Evening Mail*, and *Saunders' News Letter*.

Of the weekly newspapers, the largest circulation is claimed by the *Weekly News*, the *Flag of Ireland*, the *Irishman*, the *Nation*, and the *Weekly Freeman*.

The street sale of newspapers in Dublin is an institution of very long standing, much longer than in England. At the corner of the chief streets there are regular newsvendors, with or without stalls or chairs. Newsvending as a shop trade is quite of recent introduction. Since 1860 news shops have multiplied, but prior to that date there were only two or three newsagents in Dublin, and most of the towns were wholly without this branch of trade. At the railway stations there is now a large sale. On most of the lines there are book-stalls, where papers are sold. On the chief lines the trade is in the hands of our great English newsagent, Mr. W. H. Smith. On some of the lesser lines there are independent contractors or speculators.

The non-political literature on the Irish book-stalls is not of a high order. The books are much the same class as on English railways, with the addition of Irish national reading; but the periodical literature is inferior. The largest sale at several stations where I made inquiry, was of periodicals which have little reputation in England, in fact, the poorest London periodicals. They are supplied at a reduction of price, which more respectable literature does not emulate, and the Irish penny purchasers take what is provided, without knowing the difference. Still the taste is improving, and the habit of reading becoming more universal; another generation will be lifted above the present level, and be ripe for better intellectual food.

Which of the newspapers are the most influential? it may be asked. The *Daily Express* is the best informed organ of the Conservatives, and as such has great weight. The *Freeman's Journal* is in a certain sense a Government and Liberal organ, but it runs crooked when the views of the Government are at variance with the Catholic clerical party. Then it is *their* organ, and fairly expresses their views. The *Irish Times* and *Saunders' News Letter* are also influential papers, and represent large sections of public opinion.

The *Weekly News* and the *Nation* are published at the same office, and are "national" papers, taking strong Irish and anti-English tone on most questions. The *Nation* was originally an independent national paper, and was the organ of the Young Ireland party. Latterly it seems to be most identified with the interests of the Romish or Ultramontane Catholics. The *Irishman* and the *Flag of Ireland* are published in the same office, both of them are more intensely national than the *News* and the *Nation*, but with less subservience to the Catholic priesthood.

The Catholic hierarchy have no organ professedly belonging to them, nor any paper in which they wholly confide. They part from the political "national" papers as yet on the Home Rule question, to which they are all professedly hostile. But the national papers know that much of their influence would be lost if they openly opposed Cardinal Cullen's views, and they trim their articles to retain all adherents possible.

The circulation of all the papers, especially the Irish or national ones, is very uncertain as to amount. Any event which can be magnified into an Irish grievance, and become the subject of strongly-written articles, causes the circulation to bound up rapidly, so that the proprietors of the papers have interest in fostering political excitement. There is this to be said, residents in Ireland think far less of the strong writing, than is usual on this side of the water. It is only Irish "bunkum," and means little beyond. Keogh and Froude helped greatly during last year to keep up public excitement, and gave ample scope for sensational articles in the national papers.

On leaving Dublin, it was curious to notice, either in travelling to the north or the south, the contrast of tone in the press. The Dublin dailies are carried everywhere along the lines; but the local papers show distinctive features in north and south. On entering Ulster, the strong Protestant papers of Belfast make their influence felt, and the smaller local papers are even more intense in their politics. In the south, the local journals in their general politics are less independent, and are mere echoes of the Dublin papers.

The contrast between Protestant and Catholic papers is seen in nothing more strikingly than in the advertisement columns. In the Catholic papers are numerous notices of ecclesiastical affairs, conspicuous among which are announcements of lotteries for chapels and schools and seminaries. These lotteries one would suppose are scarcely legal, but they are an institution in Ireland, as in other popish countries, and the end seems to be taken to justify the means. The lotteries are not confined to local patrons, but the coupons are very largely circulated by post throughout the kingdom, and many chapels have been greatly indebted to English credulity for the funds by which they were built. Books of coupons are transmitted to trusty Catholic correspondents, who distribute them, with tempting baits of prizes, few, if any, of which are ever heard of falling to the lot of English purchasers of tickets.

Of the Irish newspapers, so far as they belong to party politics, I say nothing, but in studying the disturbing forces of public life, the national press calls for special notice. The principal papers of this class I have already enumerated. The oldest of them, and that which chiefly contributed to the establishment of the National party, is the *Nation*, which has now been in existence above thirty years, being established in 1842.

Charles Gavan Duffy was the first editor of the *Nation*. Born of humble parentage in county Monaghan, he went to Dublin in his eighteenth year, and found employment on the newspaper press. He was editor of a Belfast paper for some time, returning to Dublin in 1841, and in the following year became a leading spirit in the "Young Ireland party," by whom the *Nation* was founded, in order "to create and foster public opinion in Ireland, and to make it racy of the soil." The Repeal agitation was then at its height, and the rule of O'Connell was supreme. In 1844 Duffy was O'Connell's fellow-prisoner in Richmond gaol, being convicted of sedition. He acted with O'Connell till 1847, when he seceded from the Repeal Association, and was one of the founders of the Irish Confederation. He was tried for treason-felony in 1848, but the prosecution was abandoned. He then resumed the editorship of the *Nation*, the publication of which had for a time been suspended, confining himself more to social subjects, such as the landlord and tenant question. He was elected member for New Cross in 1852, and held his seat till 1856, when he resigned to go to Australia. His career there has been honourable and distinguished, he having twice held the office of Prime Minister of the colony of Victoria. He has lately received the honour of knighthood.

The name of Charles Gavan Duffy will live in Irish literature as the editor of the "Ballad Poetry" of Ireland. This work, first published in 1845, had in twenty years passed through thirty-eight editions, amounting in all to 76,000 copies. In the following year, during a visit to Europe, after ten years' absence, he was asked to prepare a new edition. Some omissions there are, but no additions to this collection of national ballads. A few explanatory or illustrative notes are appended. This thirty-ninth edition was dedicated to Mr. Justice O'Hagan, now Lord Chancellor of Ireland, as the first edition had been inscribed to the same friend, then a rising barrister. The preface contains brief references to some of the song writers who had passed away since the first appearance of the work: "John Keegan, the peasant poet, who left us, almost for the first time, genuine songs of the field and the cabin;" D. J. Fraser, "the poet of the workshops;" Edward Walsh, "whose tender and passionate genius interpreted so successfully between the Celtic brain and the English tongue." But the most touching and graceful of these brief biographical references is "to the master and chief, whom they all cheerfully accepted and acknowledged in that character, Thomas Davis. In the original introduction there is no allusion to him beyond the slightest and most casual; not because he was living, and apparently destined to a long and distinguished career, for I attempted some estimate of the genius of others in kindred circumstances, but literally because he shrank painfully from any public recognition of his labours by his friends and associates. To have written of him as I felt, would have rudely wounded his modest and sensitive nature. But I may now declare, that though he was foremost among the young poets of his day, his greatest poem was his life. It never has been my good fortune to meet so noble a human creature; so variously gifted, so unaffectedly just, generous, and upright; so utterly without selfishness and without vanity; and I never expect to meet such another," A tribute this, honourable alike to the writer and to his departed friend.

The original introduction to Sir Charles Duffy's book gave a very interesting historical account of Irish ballad poetry. The spirit in which this work was undertaken may be seen in the following passage, expressing the author's desire to make it not a party or sectarian but a national collection. "Whatever could illustrate the character, passions, or opinions of any class of Irishmen, that we gladly adopted. Our duty is to know each other; to learn how much is mutually to be loved, that we may love it; how much is mutually to be disliked, that we may forgive it. Everything contributing to this end ought to be regarded as precious. Some of the Ulster ballads, of a restricted and provincial spirit, having less in common with Ireland than Scotland; two or three Orange ballads, altogether ferocious or foreign in their tendencies (preaching murder or deifying an alien), will be no less valuable to the poet or the patriot on this account. They echo faithfully the sentiments of a strong, vehement, and indomitable body of Irishmen, who may come to battle for their country better than ever they battled for their prejudices or bigotries. At all events, to know what they love and believe is a precious knowledge." But I must not be tempted to enter the broad field of Irish ballad poetry. My only purpose in here alluding to it is to note its influence on the existing political views of the people, and especially the use that was made of it by the Young Ireland party. To this party I think scant justice has been done in England, or even by their own countrymen of different politics. Other of the leaders I might name, such as Michael Joseph Barry, editor of "The Songs of Ireland," and Meagher, "Meagher of the Sword," who in America has had a career as distinguished as that of Duffy in Australia. The representative man of the movement was Thomas Davis, whose poetry has been a power in Ireland, and still keeps up the enthusiasm of the National party. In literature he will rank with Ireland's best poets, yet I have found his poetry ignored by many Irishmen, some of whom ask, "Who is Thomas Davis?"

There was a ring of fresh young patriotism about

the first years of the *Nation* newspaper, which made it popular in Ireland and respected abroad. At one of the early meetings of the conductors—they used to have weekly suppers—it was resolved that by political songs and ballads the popular mind might be most influenced. Fletcher of Saltoun's familiar saying was quoted, " Let who will make a country's laws, let me make its ballads." Davis had never attempted anything in verse, but he tried, and was successful. Charles Duffy, however, led the way with this new political weapon, his song "Faugh a Ballagh," or more correctly, "Fag an Bealach," "Clear the Road," being printed in the third number of the *Nation* as the charter-song of the contributors:—

>Hope no more for fatherland,
>　All its ranks are thinned or broken;
>Long a base and coward band
>　Recreant words like these have spoken:
>　But *we* preach a land awoken;
>Fatherland is true and tried,
>　As your fears are false and broken;
>Slaves and dastards, stand aside—
>　Knaves and traitors, Faugh a Ballagh!
>　　＊　　＊　　＊　　＊
>Fling our banner to the wind,
>　Studded o'er with names of glory;
>Worth and wit, and might and mind,
>　Poet young, and patriot hoary,
>　Long shall make it shine in story.
>Close your ranks—the moment's come—
>　*Now*, ye men of Ireland, follow!
>Friends of freedom, charge them home—
>　Foes of freedom, Faugh a Ballagh!

The first ballad written by Davis was a "Lament for the Death of Eoghan Ruadh O'Neill," or Owen Roe O'Neill, as he is commonly called, who is supposed to have been poisoned when marching to meet the forces of Cromwell in November, 1649. One of his veterans chants the lament:—

> Sagest in the council was he, kindest in the hall:
> Sure we never won a battle—'twas Owen won them all.
> Had he lived, had he lived, our dear country had been free;
> But he's dead, but he's dead, and 'tis slaves we'll ever be.
>
> Wail, wail him through the island! weep, weep for our pride!
> Would that on the battle-field our gallant chief had died!
> Weep the victor of Beinn Barb—weep him, young men and old!
> Weep for him, you women—your Beautiful lies cold!
>
> We thought ye would not die—we were sure you would not go,
> And leave us in our utmost need to Cromwell's cruel blow—
> Sheep without a shepherd, when the snow shuts out the sky—
> Oh! why did you leave us, Owen? why did you die?

Thomas Davis was of Welsh extraction, and, though devoting most of his poetic enthusiasm to Irish subjects, took warm interest in the land of his forefathers. In one of his political essays this sympathy is expressed. Finding slight information about Wales in a standard book of reference, M'Culloch's Geographical Dictionary, he exclaims, "And has time, then, mouldered away that obstinate and fiery tribe of Celts which baffled the Plantagenets, which so often trod upon the breastplate of the Norman, which sometimes bent in summer, but ever rose when the fierce elements of winter came to aid the nation? Has that race passed away which stood under Llewellyn, and rallied under Owen Glendower, and gave the Dragon flag and Tudor kings to England? Is the prophecy of twelve hundred years false? Are the people and tongue passed away? No! spite of the massacre of bards and the burning of records, spite of political extinction, there is a million of these Cymri in Wales and its marches; and nine out of ten of them speak their old tongue, follow their old customs, sing the songs which the sleepers on Snowdon made, have their religious rites in Cymric, and hate the Logrian as much as ever their fathers did."

Fired with the remembrance of old Welsh struggles for independence, he wrote a song to his favourite Welsh tune, "The March of the Men of Harlech," entitled, "Cymric Men and Cymric Rulers," of which here is the first stanza:—

> Once there was a Cymric nation,
> Few its men, but high its station—
> Freedom is the soul's creation,
>   Not the work of hands.
> Coward hearts are self-subduing;
> Fetters last by slaves' renewing—
> Edward's castles are in ruin,
>   Still his empire stands.
> Still the Saxon's malice
> Blights our beauteous valleys;

> Ours the toil, but his the spoil, and his the laws we writhe in ;
> Worked like beasts that Saxon priests may riot in our tithing ;
> > Saxon speech and Saxon teachers
> > Crush our Cymric tongue !
> > Tolls our traffic binding,
> > Rents our vitals grinding,
> Bleating sheep, we cower and weep, when by one bold endeavour
> We could drive from out our hive these Saxon drones for ever.
> > "Cymric rule and Cymric rulers"—
> > Pass along the word.

This is a characteristic specimen of the visionary yet mischievous genius of the man. It is visionary, because an appeal to Cymric patriotism as a political force is simply ridiculous. He might as well call upon the descendants of Gurth and Wamba to repossess their ancient forests, or the scanty remains of the black rats to make a stand against their brown Norwegian conquerors. But there is mischief with the folly, because in raising questions as to the righteousness of tolls and rents, and the rights of labour against capital, the ignorant part of the population is incited to crimes against property and law. But in his prose essay Mr. Davis contents himself with urging the Welsh members to unite in agitating for home rule. "Let them agitate," he says, "for a local council to administer the local affairs of the Principality. Localization, by means of Federalism, seems the natural and best resource of a country like Wales, to guard its purse and language and character from imperial oppression, and its soil from a foreign invasion. As powers run, it is not like Ireland, quite able, if free, to hold its own; but it has importance enough to entitle it to a local congress for local affairs."

As for Wales, so for Ireland, nationality was the master idea of Davis in the political songs which for years, through the pages of the *Nation*, stirred the Irish with patriotic passion. The historical ballads were the best. Beranger himself never wrote a war-song more stirring than the "Fontenoy" of Davis is to Irishmen. The day was almost lost to the French, and a massive column of troops, English veterans of the Marlborough wars and Scotland's famous "Black Watch," were advancing:—

On through the camp the column trod ; King Louis turned his rein.
"Not yet, my liege," Saxe interposed ; " the Irish troops remain."
And Fontenoy, famed Fontenoy, had been a Waterloo,
Were not those exiles ready there, fresh, vehement, and true.
"Lord Clare," he says, " you have your wish ; there are your Saxon foes."
The Marshal almost smiles to see, so furiously he goes !
How fierce the look these exiles wear, who're wont to be so gay ;
The treasured wrongs of fifty years are in their hearts to-day—
The Treaty broken ere the ink wherewith 'twas writ could dry,
Their plundered homes, their ruined shrines, their women's parting cry,
Their priesthood hunted down like wolves, their country overthrown,
Each looks as if revenge for all rested on him alone.
On Fontenoy, on Fontenoy, nor ever yet elsewhere,
Rushed on to fight a nobler band than these proud exiles were.

The sad story of Fontenoy need not hinder any

generous English reader from admiring patriotic strains like this, any more than a Scotchman need be less loyal now for the story of Flodden. The song of "The Geraldines" and "A Rally for Ireland" are grand historical ballads, which may make all Irishmen proud of Thomas Davis.

Clarence Mangan, one of the stars of the *Dublin University Magazine*, and one of the best of recent native poets, wrote a humorous but congenial ode on the *Nation's* "first number," of which here are two out of many stanzas :—

> 'Tis a great day and glorious, O public, for you!
> This October fifteenth, eighteen hundred and two!
> For on this day of days, lo! THE NATION came forth,
> To commence its career of Wit, Wisdom, and Worth.
> To give genius its due, to do battle with wrong,
> And achieve things undreamed of as yet, save in song.
> Then arise! fling aside your dark mantle of slumber,
> And welcome in chorus THE NATION's first number.
>
> Though we take not for motto *nul n'a de l'esprit*
> (As they once did in Paris), *hors nos bons amis*,
> We may boast that for first-rate endowments our band
> Forms a phalanx unmatched *in* or *out* of the land—
> Poets, patriots, linguists, with reading like Parr's;
> Critics keener than sabres, wits brighter than stars,
> And reasoners as cool as the coolest cucumber,
> Form the host that shine out in THE NATION's first number.

Sir C. Duffy wrote the ballad entitled "The Munster of the North," a shameless pæan on the atrocious massacres in the rising of 1641. A few stanzas will show the spirit of this poem :—

Joy ! joy ! the day is come at last, the day of hope and pride,
And see ! our crackling bonfires light old Bann's rejoicing tide,
And gladsome bell and bugle-horn from Newry's captured tower.
Hark ! how they tell the Saxon swine this land is ours, is ours.

   * * * * *

Come, trample down their robber rule, and smite its venal spawn,
Their foreign laws, their foreign church, their ermine and their lawn,
With all the specious fry of fraud that robbed us of our own,
And plant our ancient laws again beneath our lineal throne.

Our standard flies o'er fifty towers, o'er twice ten thousand men ;
Down have we plucked the pirate red, never to rise again ;
The green alone shall stream above our native field and flood,
The spotless green, save where its folds are gemmed with Saxon blood.

In this strain the poor Irish of the nineteenth century are taught to celebrate the cruel massacre of their Protestant fellow-countrymen in Ulster. No wonder that this poem was denounced as an attempt to perpetuate civil discord, and to encourage the ignorant populace to make light of assassination and murder. Mr. Duffy's defence was that he meant no apology for the excesses of that rising, the result of desperate provocation. "The ballad," he said, "was meant as a true representation of the feelings of the insurgents in the first madness of success. 'There would have been no sense or propriety in making these men talk coolly, and exhibit the horror of spilling one drop of human blood into which O'Connell trained this generation." This was a poor and untenable excuse, which Mr. Duffy would now hardly offer. The want of sense and propriety is shown in making a song of triumph over scenes which a true patriot would willingly allow to rest in oblivion. The same sanguinary spirit revels in many of the ballads of the *Nation,* as in "Inis-Eoghain," or Inishone, "The Ballad of Freedom," "Oh, for a Steed," "The Lament of Iraiune Maol," and a score beside. Well might the men of Ulster indignantly ask if this was true patriotism or true nationality, to stir up the worst passions of *Irishmen* against *Irishmen.*

The folly of the thing became apparent even to the hot-headed poets of the *Nation,* and a better class of ballads found place in its pages. Such was the song by Thomas Davis, "Orange and Green will carry the day," to the tune of "The Protestant Boys," though still marked by the insane hatred of England :—

> Rusty the swords our fathers unsheathed;
> William and James are turned to clay;
> Long did we till the wrath they bequeathed,
> Red was the crop, and bitter the pay!
> Freedom fled us!
> Knaves misled us!
> Under the feet of foemen we lay;
> Riches and strength
> We'll win them at length,
> For Orange and Green will carry the day!
> Landlords befooled us,
> England ruled us,
> Hounding our passions to make us their prey:

> But in their spite
> The Irish unite,
> And Orange and Green will carry the day.
>
> Fruitful our soil where honest men starve,
>   Empty the mart, and shipless the bay;
> Out of our want the oligarchs carve,
>   Foreigners fatten on our decay!
>   Disunited,
>   Therefore blighted,
> Ruined and rent by the Englishman's sway;
>   Party and creed
>   For once have agreed—
> Orange and Green will carry the day!
>   Boyne's old water,
>   Red with slaughter,
> Now is as pure as an infant at play;
>   So in our souls
>   Its history rolls,
> And Orange and Green will carry the day!

Unhappily, the same pen wrote another song, "The Green above the Red," breathing the spirit of strife and defiance, instead of peace and union:—

> Full often, when our fathers saw the Red above the Green,
> They rose in rude but fierce array, with sabre, pike, and skean,
> And over many a noble town, and many a field of dead,
> They proudly set the Irish Green above the English Red.
>
> But, in the end, throughout the land, the shameful sight was seen,
> The English Red in triumph high above the Irish Green;
> Yet often by the healthy hope their sinking hearts were fed,
> That in some day to come the Green should flutter o'er the Red.
>
> And 'tis for this we think, and toil, and knowledge strive to glean,
> That we may pull the English Red below the Irish Green,
> And leave our sons sweet liberty, and smiling plenty spread,
> Above the land once dark with blood—the Green above the Red.

We'll trust ourselves, for God is good, and blesses those who lean
On their brave hearts, and not upon an earthly king or queen;
And freely as we lift our hands, we vow our blood to shed,
Once and for evermore to raise the Green above the Red.

A more practical way of "spiting the Government" was an attempt to check enlistment in the British army, by the song of "The Saxon Shilling." The author was Mr. K. T. Buggy, for some time editor of the *Kilkenny Journal*, and an active agitator in the Repeal movement. He succeeded Mr. Gavan Duffy as editor of the *Belfast Vindicator* :—

>Irish hearts! why should you bleed
>   To swell the tide of British glory,
>Aiding despots in their need,
>   Who've changed our green so oft to gory?
>None, save those who wish to see
>   The noblest killed, the meanest killing,
>And true hearts severed from the free,
>   Will take again the Saxon shilling!
>
>Irish youths! reserve your strength
>   Until an hour of glorious duty,
>When freedom's smile shall cheer at length
>   The land of bravery and beauty.
>Bribes and threats, oh! heed no more,
>   Let nought but justice make you willing
>To leave your own dear island shore
>   For those who send the Saxon shilling.

In keeping with the anti-loyal and anti-British feeling we have songs in praise of Louis XIV., of Akbar Khan, and the robber Affghans, of the Canadian rebels, and all foes of England. The greatest tyrants and most worthless scoundrels are all saints and "friends of freedom," if they are only anti-English :—

> Viva la the New Brigade !
> Viva la the Old one too !
> Viva la, the Rose shall fade,
> And the Shamrock shine for ever new !

This is the burden of the poetry of the *Nation*.

I have given these snatches of song as the truest exponents of the spirit of the National party in Ireland. No specimens of the editorial articles in the *Nation* would more fully express the principles of that journal, and of the class of papers of which it is the representative. The political songs are published in a little volume, of which I have the fiftieth edition, published in 1870. Above a hundred thousand of the earlier editions had been sold, and as the price of the new stereotyped edition is only sixpence, the circulation will be immense. No wonder that the people are imbued with national feeling, in the sense of antipathy to English rule and institutions. The depth and extent of this feeling should not be ignored but respected, for it may turn to an element of strength in the United Kingdom. No uneasiness is caused by the wildest manifestations of nationality among Welshmen or Scotchmen, and it will be so yet with Irish national enthusiasm. Even Mr. Lowe may come to praise it as much as he did that of Scotland at the St. Andrew's dinner.

One thing to be noted about the songs and ballads which I have quoted from the *Nation* is, that they belong to the early years of the paper. It did then represent the earnest, though misguided, and sometimes violent aspirations of a National party. In late years the spirit of the *Nation* is less purely national, and more papal, or in other words, hostile to Irish independence as well as British rule. There is a purer tone of nationality in the *Irishman* or the *Flag of Ireland*, and to these papers we must look for the maintenance of Irish as opposed to Romish influence. If the conductors of the National papers would only contend for their own Irish interests, without alienating by their coarse violence all men of moderate principles, they would have more influence on the public opinion of the empire, without losing any popularity among their supporters. The refusal to support the Italian bishops in their hostility to united education has been honourable to the *Irishman* and the *Flag of Ireland*. If the leaders of the National party were true patriots, they would see, with Judge Keogh and Father O'Keeffe, that the rule of Cardinal Cullen is far more injurious to their country than the rule of any English Government.

One word as to the prosecutions of the National

journals. The seditious articles which constantly appear, I have already hinted, are not to be measured by English newspaper standards. They are often mere sound and fury, and are taken in Ireland itself at their worth, for any political influence. The same literary rowdyism is common in America, especially at election seasons. In Ireland, the real mischief of these articles, as lately on occasion of the Dillon demonstration at Cork, is that they incite poor ignorant Irishmen to crimes which bring them under the penalties of the law. The daring defiance of authority and the open treason, often allowed to pass uncensured, in the Irish papers, prove the mild tolerance and the much-enduring patience of "the Saxon oppressors." In no other country of Europe would such license be permitted. But when legal limits are passed, the duty of the Government is to make the prosecution more than a form. If the editors and writers are now called to account, the trial and punishment only serve to give them the prestige of political martyrs, and the papers flourish more than ever. The ordinary procedure of courts of law and trial by jury will not meet the difficulty. As in troublesome times the suspension of the Habeas Corpus Act is submitted to with the assent of all peaceable men, so the suspension of the common law as to the "liberty of the press" would meet with the sympathy of all true patriots, when that liberty degenerates into criminal license. A strict law on the press, carried out with firmness, would soon teach a useful financial lesson to the proprietors of papers which publish treason and incite to crime. They would learn that "loyalty is the best policy," and would be less anxious to increase the occasional sales of their papers by articles abusive of the Government.

CHAPTER XXII.

THE DUBLIN EXHIBITION.

National Portrait Gallery—The Leinster Hall—National Exhibition.

OF the Dublin Exhibition of 1872 so much was written and published, on both sides of the Channel, that I content myself with setting down only some brief notes of impressions made by it, without any descriptive details.

In the first place, looking at the names of the chief promoters of this national display, and of the distinguished and patriotic men who formed the executive council and committee, Catholics and Protestants, Liberals and Conservatives, men of all creeds and political opinions, there was here a practical illustration of the kind of "Home Rule" which might safely and usefully be inaugurated in Ireland. Out of the men who worked harmoniously together for this great national undertaking, surely there might be formed a council—call it council rather than parliament—to which the work might be entrusted of developing the resources and administering the affairs of the sister kingdom, without any interference with matters of imperial government. There was no strife in that Exhibition Council, except emulation in carrying out what tended to the well-being and honour of the common country. And there are many affairs in which a council containing elements as diverse, could unite in peaceful consultation, upon all the subjects which could be legitimately delegated to a national home rule assembly.

Another thought of similar tone was suggested in walking through the magnificent National Portrait Gallery of Irish worthies. Here were the representatives of all times and all parties in Irish history; the descendants of Celts, Saxons, and Normans, Royalists and Rebels, statesmen who had led opposing factions, and soldiers who had led hostile armies in civil wars; yet every Irishman, and every stranger, who visited the gallery, could not but feel a common pride and interest in the collected portraits of those who belonged to the national annals. Any maniac who might have given vent to his feelings by slashing at pictures with which he had least sympathy, would fitly represent the Irishman who would allow bygone animosities of history to interfere with common efforts for the present and future welfare of the country. If there were a permanent national portrait gallery in Dublin, it could not but have a peaceable as well as patriotic influence, in accustoming men of different creeds and parties to think less of old divisions and strifes, and more of the common honour and interest of their native land. Surely all may be both loyal and "united Irishmen" now.

This feeling impressed itself strongly on seeing among the portraits that of Robert Emmett, and learning the circumstances under which it appeared. It was sent from New York by the Hon. Judge Emmett, nephew of the revolutionary chief, with a letter expressing his wish "to contribute to an object of such national interest to his native land, and gratefully appreciating the feeling which dictated the request of the committee of the Exhibition." It was a generous message from the venerable judge, considering the sad history of Robert Emmett, who was executed for the attempted rebellion in 1803. "Let me assure you," said Judge Emmett, now in his 81st year, "from a vivid recollection of my uncle, that it is a most exact and expressive likeness. He was my instructor in my early boyhood, and condescended in many ways to be my playmate, and his features never have been, and never can be, effaced from my memory."

Next to the portrait of Robert Emmett was that of Thomas F. Meagher, one of the exiled leaders of the rebellion of 1848, who has since so distinguished himself as a general in the United States army in the great war. Close by was the portrait of Thomas Davis, the poet of the "Young Ireland" party, whose genius and patriotism have raised him to so high a place in the literature of Ireland. The appearance of men like these in the collection gives proof of the true national spirit in which the Exhibition was planned, and may well be an augury of happier times, when past political strifes will be merged in a common patriotism.

Of the four hundred portraits which formed the collection, a few were not of natives of Ireland, but of those who were associated with its history in public transactions. Such were Edmund Spenser, Sir Walter Raleigh, Oliver Cromwell and his son Henry, Charles I., Strafford, Schomberg, William III., and others of later times. But of Irish worthies what an illustrious host! Fitzgeralds, Boyles, Plunketts, Talbots, Wellesleys; Ussher, Berkeley, Burke, Goldsmith, Canning; Edgeworths, Sheridans, Lawrences, Drummonds; Grattan, Flood, Curran, Shiel, O'Connell, Moore, Lover, Maclise, Doyle, and a hundred more whose names are distinguished in British as well as in Irish annals, in arms or arts, in literature or statesmanship. Irish beauty also was represented: Elizabeth Gunning, one of the three Roscommon beauties; Fanny Jennings,

Duchess of Tyrconnel; the Duchess of Leinster, mother of Lord Edward Fitzgerald, and his wife Pamela; the mother of the Wellesleys; and many more of lesser fame. For historical interest, rather than for artistic value,—though there were masterpieces of Vandyck, and Lely, and Kneller, and Reynolds,—this portrait gallery was a truly national triumph, such as Ireland has not before witnessed.

Not less interesting in its way was the collection of Irish arts, industries, manufactures, and natural products, which occupied the "Leinster Hall," and formed another specially Irish department of the Exhibition. The general collection and the loan museum contained many valuable articles, paintings, and works of art of every description, such as we have been accustomed to see in the South Kensington exhibitions. But the Leinster Hall was the place of attraction to those who wished to study the products and the industries of Ireland. No one could examine this collection without feeling assured of great future development of the resources of the country. The natural products were there, and the knowledge, skill, and ingenuity of the people were never better displayed than in this exhibition. Of the mineral wealth of the country the specimen cases exhibited by the Irish Mining Company gave visible proof. Of the textile fabrics, lace and fancy work, for which Ireland is justly distinguished, there was a wonderful display: woollen friezes, tweeds, and terries; Balbriggan hose; silk brocatelles and poplins; and every variety of the great flax and linen manufacture of the country. In the lace and needlework exhibition it was pleasant to see how much work came from industrial schools and reformatories and other institutions, telling of Irish charity as well as of Irish industry.

In other departments, the specimens of metalwork, leather-work, bog-oak and other wood-work, furniture, coach and car building, jewellery, porcelain and pottery, chemical products, not omitting stout and whisky, all attest skilled industry and varied resources, with the possibility of large increase of national wealth. Yet, in looking more carefully into the origin of the articles here collected, the sanguine feeling is checked in noting that they come from comparatively few places, not from all parts of the country. In some parts of the island there are busy sounds of industry, telling of manufacturing prosperity; in others, even where natural resources are not wanting, there are few signs of industrial life. There is no reason in the nature of things, in the sky above or in the soil below, why there should not be prosperity and progress in Munster as much as in Ulster, and it is to be hoped that the Irish will some day discover the cause of the difference.

CHAPTER XXIII.

STATE PURCHASE OF IRISH RAILWAYS.

Arguments for and Against—Imperial Grants to Ireland.

THE purchase of the Irish Railways by the State has been for some time proposed, and a motion is to be again brought before the House of Commons by Sir R. Blennerhasset. It is a question upon which there is much to say on both sides. Reduction of fares, public convenience, and developing of the resources of the country, are the pleas for the purchase and management by the State. There are no less than fifty-six separate lines, the average length of each not above forty-eight miles. Of course there is a great amount of needless expense in management, with so many separate boards of directors, secretaries, managers, engineers, accountants, and office officials, most of which would be saved by a central united management. The reply to these pleas is, that the numerous companies ought themselves to combine or amalgamate, thereby saving the useless expenditure in management, and dividing the profits of the united lines, in the ratio of the actual present profits. As to reduction of fares and freights, the Government could control such matters, if it is to interfere at all, without taking the responsibility of management. The principle of interference is already maintained in requiring parliamentary trains to be run at fixed rates.

There is no risk of great loss if the experiment is to be made, the estimated purchase price being about £30,000,000. It is estimated that at least £60,000 would be realized as net profit after paying all working expenses and interest. This is a small margin, which increased wages, increase of price of fuel, and other contingencies could easily turn to the wrong side of the account. However, there seems little objection on financial grounds. On grounds of political economy the precedent of the post-office and the telegraphic service can fairly be urged.

From what I could learn on the lines, the few which are prosperous have no wish to be interfered with; the less prosperous are anxious for the purchase. It is the shareholders of these lesser lines who chiefly keep up the agitation, though the public proposers of the purchase are no doubt actuated by patriotic motives, believing that the change will be for the benefit of the country. It is not apparent how this is to be effected by the mere transfer of the lines to different management. The Government cannot undertake mining operations and other works for the sake of increasing the traffic. The Midland Great Western, one of the best managed of the lines, has reduced the freight of coal to a halfpenny per ton per mile. If this rate of carriage, with the extraordinary value of coal in the market, does not develop the resources of the coal region round Lough Allen, the Government management could effect no industrial charm. The Midland has also led the way in attaching third-class carriages to every train, and an increase in passenger traffic returns has rewarded the liberality of the directors. The returns of the Great Southern and Western, and of the Ulster railway, also among the best managed lines, have shown steady increase. The details on all disputed points will be brought out in the debate.

As far as I can judge, the public advantage of the purchase of the railways cannot be great, but the risk is also small. If the measure is sought for the benefit of Ireland, and not of the shareholders, its adoption would do no harm, and would furnish additional experience in case the greater question of the purchase of all English railways should arise. This would involve a sum at least twenty times the amount of the Irish investment. It is the old story of the *experimentum in corpore vili*. The precedent of the railways may prove as remote from practical use as that of the disestablishment of the Church, or the interference with contracts about land tenure. I should like to know whether a home Parliament in Dublin would buy the Irish railways, or whether it is only proposed because the imperial exchequer will furnish the money.

The large amount of patronage is another point to consider. There would need to be stringent rules as to qualifications and appointments, for political recommendations would not here be of the same unimportance as in the post-office service, and other departments not involving safety of life.

"Nothing ask, nothing get," seems to be the practical proverb with Irishmen of all grades, from beggar to cardinal. Few people are aware of the enormous sums already granted to Ireland. For the police alone (Dublin and Constabulary) the grant from public revenue is above a million sterling; and the education grant, for national and industrial schools, is about half a million. An amusing illustration of the continual attempts to get grants from public revenue in aid of local taxation was recently reported. An influential deputation came to ask that pensions as well as salaries of poor-law medical officers should be paid by Government. Lord Hartington fenced off the application by humorously suggesting that this might lead to frequent and early retirements from service.

Of Ireland and the Irish character in the matter of "jobbery" Charles James Fox had a decided opinion, which he thus expressed in a letter to Lord Northington in November, 1783: "This country is reduced low enough, but depend upon it we shall be tired if, year after year, we are to hear of granting something new, or acquiescing in something new, for the sake of pleasing Ireland. I am sure you must feel as I do upon this subject, but situated as you are among Irishmen, who, next to a job for themselves, love nothing so well as a job for their country, and hardly ever seeing anyone who talks to you soundly on our side of the question, it is next to impossible but you must fall insensibly into Irish ideas more than we do, who see the reverse of the picture, and who of course are much more sensible to the reproaches of this country than of that. Ireland appears to me to be like one of her most eminent jobbers, who, after having obtained the Prime Sergeantry, the Secretaryship of State, and twenty other great places, insisted upon the Lord-Lieutenant adding a major's half-pay to the rest of his emoluments."

CHAPTER XXIV.

IRISH NATIONAL EDUCATION.

Historical Sketch—Origin and History of the National Board—Grants now Denominational more than National—Christian Brothers, Schools—The National School Teachers.

A FEW days before the opening of Parliament an educational meeting was held at Exeter Hall, by the Birmingham League, at which reference was made to the Irish National Schools. One of the speakers said, "he had opposed the principle of denominational education in England, and he should oppose the principle if it were attempted to be carried out in Ireland." Such a statement, from a member of Parliament too, reveals a strange ignorance of the real conditions of the national system in Ireland, which was probably shared by the crowded audience who applauded the sentiment.

Lord Hartington, on the part of the Government, has stated that no essential change is at present proposed in the Irish system, but it is a question the discussion of which cannot be long postponed, and a brief statement of the history and actual position of the primary education of Ireland may be useful for reference.

Education in Ireland has taken a wonderful start within the present generation. So far as primary schools are concerned, Ireland is now abreast of the most advanced countries of Europe, at least as to the number of schools to the population, and of pupils on the school rolls. There are now not much under 7,000 National schools, with above a million of enrolled pupils. The average actual attendance, however, is not greatly above a third of the enrolled number. More can be said also in favour of the quantity than the quality of the education. The results can hardly be said to be commensurate with the extent of the organization of the national system, or with the vastness of the sums placed at the disposal of the Board of Commissioners. The parliamentary grants in forty years have been nearly seven and a half millions sterling. This large amount of money is supposed to be applied to purposes of *National* education ; but, in point of fact, the great proportion of it has been under denominational control. In a large portion of the country the schools are wholly under the control of the Roman Catholics.

That this result has been the fault of Protestants themselves is well known. With the exception of a small minority, who shared the patriotic and liberal views of the late Earl of Derby and of Archbishop Whately, the Irish Church as a body set itself from the first in opposition to the National schools. They took up the watchword of Sir Robert Harry Inglis, and denounced "the godless system of education." Because the Church catechism could not be used, and the entire English version of the Bible, they would have nothing to do with the schools. The result was that the control of primary education was left mainly in the hands of the representatives of the Romish Church, and of the worst section of that church, who gradually ousted the Protestants and liberal Catholics, who had inaugurated and organized the system, under the rule of Archbishop Whately and Archbishop Murray. Their principle was to give good secular education, with as much moral and religious teaching as could be given on common ground agreed on by both churches. By refusing to work on this ground, the Irish Church left the minority of their body to carry on an unequal contest with the Romish hierarchy.

The Presbyterians at first were much divided as to the support of the National schools. When they saw the schools in Catholic districts wholly under direction of the Romish clergy, and even convent schools and Christian Brothers recognized as National Board schools, they determined to assert their right to similar recognition for their schools. After much battling and bargaining, in 1839 they gained their point. The Presbyterian schools in Ulster were adopted by the Board, and on the terms insisted on by the sturdy Protestants of the north. It was a triumph of the denominational over the national principle. The Presbyterians have now as much control over the schools in the districts where they prevail as the Catholics have in other districts. They have given their complete adherence to what is called the National system, so much so that at the last meeting of their General Assembly a resolution in its support was carried without a dissentient voice.

The majority of the Irish Episcopal Church is now also understood to be in favour of the National system, the Primate and several of the bishops having given their adherence since the disestablishment of the Church. An influential minority, however, headed by Archbishop Trench, refuse to co-operate with the Government in the National system. They continue to support their own schools, and in this show a consistency and loftiness of principle which can only excite admiration, so far as the action arises from jealousy of lowering the standard of Scriptural and Protestant truth. The pupils at these schools are sure to be trained in the faith and spirit of the Irish

Church, and the same or higher praise must be bestowed on the schools supported by the Irish Church Mission Society, and other associations which regard the religious element as the most important in primary education.

The Church Education Society was instituted in 1839 for the establishment of schools and the education of pupils in the principles of the then Established Church. At that time the dissatisfaction of the Irish Church with the National schools was at its height, and the inadequacy of the old parochial and local schools was generally felt. Up to 1868 the average funds contributed by voluntary subscriptions and donations amounted to about £45,000 yearly. The number of pupils in that year on the rolls was 61,612, in the proportion of 43,241 of the Episcopal Church, 12,169 of Protestant dissenters, and 6,202 Roman Catholics. In 1861 the number of pupils had been as high as 74,583, in the proportion of 49,864 Episcopalian, 14,537 Protestant dissenters, and 10,162 Roman Catholics. In 1870 the numbers had fallen to 52,166, of whom 44,602 were Episcopalians, with only 3,747 Protestant dissenters, and 3,757 Catholics. These numbers seem to show that the difficulty of maintaining these schools will increase, and that there is a larger adhesion to the National system, within as well as without the communion of the Irish Church.

I have met Irish Churchmen who declared they would sooner see Catholics without any education than attending a National school! This will hardly be credited, but I have had discussion with such men, and of high position too. Unable to agree with them, I yet am fully aware of the strength of the objections to the National system as at present worked, and of the necessity for the whole subject being reconsidered by the English Government. The annual parliamentary grant is gradually creeping up to half a million sterling, and a large proportion of this is virtually a gift for the benefit of the Romish Church. It is, in fact, an indirect endowment of that Church. The management of the schools being in their hands, the priests appoint as teachers those who are utterly subservient to them, and who are really the trainers of the young in the tenets of Popery, as well as in the subjects for which the National schools were intended. I speak of what I have myself seen. I have asked teachers if Father so-and-so, the manager of the school, came to give the religious instruction, and how often? In some instances (and I take them to be examples of what is common) the visits of the priest are only occasional, the teacher being left to give the religious as well as secular teaching, of course only at the time provided under the Conscience Clause. But I am satisfied that there is too much ground for the complaints of Irish Churchmen, that the National schools in Catholic parts of the country are too much in the hands of the priests. The priest is too commonly the manager, and the master is entirely under control of the manager, and removable at his pleasure.

If there were the smallest hope of remodelling the Irish national system in the direction of the American system of Common schools,* I would agree with those Irish Protestants who withhold their support from the National Board. But this is impossible where the numerical majority of Catholics is so excessive. The proper course of action is for all Protestants to unite in seeking such modification of the existing system as to diminish the paramount power now wielded by the Romish hierarchy and their supporters in the National Board. That Board is not carrying out the original intention of Lord Derby's system of national education. It was intended that in every district the different denominations should unite in the management of the schools, having common ground in secular teaching, and leaving the denominational or religious teaching to the several churches. Such united boards are not to be found in Ireland, but the schools are

---

* I have given an account of the American Common Schools in "Across the Ferry, or First Impressions of America." In most of the States of the Union all the great educational problems have been happily solved, and also the "religious difficulty" which afflicts us here.

almost everywhere appendages of denominational churches. I believe that this state of things can be to some extent remedied, and at all events that the National Board of Commissioners could be made to carry out more faithfully the design of the system. But, before giving some practical suggestions on this matter, a brief review of the past history of Irish education will be useful.

There are numerous Acts of the Irish Parliament, from the reign of Henry VIII. down to George III., relating to the establishment or support of Parochial, Charter, and Local schools.

The Charter Schools were so called after a society incorporated by charter of George II., in 1733, "for the encouragement of Protestant schools in Ireland." Ample funds were provided both by the Irish and English Parliament, a grant of £20,000 yearly being continued after the Union, which, with endowments and other resources, made up an income of about £60,000 a year. Management of the schools was under a Board of fifteen Commissioners in Dublin. The whole system was bad, and was grossly mismanaged, till, in a report of inquiry in 1816, it was stated that this society, "with funds sufficient for the instruction of 200,000 children annually on the plan of daily schools, had been expending all on 33 boarding schools, with little more than 2,000 children." Upwards of a million and a half of money was expended on these Charter schools without any impression being made on the condition of the poor Irish. A more deplorable instance of the abuse of charity and public funds could not be found than in the history of these chartered schools, up to the time of the parliamentary inquiry.

Of parochial schools there have nominally been between seven and eight hundred at once in operation, but many of these were small and inefficient. A fund was established by Erasmus Smith so long ago as 1669, but the greater part of the endowments were in course of time shamefully misappropriated. Here and there flourishing schools and able teachers were found even in the darkest time of last century, but the real work of Irish education on any appreciable scale does not date from more than seventy or eighty years ago. Several voluntary associations then were at work. In 1792 the "Association for Discountenancing Vice" had been formed, and in these schools about sixteen thousand children were taught. The "Society for Promoting Christian Knowledge" had a large number of schools, but fewer pupils. The "London Hibernian Society" came into the field in 1806, and claimed at its most prosperous time to have above 900 schools, with about 30,000 Catholic, and 50,000 Protestant children. The "Sunday School Society," though chiefly intended for religious instruction, as its name implies, gave also week-day teaching in many of its schools. At a later period Erasmus Smith's fund gradually came into better use, and inspectors were appointed, through whose reports many of these endowed schools were restored to proper efficiency. But the greatest step in these educational movements was the formation of the Kildare Place Society in 1812. For the few first years the scholars were only numbered by hundreds, but by liberal subscriptions and large parliamentary grants the schools were numbered by hundreds, and the pupils were nearly 140,000 in 1831, when parliamentary aid was unhappily withdrawn. In 1818 the Irish Society was formed, for the education of the native Irish in their own language. At its most prosperous time this excellent society had nearly six hundred teachers and seventeen thousand scholars, some hundreds of them upwards of fifty years of age.

Through all these agencies there had been a steadily progressive desire for education throughout Ireland. The Catholic clergy had not given special heed to the movement, till the amount of light gave alarm. The Kildare Place Society was the chief object of hostility. The use of the Bible was denounced as an agency of proselytism, though many Protestants had blamed the Society for using the Scriptures too little. The influence of the Romish party obtained the removal of the parliamentary grants. The National Board of Education was then appointed, the chief of the seven Commissioners being the Duke of Leinster, the Archbishop of Dublin, Dr. Whately, and the Roman Catholic Archbishop of Dublin, Dr. Murray.

It was said at the time, and has been said often since, that the formation of the National Board was the result of a deeply-laid design of the Romish clergy. They saw it was too late to arrest the progress of education, and they therefore directed their efforts to obtain a system which could be worked so as to fall under their own control. By apparent conciliation and concession, there could be no reasonable ground for Protestants refusing to meet them, and the system once established, the control of National Education could be afterwards contrived. This may have been the design; but we are not the less satisfied that the English Government, and especially the late Earl of Derby, then Mr. Stanley, to whom the measure was mainly due, were actuated by a sincere and earnest desire for the welfare of Ireland. The formation of the National Board was no political compact, but an honest plan for securing the best help of the Government in the education of the Irish people.

More than this, I believe that Dr. Murray was as sincere and earnest as Dr. Whately in carrying out the intentions of the Government. In a conversation with Mr. Senior, recorded in his "Journal," Dr. Whately said, "Archbishop Murray and I agreed in desiring large portions of the Bible to be read in our National schools; but we agreed in this because we disagreed as to its probable results. He believed that they would be favourable to Romanism: I believed that they would be favourable to Protestantism; and I feel confident that I was right. . . . Though the priest may still, perhaps, denounce the Bible collectively as a book dangerous to the laity, he cannot safely object to the Scripture extracts which are read to children, with the sanction of the prelates of his own Church. But these extracts contain so much that is inconsistent with the whole spirit of Romanism, that it is difficult to suppose that a person well acquainted with them can be a thorough-going Roman Catholic. The principle upon which that Church is constructed, the duty of unenquiring, unreasoning submission to its authority, renders any doubt fatal. A man who is commanded not to think for himself, if he finds he cannot avoid doing so, is unavoidably led to question the reasonableness of the command. And when he finds that the Church which claims a right to think for him has preached doctrines, some of which are inconsistent with, and others are opposed to what he has read in the Gospels, his trust in its infallibility, the foundation on which its whole system of faith is built, is at an end. The education supplied by the National Board is gradually undermining the vast fabric of the Irish Roman Catholic Church."

Dr. Whately has here given his private reason for approving the use of the "Scripture Extracts." Of course he could not openly profess these views. He could not praise the National Board as an instrument of conversion from Popery. But he strongly felt that the National schools, as at first established, were the most powerful instruments for the saving of souls as well as for mental education.

Dr. Murray was not less outspoken in his approval of the "Scripture Extracts." In a letter dated October 21st, 1838, addressed to the Irish Catholic prelates, he said of them, "They are so constructed that they may be used in common by all the pupils. It would be unfair in us to expect that a book to be used at the time of joint instruction should unfold any peculiar views of religion. The sacred text which it contains supplies much of sacred history, and much of moral precept, with which it is highly important that all should be acquainted; while the notes which are added are such as can give no just cause of offence to any other denomination of Christians." Such were Dr. Murray's views of the "Scripture Extracts." And the request made by the whole of his brother prelates (with one exception) that he should continue to act as commissioner, in reply to his proposal of resigning, did, in fact, commit them all to the same view. The "Scripture Extracts," and Dr. Whately's "Easy Lessons on Christian Evidences," remained as class-books; and no book could be so used without the unanimous sanction of the members of the National Board.

It is important also to hear the views of the Commissioners as officially expressed in the first report presented by them to the Lord-Lieutenant. In order to meet the objections which many Protestants urged against the National system, the following observations were introduced: "It having been imputed to us that we intended to substitute these extracts from the Scriptures for the Scriptures themselves, we deemed it necessary to guard against such misrepresentation by annexing to them the following preface: 'These selections are offered, not as a substitute for the sacred volume itself, but as an introduction to it, in the hope of their leading to the more profitable perusal of the Word of God. The passages introduced have been chosen, not as being of more importance than the rest of Scripture, but merely as being more level to the understandings of children and youth at school, and also best fitted to be read under the direction of teachers not necessarily qualified, and certainly not recognized as teachers of religion. No passage has either been introduced or omitted under the influence of any particular view of Christianity, doctrinal or practical.'

"It has been further imputed to us that we denied to children the benefits of religious instruction, and kept the Word of God from them. To guard against this extraordinary misrepresentation, we have introduced the following notes into our regulations. (These notes give explanation as to the familiar time-tables and Conscience Clause; but the first of the notes deserves especial notice, as meeting the charge of the education being intended to be exclusively secular.) 'The ordinary school business, during which all the children, of whatever denomination they may be, are required to attend, is to consist exclusively of those branches of knowledge which belong to literary and moral education. Such extracts from the Scriptures as are prepared under the sanction of the Board may be used, and are earnestly recommended by the Board to be used, during the hours allotted to this ordinary school business.'"

Such was the spirit in which the Irish National Schools were established, and were first carried on. But a change came over the spirit of the system. On the death of Archbishop Murray a new Primate was appointed, and a different attitude was at once assumed by the Church of Rome towards the

National Board. There is no doubt that the feeling of hostility had been gathering, and this was made the occasion for its being avowed. A painful and in some ways a disgraceful conflict was raised in the Board, the attack being first made on the "Scripture Extracts," and the "Lessons on the Evidences." Dr. Whately intimated that he would take no part in the discussions, and even avoided attending the meetings till the decision on these books was made. They were voted prohibited books, and the use of them forbidden to Roman Catholics, children and teachers. After the sanction unanimously given to these books for years, the removal of them denoted an absolute change of principle and of policy in regard to national education, and there was no honourable course apparent to Dr. Whately but to withdraw his connection with the Board.

The Lord Justice of Appeal (the Right Hon. F. Blackburne), and Baron Greene, retired from the Board with the Archbishop. The former, in his evidence before the Lords' committee in 1856, says, "I consider the expunging of the books from the list as a breach of faith," and gives this as the reason for his having resigned. The Government subsequently caused the Board to draw up and insert among their fundamental rules the following: "The Commissioners will not withdraw, or essentially alter any book that has been or shall be hereafter unanimously published or sanctioned by them, without a previous communication with the Lord-Lieutenant."

This was a tacit admission on the part of the Government that the course which led to the withdrawal of Dr. Whately was unjustifiable. But the mischief was irreparable. After the first breach in the Board, the confidence of all moderate men and the best friends of Ireland was at an end. Even in Dr. Murray's time, it was said that the Protestant members of the Board would need all the wisdom of the serpent, as well as the innocence of the dove, to save them from the machinations of the Romish Church. But under the new *régime* there was no hope of successful resistance to the Romish party. The result has been, that over a large part of Ireland the National Education is wholly under the control of the priesthood. The schools are mere appendages of the Romish chapel, the manager of each school being in the vast majority of cases the parish priest, and the schoolmaster a mere tool and agent of the manager. In places where the funds for the establishment of the school have been advanced by a Protestant landlord, he may appoint his agent, or the Protestant clergyman as manager, but the result would generally be that Roman Catholics would not be suffered to go to the school. In the northern and Protestant parts of

Ireland the National schools are less under priestly control, but taking the whole country, it is an admitted fact that the National system is really denominational, and that the funds are applied for the education of the young, under the control of the Romish Church. According to rule, religious instruction can only be given at a fixed time, and the teachers of various denominations have access for this purpose. But in most schools in the Catholic parts of Ireland, the priest is the sole giver of this instruction. He does not even need to attend except on rare occasions. The teacher, being appointed by him and under his control, is left to indoctrinate the children in the Roman Catholic faith. Indeed, in many places, since the National schools have fallen into discredit with the Ultramontane party on account of the principle of mixed attendance, the priests are discouraged from attending, and the religious instruction, if any, is left to the teachers. Of what kind this is, may be anticipated from the creed and position of most of the teachers. One traveller happening to enter a school when the religious lesson was being given, heard the phrase "faithful unto death" explained to mean, that "we must die sooner than become a 'Jumper'" (Protestant). This is a suggestive sample of "religious training."

In towns, and in country districts where there is a

mixed population, if the National schools cannot be retained wholly under priestly influences, separate schools are established, where the order of the Christian Brothers hold undisputed sway. What their training of the young is may be guessed from an examination of their educational books, compared with those of the National Board and in use in Church schools. I have before me the series of class-books in use in these schools. I might quote many instances, but one will suffice: *ex uno disce omnes.* In the Third Book of Reading Lessons, which professes, in the preface, to present " impressive appeals of religious truth, which, apart from their moral effects, possess a paramount influence in giving a reflective tone to the mind," I find the following choice extract. It is the story of St. Brigid, or Bridget, " the great patroness and brightest ornament of Ireland." We are told that " in all things she was a model of perfection. She knew nothing but Jesus Christ, and Him crucified; and her only desire was to promote the glory of God among men. She induced innumerable virgins to join her in the profession of the evangelical precepts of poverty, obedience, and chastity; she founded monasteries in every part of Ireland; and by her teaching and example she so moulded the character of the females of Ireland that they have ever been remarkable for their love of the purity of virtue, and their anxiety in every age to devote themselves to a religious life, and the *service of God in the cloister.* Our forefathers were so filled with admiration of the virtues and good works of St. Bridget, and formed so exalted an idea of her dignity, that in their writings *they frequently compare her to the great Virgin Mother of God*, whom they were accustomed to invoke as the glory of Jerusalem, the beauty of the world, the powerful mistress of heaven and earth; and they did not hesitate to call her the Mary of Ireland. In the life of our saint several facts are recorded which cannot fail to edify those who meditate on them. One night, says St. Cœlac, whilst the Sisters were engaged in prayer, St. Bridget was wrapt in ecstasy, and saw the earth and heaven filled with youths, who were dressed in garments of angelical whiteness. Christ, the King of kings, was enthroned on high, whilst the assembled multitude gathered round His throne, and intoned the sacred canticle, 'Holy, holy, holy is the Lord of hosts.' Heavenly music accompanied this hymn of praise, and the angelic choirs re-echoed the respective alleluias. This vision filled our saint with spiritual joy, and at the dawn of day its meaning was unfolded to her, when the holy bishop Ibar *came to her cell to offer up the Holy Sacrifice of the Mass, in which the King of kings, surrounded by myriads of angels, condescends to come and dwell on our altars*, and those scenes are repeated on earth which were presented to our saint as occurring in heaven!

"Since the days of our great patroness, Ireland has had to undergo many vicissitudes of fortune, such as the Danish and Norman invasions, the devastations of the sixteenth century, penal laws and persecutions, . . . but all the efforts of the powers of darkness have been in vain; the faith of Ireland has never been shaken; *St. Bridget and St. Patrick have watched over it;*——"

Enough, enough! And who does the reader suppose is the author of this silly and profane nonsense? No less a personage than Cardinal Cullen! to whose praises there is an extravagant "Ode" among the poetical pieces in the same volume. This is the teaching, and these are the teachers to whom the Government is asked to hand over the education of Ireland!

But now for the practical question of what ought to be done. Some change in the National school system is necessary. It cannot be in the direction indicated by Cardinal Cullen. If all Protestants and liberal Catholics would unite, as in the days of Whately and Murray, the system might be made more truly national and efficient. All the machinery is present; the only change is wanted in its working.

The total number of National schools in Ireland in 1871 was 6,914, the number in 1870 having been 6,806, and in 1869, 6,707. The number of pupils on the rolls were, in these three years, 1869, 991,335; in 1870, 998,999; and in 1871, 1,021,700. The average daily attendance, however, was only 363,850 in 1871; 359,199 in 1870; and 358,560 in 1869. The number of teachers and monitors were, in 1871, 13,873, against 13,378 in 1870, and 13,319 in 1869. The salaries and allowances paid to teachers and monitors out of parliamentary grants were, in 1871, £296,136. The local contributions to teachers in the same year were £63,561, of which £50,242 came from fees, and £13,319 from endowments and subscriptions.

The total expenditure of the Board of National Education in 1871 was £474,055, to which amount it has gradually risen from £406,307, in 1870, £395,124 in 1868, and £363,536 in 1866. The total amount of parliamentary grants, since the commencement of the system in Ireland in 1831, up to the close of 1871, has been £7,342,356.

At the close of 1871 the National Board had in their service 6,476 principal, and 2,556 assistant teachers, and 396 junior literary and industrial assistants, making in the whole 9,428, of whom 3,461 are trained; and at the same period 440 workmistresses and teachers of the higher industrial branches. The total number of male and female teachers trained from the commencement in 1833 to Dec. 31, 1871, was 8,929; the number trained in 1871 was 251—116 males and 135 females.

The average income from all sources of classed male principal teachers was £42 0s. 4d., and of classed female principal teachers £34 10s. 3d. The classed assistants received respectively — males, £22 5s. 8d.; females, £19 1s. 1d. The total emoluments, from all sources, available to the teaching staff of the schools in connexion with the Board, including model and training schools and other establishments, for 1871, was £359,698, of which 82·3 per cent. was derived from the State funds, only 17·7 having been locally provided from fees or from subscriptions. The amount paid for the ordinary teachers' salaries was £273,216. The payment of teachers is miserably small, and the wonder is that so many are found with respectable qualifications, to labour for such a pittance.

The vote, taking in the supplementary estimate at the close of last session of Parliament, for increase of pay to the Irish National school-teachers, was a small but acceptable boon, and gave general satisfaction. But more is required than a slight increase of pay. The teachers must be made independent of local influences, and not subject to dismissal at the will of the patrons and managers of schools, without the sanction of the Board. At present, the inspector can report on the incompetency or faults of a teacher, but the most competent and faultless teacher can be dismissed without reason by the patron or manager.

At present, there are two classes of schools under the control of the National Board—vested and nonvested. The first are directly under the control of the Board, the others are under control of trustees and managers, local and denominational. There is scarcely, as I have already said, an instance of the people of all denominations joined together forming a united committee, appointing patrons or managers, as is done in England under the new School Board, and as is the universal practice in the United States. In the Roman Catholic parts of Ireland the non-vested schools are nearly all under the control of the priests, who are the patrons and managers. They appoint the masters, and so control the education. If another school is established in the place by the private means of those who object to this control, their priests will denounce from the altar those who send their children to the school. Practically, the large bulk of the parliamentary grant for education is given to the Romish Church. The model schools, and those vested in the Board, are alone undenominational. The remedy is to give the National Board larger power than it now possesses, making it independent in its patronage and superintendence of teachers, or else to organize a new Board, under the Minister of Instruction, which shall be National in reality as well as name. If the local patrons and managers protest against this centralization of authority, let them take the whole matter into their hands. Let them have school-rates in their several districts, and let them represent the ratepayers. But do not let them interfere with the Board as long as the money is given by parliamentary grant, not for denominational but national use. The remarks of the *Times* on the passing of the Supplementary Estimates for National Education in Ireland, at the close of last session, contain some points well worthy of attention:—" The pecuniary aspect of the affair is that which first presents itself, and we cannot be surprised at the sense of injustice avowed by those who are receiving no aid from the State, or very little aid, guarded by many stringent conditions, in particular the condition of large private and local expenditure. Ireland is the 'pet' child of the State. To her it is all outgoing, all liberality and confidence, without corresponding effort or sacrifice being made. It is certainly something exceptional to see Ireland receiving for education £430,390 in one year, sufficient, by supposition, for the whole education of the Irish peasant and working classes, with but trifling stipulations, and these much set at nought. It is notorious that a very large part of the education thus given out of the imperial revenue is virtually and wholly under the management of a clergy who only work on the condition of having entirely their own way. There are people in this country who choose to have entirely their own way, but then they pay for it out of their own pockets, or out of the pockets of the friends whom they can infect with their own zeal. In Ireland the luxury is without cost, and is largely enjoyed."

The injustice of paying for Irish education out of imperial funds, while English and Scotch education of the same class is to be paid for out of local rates, is manifest; but the *Times* pronounces "that imperial policy for a time requires the inequality and unfairness. In the midst of immense waste of public money which is inevitable, yet deplorable, we need not grudge an annual payment still considerably short of half a million, and less than 10s. a head for the total number of children for whom education has to be provided. The special object of this year's supplementary estimate is to afford better pay to the third class of probationary teachers. As Irish teachers in general receive only a half or a third of that easily obtained by English teachers of the same class and attainments, for the same work, these third-class probationary teachers, whose case was thought 'crying,' must, indeed, have been poorly paid. Whatever we do, or fail to do, with Ireland, let not money stand in the way of its education."

Now see the response made in Ireland to this generous spirit expressed on the part of England. The National Board having directed the inspectors to require the signatures of managers of schools to a form of agreement, by which the teachers will be entitled to receive payment by results, and be protected from arbitrary dismissal, Cardinal Cullen has addressed a circular to the clergy, advising them not to sign any document until further explanation. The real cause of this order was the check which the Government sought to interpose on arbitrary dismissal of teachers by managers. The Board required three months' notice or three months' salary, if no sufficient cause of dismissal could be shown. Not only have the managers of Roman Catholic schools generally obeyed Cardinal Cullen's mandate, by refusing to sign the agreement, but the poor dependent teachers have petitioned the Board not to carry out the new arrangement on their behalf. That they act under terror and compulsion is evident, although their memorial represents that the new arrangement would excite hostility to the National system.

It is plain that interference with the existing tyranny

must be made by Parliament, and when the question is brought up, let us hope that the *Times* will repeat the note of warning given last August: "If the Roman Catholic clergy insist too much on their own way, they will find themselves drawing near to a grand re-adjustment of the Education question. Nothing is so contrary to all the traditions of this people and Empire as to go on paying money, and that more and more, without any account of it, or even share in its expenditure. It is a practice which really cannot last, and will not last, for any considerable time. Ireland will be reminded that she has land, and that she is able to levy rates upon it for roads and a few other purposes. She will be told that if she wants more for education she can obtain it nearer home, and in that case it will be necessary to have School Boards."

To this I only add, that if the present Board of Commissioners is so irreclaimably under the power of the Romish hierarchy as it has shown itself in the case of Mr. O'Keeffe and the Callan schools, it has become unfit for directing the national education. A new central Board, under the Minister of Public Instruction, with independent Inspectors, reporting to Parliament, is what the case requires. In granting half a million of money annually, Parliament has claim to the service of such a Board.

CHAPTER XXV.

IRISH UNIVERSITY EDUCATION.

Existing Institutions—Trinity College and Dublin University—The Queen's Colleges and University—The Catholic University—Ultramontane Claims—The Synod of Thurles—The Government Plan.

THE Irish University question has been put off from year to year, and at length presses for settlement.

Leaving out of view colleges which are wholly or mainly "schools of the prophets," institutions for training students for the ministry of the churches, the present academical system comprises (1) Trinity College, or the Dublin University; (2) the Queen's Colleges of Cork, Belfast, and Galway, constituting together the Queen's University; and (3) the Roman Catholic University, St. Stephen's Green, Dublin.

It is said that something more is required, and that there ought to be an Irish National University, not superseding, but overtopping the existing academical institutions; to be established, chartered, and endowed by the British Government. Whether this new University is to be in substance only an Examining Board, granting degrees and honours, or whether it is to be a great teaching seminary; whether it is to be established on an entirely new basis, or on old foundations, extended to meet the demands of the times; whether the endowment is to be by national grant, or by appropriation of part of the funds of Trinity College; these and other questions remain yet open.

There are difficulties which at the outset face the Government. It is not a difficulty for Liberal or Conservative, for Mr. Gladstone or for Mr. Gathorne Hardy; whichever party is in office this Irish University question puts the Government in an embarrassing and humiliating position. There is no spirit of high statesmanship apparent, as when the late Lord Derby took the lead in introducing the system of national education. Patriotic principle is kept down by considerations of political expediency. The Ministry have to try to pacify and please the Romish hierarchy of Ireland, without rousing the hostility of the Protestantism of the empire. It is impossible to satisfy both sides, and the choice between the irreconcilables must sooner or later be made. "Religious equality" is the watchword of that shifty expediency which will try to make concessions to the Romish party under the guise of a national University.

So far as the question concerns University education, the problem could be easily solved. The extension and reconstruction of Trinity College, as the Dublin University, along with the Queen's Colleges, would meet all the requirements of higher education. There is a very general desire among Protestants, even those who have traditional reverence for the old associations of Trinity, to make concessions in accordance with the spirit of the times. That the Catholic laity would gladly hail such concessions, is known from the large advantage already taken of the institutions which are now open alike to all denominations. The Ultramontane party alone offers obstruction to the settlement of the question. How far it is entitled to be heard will appear from a brief consideration of the origin and history of the denominational University which now stands as a bugbear in the way of a national University system.

The Roman Catholic University in Dublin sprang from no spontaneous zeal for academical education, or for the training of the Irish youth in higher learning. It was purely the result of hostility to the "mixed education" offered to the youth of all denominations by the Queen's Colleges. Before the Queen's Colleges were established, and when Trinity College was the only academical institution in Ireland, there was no movement for a separate University for Catholics.

A sufficient supply of youths educated for the Church was all that was desiderated, and these were supplied by Maynooth and other seminaries. The zeal now shown for the academic training of Catholic students was then never heard of. Ireland was more populous then than now, and no anxiety was shown to provide for the "twenty thousand youths thirsting for college education" of whom we now hear!

When the Queen's Colleges began to attract non-theological students, the alarm of the Ultramontane party began. "In founding these Colleges," said Sir Robert Peel in 1845, "we shall promote social concord between the youth of different religious persuasions, who, hitherto too much estranged by religious differences, will acquire new methods of creating and interchanging mutual esteem. I sincerely believe that, as well as receiving temporal advantages, so far from preventing any advantages with respect to Christianity, the more successfully will you labour to make men good Christians the more they are imbued with that great principle of our faith—a principle which, I grieve to say, many individuals are too apt to forget—the principle, I mean, of reciprocal charity." This was the very principle which the Church of Rome dreaded, and accordingly the Queen's Colleges were from their very foundation viewed with dislike and fear. The reports sent to Rome called forth, as early as 1847, only two years after their foundation, in a papal rescript, a formal condemnation of "the godless Colleges." The institution of a denominational University was then first recommended, in direct opposition to these national institutions. In 1850 the bishops assembled at the Synod of Thurles appointed a committee of eight prelates, eight priests, and eight laymen, "to take steps to form and organize a Catholic University." The University of Louvain was taken as a precedent and model, that University having been founded, in 1833, by the Belgian Ultramontane prelates, in opposition to the national Universities of Ghent and Liege.

The Irish prelates, if we may judge by their repugnance to admit a fair lay element in the governing body of their University, would have dispensed with lay aid in the foundation, but for the necessity of appealing for voluntary contributions. Before the end of 1851 the committee reported that £21,000 had been received; and it is stated that up to 1871 about £150,000 in all had been contributed. This represents an annual average collection of about £7,500 during twenty years. A building was secured in St. Stephen's Green, and the new institution was inaugurated, with a cardinal for its chancellor, a governing council consisting of four archbishops and eight bishops, and a large staff of professors for the five faculties into which it was divided. How many students have availed themselves of the educational advantages of this imposing establishment, how the funds have been distributed and applied, and other information usually given as to public institutions, it is in vain to ask. An air of mystery and reserve has always shrouded the proceedings, no official reports or statistics being published.

In 1865 the O'Donoghue brought forward a motion in the House of Commons, praying for a Charter of Incorporation, with the power of conferring degrees. He disclaimed the intention of asking for any grant of public money, the same position being for the moment taken up by the prelates in their communications with the Government.

There are two parliamentary papers which contain the negotiations of the Roman Catholic bishops with the British Government, and the state of the question as it stood when these negotiations were closed. The first contains the correspondence between Sir George Grey and the Bishops in 1865; and the second contains the correspondence between the Bishops and Lord Mayo in 1867 and 1868. Dr. MacHale, Archbishop of Tuam, wrote to Sir George Grey, 9th August, 1865, saying it was generally understood that the Government intended to introduce modifications in the system of University education, and inquired what they were. Sir George Grey, in reply, referred to his speech in the previous session of Parliament, and said that the principle on which they intended to act was that facilities for obtaining a University degree should no longer be restricted to students of Trinity College or the Queen's Colleges, and that this would involve some modification of the Queen's University charter, and some alterations in the composition of the senate. After consultation on this reply Cardinal Cullen wrote a letter, in which he said, "The archbishops are instructed to state that the Roman Catholic episcopal body, while declining to accept as satisfactory any arrangement which will leave preponderating advantages to existing State institutions, collegiate or university, will not refuse for themselves or their flocks concessions that may diminish the evils and injustice of which they have had so long to complain; it being, however, distinctly understood that such acceptance is not to be construed as an acquiescence in any form of mixed education."

In plain words, the Ultramontanes denounce mixed education, and demand an endowed Catholic University, but meanwhile will take what they can get in the way of concession as to existing institutions.

In January, 1866, Dr. Cullen forwarded two memorials, one to the Government and the other to the Queen, signed by the twenty-nine Roman Catholic bishops. In these they asserted the right of the Roman Catholic University to a charter enabling it to grant degrees; and they declared the concessions indicated by Sir George Grey as unsatisfactory, " if unaccompanied by an endowment of the Catholic University, and a reconstruction of the Queen's Colleges." On the principle, however, of "not refusing concessions," they proposed, 1st, that the Roman Catholic University should be chartered as a college within the new university; 2nd, that this college should have a suitable endowment; 3rd, that burses and scholarships should be provided, either by the application of existing or the creation of new endowments; 4th, that the Catholic University College should be empowered by charter to affiliate colleges and schools to itself; 5th, that the tests of knowledge should not be such as to identify, even by name, the newly-chartered college with any system condemned by the Roman Catholic religion; 6th, that the tests of knowledge be guarded against every danger of abuse, or of the exercise of any influence hostile or prejudicial to the religious principles of Roman Catholics; that they may be made as general as may be, consistently with a due regard for the interests of education; the time, matter, and manner of examination being prescribed, but not the books, or special authors, at least, in mental and social science, in history, or in cognate subjects; and that, in a word, there be banished from them even the suspicion of interference with the religious principles of Roman Catholics; 7th, that the Queen's Colleges be re-arranged on the principles of the denominational system.

These seven propositions exhibit the whole question as viewed by the Ultramontane party. The main attack is upon mixed education. It is gall and wormwood to the bishops to find that, in spite of their denunciations, Roman Catholics continue to avail themselves of the advantages of Trinity College and the Queen's Colleges. The scholarships and prizes of these institutions "hold out so many bribes to Roman Catholic young men to induce them to become disobedient children of their own Church." They wish the Queen's Colleges to be made denominational and not national. Their own Catholic University not being prosperous, they demand endowment for it, with scholarships and burses, and affiliated colleges and schools. In short, another greater Maynooth is demanded, an endowed University for general as that is for theological training. The fifth proposition is not clear in its object, but a little consideration shows that the clause *even by name* points to the word *Queen's* College as objectionable.

This new college is to be the Pope's, not the Queen's, College, though endowed by public money. The sixth proposition proves the impossibility of even having a central University by which degrees could be granted in competition to students from the various colleges in Ireland. The standard of examination would have to be lowered to that of the Catholic College, where "books and authors in mental or social science, history, and cognate subjects" are chosen by the Romish authorities. Let them grant degrees of their own, and they will be pleased; but if there is to be a central Irish University, the standard of examination for degrees must be degraded to the level of the Romish College.

Anxious as the Government of that day was to propitiate the Roman Catholic bishops, these demands must have astounded them. Sir George Grey replied that Her Majesty's Government were willing to grant a charter of incorporation to the Roman Catholic University as a college, but that the terms and provisions would require consideration. In another letter, 30th January, 1866, Sir George Grey said that the Government proposed to assimilate the Queen's University in Ireland to the University of London, with power of granting degrees, and to give a charter to the Roman Catholic University as a college. The charter for that college must, however, be different from that proposed by the bishops. The four Roman Catholic archbishops might be constituted visitors, but the governing body should not be wholly ecclesiastical. As to endowment, the Government declined to promise anything for the Roman Catholic College, but would be willing to propose a grant for burses and scholarships open to competition to all students, without distinction, members of the Queen's University, if established. The Roman Catholic bishops were thus foiled in their attempt to obtain a separate University, endowed with State money, yet not under State control, and "not even by name" identified with the nation from which they were begging the charter and the money.

They tried again what they could do with another Government. The plan of reconstituting the Irish Colleges, and combining them in a degree-granting University, like that of London, was in abeyance. The bishops sent a memorial to the late Earl of Derby asking for "a charter and endowment for the Catholic University," and also asking for "such ulterior concessions as shall place the Roman Catholics of Ireland on a perfect equality with their fellow-subjects of other denominations as regards academical education." This was in October, 1867. Lord Derby's Cabinet was no doubt puzzled as to how this application was to be met. The Ministry had been nearly a year and a half in office, and had staved off the troublesome question. Now the matter was thrust upon them by the memorial of the importunate Dr. Cullen and the bishops. No reply was sent till March, 1868, when a "confidential memorandum" came from Lord Mayo. He referred to the correspondence with Sir George Grey and to the supplementary charter scheme, the unsuccess of which had by this time been tested. He proposed "the formation of a new University, to stand in the same relation to Roman Catholics that Trinity did to Protestants." This was indeed a concession, an admission of the Catholic objection to mixed education. But Lord Mayo's correspondence affirmed as "indispensable that a lay element of much power and influence should be introduced into the governing body." The State would not exercise control, but the institution would be "subject to the constant influence of public opinion, and be governed by a body acting in the light of day." As to endowment, Lord Mayo advised the question to be "postponed until the Colleges are firmly established. It is a question of great difficulty, and need not form an indispensable portion of the plan." As Sir George Grey had proposed to give burses and scholarships, open to the students of the new Roman Catholic College as to others, Lord Mayo, not to be outdone in the spirit of concession, said "it might be necessary to ask Parliament for a sum for the payment of the expenses of examination, the foundation of a certain number of University scholarships, and the giving of prizes ; also payment of the salaries of certain officers and servants of the University, and perhaps some provision for a university hall and examination rooms." The bishops made numerous objections to the proposed constitution as sketched by Lord Mayo, especially to the proposal as to "the lay element of much power and influence in the governing body," amenable to public opinion. The postponement of the Endowment question was still more disliked, but this they could not decently urge among their grounds of dissatisfaction. The objections were so decided that the Government closed the negotiation, and Lord Mayo wrote, and it was the last thing he wrote on the subject, "The object of the Government was to create an institution which, although denominational in its character, would be thoroughly independent, self-governed, and free from any external influence, political or religious. The proposals made in your letter would strike at the very root of these principles, and I am, therefore, with extreme regret, obliged to inform you that the recommendations contained in that letter cannot be entertained."

The Catholic University, then, in St. Stephen's Green, which was inaugurated with so much vaunting, has proved a melancholy failure as yet. There was some hope while Dr. Newman was connected with it, but since Cardinal Cullen and his party brought their full influence to bear, the reign of incompetency and bigotry commenced. The institution subsists only as an eleemosynary establishment, kept up by subscriptions and an annual collection throughout the country. I believe last year's collection was under £5,000. The laity withhold their support, excepting those of the Ultramontane party. Excluding the medical classes, there is a mere handful of students.

Primary education and University education have obtained ample consideration, but too little attention has been given to secondary schools. These are sadly inferior to the same class of schools in England or Scotland. There are few public grammar schools. Many of the sons of Protestant parents are educated by private tutors or in boarding-schools. The quality of the teaching in Roman Catholic schools is very inferior. All are in the hands of ecclesiastics, or members of religious orders under the supervision of the bishop of the diocese, and the bishops of the present day are opposed to everything that the Pope's Syllabus of Errors would regard as innovations. The whole course of study and system of discipline breathes a narrow and antiquated spirit ; and the pupils leave school with minds uncultivated and undeveloped, and wholly unfit for competition with pupils who have had better training. It would be well to have a commission of inquiry on the whole subject of secondary education, and on the present condition of intermediate schools, both Protestant and Catholic. Till we have the report of such a commission we are not ripe for any legislation including secondary education.

I had written thus far before the Government plan for University reform had been made public. The reasons for narrating the previous movements in the matter remain the same.

The new scheme is this: The University of Dublin, now practically one with Trinity College, is to be separated from it, and raised to the position of the Irish National University. It will be the only body entitled to grant degrees. To this University, as the mother of them all, will be affiliated Trinity College, the Queen's Colleges of Belfast and Cork, the Roman Catholic University on St. Stephen's Green, Magee Presbyterian College, Londonderry, and other colleges which may be determined in the first instance by Parliament, and afterwards by the governing body. The Queen's University will disappear. Trinity College is to be secularized, provision being made out of its funds for a theological college under the disestablished Irish Church. The Queen's College at Galway is to be suppressed.

The new University of Dublin is to be chiefly an examining body, like the University of London, but is also nominally to be a teaching body, with a staff of professors. Attendance at these University classes, however, is to be optional. Any one may present himself for examination, and compete for the prizes and scholarships to be founded. There will be no chairs of theology, ethics, mental philosophy, or modern history, and these subjects are excluded from examinations.

Trinity College is to retain its classic buildings, and other buildings are to be provided for the University.

The governing body of the University is to consist of a chancellor, vice-chancellor, and twenty-eight ordinary members, to be nominated in the first place by the Government, and named in the Act. All vacancies occurring within a period of ten years (1875 to 1885), to be filled alternately by the Crown and by co-optation of the Council; after which period four members will retire annually, one successor to be appointed by the Crown, one by the Council, one by the Professors, and one by the Senate. The Senate will consist of all graduates who keep their names on the books, and will include those now qualified both in Dublin and the Queen's University, with special powers during the first three years after 1875 (when the Act takes force) for the admission of persons who have resided a sufficient time in the other colleges.

Besides the twenty-eight nominated and elected members, every affiliated college having fifty members *in statu pupillari*, matriculated in the University, may elect one member of the Governing Council, and every college with 150 students may elect two members.

The estimated annual expenses of the University are £50,000, to be thus obtained : £12,000 contributed by Trinity College ; £10,000 from the Consolidated Fund ; £5,000 from fees ; and the remainder, £28,000 from the surplus of the ecclesiastical funds of the Irish Church. The distribution of the money will be thus made : £25,000 for the encouragement of learning, by institution of ten fellowships of £200 each, tenable for five years ; twenty-five exhibitions of £50 each per annum ; and 100 bursaries, each of £25, tenable for four years ; £20,000 per annum for the staff of professors ; and £5,000 a-year for buildings, examinations, and general expenses.

Such, in brief, is the "complicated yet comprehensive" plan of the Government for settling the Irish University question. The Bill is a historical document, however its clauses may be modified, or whatever may be its reception in both Houses of Parliament.

There are two lights in which it may be viewed: first, as a political move; and second, as a measure for the true benefit of Ireland.

Taking the political aspect of the case, the Bill is certainly a scheme of ingenious compromises. It tries to satisfy the Roman Catholics—with what result remains to be seen. It flatters the Presbyterians of Ulster. It is a less measure of spoliation than the friends of Trinity College feared. It avoids shocking the Protestant feeling of the nation by proposing the direct endowment of a Roman Catholic University. With the independent proposals of Professor Fawcett and Dr. Lyon Playfair in front, and the undeclared designs of Mr. Disraeli and his party in the rear, a ministerial movement appeared a political necessity. As a compromise between opposite plans, and as a measure of expediency, the Bill is a clever political movement.

But looking beyond this to the question of higher statesmanship, and the lasting welfare of Ireland, the Bill does not command the same praise. The only point unquestionably good is the removal of the theological faculty from Trinity College. I think the separation of Dublin University and Trinity College right, and in accordance with the original intention and charters. But that University was to be the mother of other colleges or halls *in Dublin*, as are the Universities of Oxford and Cambridge, not the mother of colleges of various creeds, and in different parts of the kingdom.

The establishment of a single University is a point of mere sentiment and political expediency, not of practical benefit. Scotland has succeeded better by having separate independent Universities, as England has, and the same spirit of freedom and of rivalry would be serviceable in Ireland. In this point the influence of Mr. Lowe has apparently prevailed, who is champion of the theory that a University is for examining, not for teaching purposes.

The Bill, according to the Queen's Speech, has for its object "the advancement of learning," and is "framed with a careful regard to the rights of conscience."

No man's conscience is meddled with at present. The real grievance is the fear of Catholic and Protestant students being educated together. To prevent this, the Ultramontanes founded a separate University. It has proved a failure, an utter failure in regard to arts and philosophy, and but for its medical school, is not worth keeping up.

To ask the direct endowment of such a University would be absurd. But there may be indirect endowment by burses and scholarships, as proposed by Dr. Cullen and the Bishops in 1866, and this indirect endowment Mr. Gladstone's Bill provides.

But how does this promote the advancement of

learning? The Council of twenty-eight may be nominated, and a chancellor and vice-chancellor appointed, displaying most imposing representative names. Are they to appoint the examiners? are they to prescribe the subjects of study and the books to be used at the examinations? In classics and mathematics, in law and medicine, there might be common ground; but what of logic, of mental and moral philosophy, and modern literature and history? The attempt to unite on such ground, and even on scientific ground, would be impossible, without lowering the standard to suit the Papal Syllabus and the Index Expurgatorius. So these subjects are omitted! Theology and ecclesiastical history being excluded, we have what the bishops call a "godless University," as we are now said to have "godless Colleges."

Many details of the Bill are open to objection. The suppression of Galway College would be a blunder as well as an injury. There is a new life being awakened in the west of Ireland, and there may be a bright future for the fine old town of Galway. The "appropriation clauses" will justly raise remonstrances. The permission to every college with fifty students to elect a member of the governing body will gradually throw the balance of power into the hands of Romanists. There are various small seminaries which may be easily manned, so as to take advantage of this privilege. Is it intended that

St. Kyran's College at Kilkenny, and St. Jarlath's at Tuam, and St. Patrick's at Carlow, and other colleges of smaller note, are to elect members to the Council, and Trinity and Belfast only to have the power of sending two members each? If the original Council is equally composed of Catholics and Protestants, the balance will easily be turned, and the true friends of liberal education will find their influence swamped, and will retire from their humiliating position, as Whately and his friends did from the National School Board.

The end of it would probably be, that Protestants and liberal Catholics, despising the degrees of the mediæval university—"a university without morals and without history,"—will seek the restoration to Trinity of the power of granting degrees, and the Ultramontane Papists would then be left in possession of the endowments which the Government are afraid now to ask openly.

Existing conditions, it is said, must be considered, three-fourths of the population being Catholic. But the evil is, that the existing conditions will be perpetuated by this scheme, which will retard the advancement of sound learning and liberal feeling in Ireland. Only one thing could be more disastrous, the endowment of Popish intermediate schools, which will probably be the next crafty scheme urged on the Government.

CHAPTER XXVI.

EVANGELICAL AND PROTESTANT AGENCIES.

The Irish Church—The Presbyterian Church—Archbishop Usher's Scheme for Protestant Union—Missions to Roman Catholics—Colportage—Bible Circulation.

I REFRAIN from saying anything about the disestablishment of the Irish Church, except this, that never had it displayed more spiritual life and active usefulness than at the time of its forced separation from the State. How it will succeed in fully adapting itself to its altered circumstances remains to be seen. As far as the reorganization has proceeded, it has met the hopes of its friends and disappointed the wishes of its foes. Its action as a free church has been hitherto chiefly seen in the progress of reconstruction. It is to be hoped that it will now become more than ever an evangelistic and missionary church, and so out of what seemed evil there will good be educed, both for the advantage of the State and for the advancement of true religion.

To a certain extent the Irish Church has been

disendowed as well as disestablished, for the annuities granted to the present clergy are to be regarded as compensation for loss of civil personal rights, and not as payment for spiritual services. Provision must be made by voluntary efforts for maintaining the trust fund, as the annuitants pass away, and for extending the church for wider usefulness. To remain stationary, far less to contract its sphere of operation, would be an unworthy position for a church which includes most of the Protestant aristocracy of Ireland. In view of the future it would be well if the leaders of the church would take more counsel from the experience of the other free churches, both in England and Scotland. In regard to financial affairs, for example, there seems to be too much dependence put upon the large donations of wealthy patrons, instead of seeking a broad and permanent strength in the small but regular contributions of the mass of the people adhering to it. The experience of the Wesleyan Methodist body might be usefully considered in this respect. The experience of the Free Church of Scotland might also be usefully imitated, in the formation and distribution of a central sustentation fund. The great argument against a purely voluntary church is, that while rich districts or parishes are sure to have ample support, there is no provision secured for the commencement and maintenance of

Christian worship and ordinances in poor districts, except by missionary agency. A central sustentation fund secures a sufficient maintenance for every station, by an equal dividend to each minister, which may be supplemented to any amount by local contributions in wealthier or more populous parishes.

These and other matters of government and administration will be matured and rectified in time. But there is one subject which forces itself on the consideration of any thoughtful observer of the present ecclesiastical condition of Ireland.

There are practically only three great divisions of religious creed in Ireland—the Roman Catholic Church, the Episcopal Church, and the Presbyterian Church. The whole of the other Protestant denominations form an insignificant element in the census. The Independents and Baptists have some influential churches in the large towns; but they count little in evangelistic work on the mass of the people. The Society of Friends occupy a useful position, exercising a peaceful and persuasive power among Roman Catholics, who seem to regard them with less hostility than other Protestant denominations. The Methodist bodies also are zealous and useful, but not strong in numbers; and practically the Protestantism of Ireland, and that almost equally, is divided between the Episcopalians and Presbyterians.

To Episcopalians and Presbyterians in different parts of Ireland I have said, what a pity at the time of the disestablishment there could not have been some attempt to form a closer union among Protestants! What a waste of power there is in maintaining everywhere two Protestant organizations, when in spirit, in creed, in preaching—in all but the non-essentials of government, discipline, and worship—the churches are one! Why not attempt some plan of union such as Archbishop Usher proposed, and nearly carried, with consent of both churches? The separation of the Irish Church from the State, and the surrender of the Regium Donum by the Presbyterians, have cleared away difficulties which could not have been surmounted at any previous time. Might not some attempt be made to form a strong and united Protestant Evangelical Church?

The history of the attempts to promote Christian union in the seventeenth century are deeply interesting, and have attracted too little attention. I found few people in Ireland knew anything of Archbishop Usher's "Irenicon." I can only briefly refer to it here.

Archbishop Usher laid his scheme of "Modified Episcopacy" before the House of Lords in 1637. He proceeded on the principle that bishops and presbyters differed, not in order, but in degree only (*gradu non ordine*); that among many presbyters there was one stated president or bishop; and that the whole government of the church should be by synods. The rector of each parish, with the churchwardens, was to conduct the affairs of a congregation. The churches, with each rural deanery, were to form the lowest synods, to meet monthly. Diocesan synods were to meet twice a year; provincial synods every three years; and a national synod, or assembly, on the sitting of Parliament, or on any special emergency. In these courts all matters were to be decided by majority of votes, the bishops being moderators or presidents, and appeals might be carried from inferior to higher courts or synods, the national synod being the supreme ecclesiastical court of the realm. He further admitted the validity of ordination by presbyters, even in the absence of a bishop.

The High Church and Court party were so alarmed by the decided movement toward union that they wrought upon the fears of the King, and on this ecclesiastical more than any political ground they hurried matters toward irreconcilable division.

When the Civil War broke out the attention of Parliament was diverted from these proposals. A new element also assumed greater force in the strife of opinion. The aid of the Scots was deemed essential to the success of Parliament in resisting the King, and their assistance could only be obtained on condition of the Parliament joining them in a covenanted uniformity of religion, on the ground of the divine right of Presbytery. The negotiation resulted in the well-known Westminster Assembly, which superseded the moderate counsels of Archbishop Usher and his friends.

In the conference which was held at Newport, in the Isle of Wight, in 1648, Usher again personally brought forward his scheme of union. The King seemed willing to adopt the plan, and made offer of various concessions. But the Parliament deemed them unsatisfactory, acting no doubt under the advice of the rigid Scottish Presbyterians. Soon afterwards the Republican party resolved upon the fall of the King, as well as the removal of the yoke imposed on them by their Scottish allies. The King was seized in November of that year, and taken to Hurst Castle, where he remained till brought to Windsor, and thence to London for his trial and execution.

After the Restoration a last attempt at accommodation, "according to Usher's model," was made. Sir Matthew Hale moved in the House of Commons a Bill to promote union. A few days after the first reading of the Bill he was appointed Lord Chief Baron of the Exchequer, in order that he might not oppose the designs of the Court. On the 28th November, 1660, when the second reading was moved, one of the Secretaries of State opposed the Bill, indicating the hostility of the King and his Council. On a division, it was thrown out by 183 to 157. Thus all the hopes of union, with the sanction of Parliament, were at an end.

The conference promised by the King had yet to be held at the Savoy. The meetings lasted from the 25th of March till the 25th of July, when the King's commission expired. The conference broke up without any prospect of accommodation. No reasonable concessions were admitted by the bishops, and some additional causes of division were introduced, so that, says Baxter, "the Common Prayer-book was rendered more exceptionable, and the terms of conformity much harder than before the civil war."

After the Savoy Conference the High Church party gained ground, till at length they had influence to procure the passing of the Act of Uniformity. The Bill passed the Commons by a narrow vote, 186 to 180, and also the Lords by a small majority. On the 19th May, 1662, it received the royal assent, and was to be in force from St. Bartholomew's Day, August 24th, hence commonly called "the Bartholomew Act." The result was, that upwards of 2,000 faithful and conscientious ministers were driven from the Church of England, and English Protestantism has ever since been rent by divisions.

During the discussions in Parliament, which preceded the passing of the Irish Church Act, it was argued, that if all Protestant denominations were placed on the same level, "the Protestant interest would be greatly strengthened by the union and communion of Protestant churches." No action has yet been taken by the representative bodies of the Episcopal or Presbyterian Church, but there have been individual manifestations of the right spirit. The Rev. Dr. Hannay, Vicar of Belfast, for instance, has preached in Presbyterian churches, and has invited Presbyterians to the communion in his own church, dispensing the elements in their own way to those who have scruples about kneeling at the altar. Whether there has been reciprocity as to the interchange of pulpits in Ireland I am not aware, but it will be a narrow policy if it is not carried out. From the beginning of the Reformation in England, down to the days of Heylin and Laud, the idea of not recognizing the orders of the ministers of the other reformed churches was never entertained. Even John Knox, the greatest of Presbyterians, preached regularly through the north of England, and was offered a bishopric, which, for personal, not ecclesiastical, reasons he declined.

It is to the laymen of the Protestant churches of Ireland that we must look for any movement towards the "union and communion" which many must desire. The clergy are not likely to move first, although the opinion of Archbishop Usher ought to have some weight with them. "He was," said Dr. Johnson, "the great luminary of the Irish Church; and a greater no church could boast of, at least in modern times." The manuscripts of Usher are preserved with pride at Trinity College, and a splendid edition of his works has been in recent years published. In the twelfth volume will be found Usher's scheme of conciliation and union. Dr. Elrington briefly refers to it in his "Life of Usher." "Whitlock," he says, "mentions the attempt of the Primate as if it had been authoritatively made in some shape or other. His statement is that 'The Primate of Armagh offered an expedient for conjunction in point of discipline, that Episcopal and Presbyterian government might not be at a far distance; reducing episcopacy to the form of synodical government in the ancient church.'" Dr. Elrington then dismisses the matter, which was of little practical bearing before the disestablishment of the church.* But it is different

---

* Mr. Froude, in his History of "The English in Ireland" (vol. i. 75), in describing the sad troubles of the seventeenth century, says, "The Catholics were one body; the Protestants to their misfortune were two. The bishops, Archbishop Usher especially, were so generous in their sympathies that, but for the political ties which connected the Established Churches of England and Ireland, they would have brought about of their own accord a fusion with the Presbyterian congregations."

now, and certain it is that without some union of Protestants such as Usher contemplated, the impression made on the Popery of Ireland will be feeble, compared with what might be expected from a strong and united Protestant Evangelical Church.

I must not conclude without brief reference to evangelistic agencies carried on in harmony with, but independent of, the Protestant churches. "I believe," says Miss Whately, in a recent report of the Irish Church Mission, "very few, even among the true and earnest friends of Evangelical missions in England, are aware of the remarkable character of the movement among the Roman Catholics of Ireland, which commenced at the time when, twenty-three years ago, the results of the Irish famine first opened the way to more direct effort, and which is continuing steadily to progress. Not even in the recently opened mission-fields in Italy and Spain, is there such encouragement to be found as in Ireland.

"The results would be more patent to casual observers, both in Dublin and in the country parts, did all, or the chief part of those brought out of Rome, remain on the spot; but the tide of emigration, which has been steadily flowing for so many years past, affects converts from Romanism peculiarly, both on account of the severe local persecution, which drives multitudes to seek a home elsewhere, and the increased desire for comfort, independence, and a rise in the social scale, which must always be the fruit of educational and civilizing influences. But for this widespread exodus of converts from Romanism, there can be no doubt that their proportion to the rest of the population would be much more appreciable.'"

I can bear testimony to what I have seen of the work of the Irish Church Missions. In the west of Ireland, even in wild Connemara, where there was hardly a Protestant to be found twenty years ago, I have been in churches filled with earnest worshippers. In remote stations I found flourishing churches and schools, in one place the minister and schoolmaster, formerly Papists, but now the leaders of an earnest band of Protestants. It is by the increase of good work like that of the Irish Church Missions, that the true progress of Ireland will be secured.

Until a comparatively recent time the Presbyterian Church did not take much part in aggressive evangelization or home mission work in Ireland; but since the revival of religious life in the old Synod of Ulster, and the formation of a broader church, with its Synods and General Assembly, similar in organization to the ecclesiastical system of Scotland, the influence of Presbyterians has greatly increased. They do not now content themselves with the spiritual oversight of their own people in the North, and with keeping up a few congregations in Dublin and some of the large towns, but they aim at extending their operations to all parts of Ireland. New congregations have been formed within the last twenty years in many towns even of the South, and missionary stations are established in Kerry, Sligo, the mountains of Tyrone, and the highlands of Donegal. The Connaught mission schools, which have been established for twenty-five years, at present are 45 in number, with about 1,560 scholars, of whom 390 are Presbyterians, 540 other Protestants, and 630 Catholic children. For mission work among the Romanists the Presbyterians seem less fitted, from their rigid adherence to denominational peculiarities; but their evangelistic zeal is most usefully exercised through the agency of the press.

Since 1859 a society has been in operation for the circulation of the Scriptures, and of books, periodicals, and tracts, by the agency of colportage. There are central dépôts in Dublin, Belfast, and Londonderry; there are also book-agents in various parts of the country, who undertake to receive and distribute monthly parcels of publications. Some of these agents are booksellers, or other tradespeople, who make a profit by the sale on commission, others help the distribution as a labour of love, for the good of the people.

This colportage agency is peculiarly adapted to the

present state of Ireland. The people everywhere have learned to read English, but there is little for them to read, except the cheap newspapers. There are few book-shops, and to the scattered rural population few opportunities occur of purchasing any publications. The growth of the work may be estimated from the fact that the sales and receipts at the Belfast dépôt in the last month of 1871 exceeded the entire issues and receipts in the year 1860.

Among the books sold by the colporteurs, the most important is the Douay Testament, thousands of which have been sold in all parts of Ireland, and the colporteurs and home missionaries can say to the people, "Look at your own Testament; there is nothing here about the immaculate conception, about the invocation of saints, prayers for the dead; nothing about purgatory, or the mass. If these doctrines are in it, show them. No; there is no Saviour but the Lord Jesus Christ, and 'in Him every one that believeth is justified.'" For a few pence these Testaments are sold, and numbers of Roman Catholics purchase them, if there is no priest at hand to terrify them. The diffusion of scriptural truth is what the Church of Rome most dreads.

I have given this brief notice of the work of the Irish Church Missions and of the Colportage Society of the Presbyterians, only as specimens of the kind of agencies now in operation under the Protestant churches. The spiritual results of these agencies in regard to individuals are not for public cognizance; but any view of the moral and social condition, and any estimate of the future of Ireland, would be incomplete and delusive without taking such subjects into consideration. Official reports on the resources of the country or on its material progress are useful in their way, but they do not reach the deep springs of national life and prosperity. Statistical returns leave out of view the most influential of all agencies at work, the moral agencies, by which the improvement of the people is secured. I had more hopeful certainty of the future of Ireland in seeing the progress of Protestantism throughout the country than in witnessing the wonders of the Dublin Exhibition; and the mission reports are more pregnant with promise than the best pages of Dr. Hancock's blue-books.

I venture to express my conviction that the power of Popery, which has so long oppressed Ireland, is passing away. The spread of popular education, the social and political changes at home, and the progress of events on the Continent, are all exciting a silent but strong influence in loosening the old superstition, and preparing for a new and better faith. There is a feeling abroad resembling what is reported of India, where the belief in ancient idolatries and creeds is being shaken, with an undefined and uneasy expectation of change approaching. This feeling has been strengthened within the last two years. The humiliation of France, the chief Catholic power of Europe; the decided action of the Prussian Government towards the Romish party; the progress of the reformation in Italy and Spain, and the present position of the Pope;—these and other European events are much canvassed in Ireland. The Roman Catholics admit that their Church is going down on the Continent. The spasmodic efforts of the Irish hierarchy to retain their influence, and to induce the British Government to assist them in gaining the direction of education, are made in desperation, as if knowing that their time is short. Now is the opportunity for Protestants to increase their efforts to enlighten the people, especially by means of the press. By utilizing more than has been done the secular press, by circulating religious books and periodicals, as well as by the ordinary agencies of churches, the mind of the nation can be reached, with more hope of success than at any previous time. In spite of the denunciations of the bishops, who forbid the reading of heretical books, and discourage inquiry, there is a widespread desire to know more about the Protestant doctrines. Large numbers of Catholics attend discussion classes and controversial lectures, and even by those who would not touch religious books or tracts, the Protestant newspapers are read. If the Protestant churches would only unite in evangelistic and educational work, the difficulty of attacking Romanism would be lessened, and greater results be obtained. Even with the present drawbacks, the progress of truth is evident, and at no distant time will surprise those who have looked with despair on the condition of Ireland.

PRESS NOTICES OF
"*ACROSS THE FERRY.*"

"A model in its way of what a book of American travels ought to be."—*London Society*.

"The book is more than a record of travelling experiences and impressions; it is a series of photographs of America as it was in 1870, and is full of practical interest."—*British Quarterly Review*.

"Well worth reading, as throwing a new light on many things of which we know but too little in this country."—*The Graphic*.

"It contains a large mass of information, and is full of suggestive matter."—*Spectator*.

"A very lively, entertaining, and generally accurate description of this country."—*Appleton's Journal* (*New York*).

"The best and most sensible articles on our country, that have ever appeared in England."—*Philadelphia Ledger*.

A Catalogue

OF

HENRY S. KING & CO.'S

PUBLICATIONS.

LONDON:
65, CORNHILL, AND 12, PATERNOSTER ROW.
1873.

Henry S. King & Co.'s Publications.

WHY AM I A CHRISTIAN?
By LORD STRATFORD DE REDCLIFFE.
Crown 8vo. *[Preparing.*

THE ROMANTIC ANNALS OF A NAVAL FAMILY.
By Mrs. ARTHUR TRAHERNE.
Crown 8vo. *[Preparing.*

THE SUNNY AND CLOUDY DAYS OF MDME. LA VICOMTESSE DE LEOVILLE-MEILHAN.
Crown 8vo. *[In the press.*

SHORT LECTURES ON THE LAND LAWS.
DELIVERED BEFORE THE WORKING MEN'S INSTITUTE.
By T. LEAN WILKINSON.
Crown 8vo. *[Nearly ready.*

STUDIES AND ROMANCES.
By H. SCHÜTZ-WILSON.
1 vol. crown 8vo. *[Preparing.*

THE RELIGIOUS HISTORY OF IRELAND:
PRIMITIVE, PAPAL, AND PROTESTANT,
INCLUDING THE EVANGELICAL MISSIONS, CATHOLIC AGITATIONS, AND CHURCH PROGRESS OF THE LAST HALF CENTURY.
By JAMES GODKIN,
Author of "Ireland, her Churches," etc.
1 vol. 8vo. *[Preparing.*

MEMOIR AND LETTERS OF SARA COLERIDGE.
2 vols. crown 8vo. With Portraits. *[In the press.*

LOMBARD STREET. A Description of the Money Market.
By WALTER BAGEHOT.
Large crown 8vo. *[In the press.*

65, *Cornhill; &* 12, *Paternoster Row, London.*

POLITICAL WOMEN.
By SUTHERLAND MENZIES.
2 vols. post 8vo. *[In the press.*

EGYPT AS IT IS.
By Herr HEINRICH STEPHAN,
The German Postmaster-General.
Crown 8vo. With a new Map of the Country. *[Preparing.*

IMPERIAL GERMANY.
By FREDERIC MARTIN,
Author of "The Statesman's Year Book," &c. *[Preparing.*

THE GOVERNMENT OF THE NATIONAL DEFENCE.
By JULES FAVRE.
Demy 8vo. 1 vol. *[Preparing.*

'ILÂM ĔN NÂS. Historical Tales and Anecdotes of the Times of the Early Khalifahs.
TRANSLATED FROM THE ARABIC ORIGINALS
By Mrs. GODFREY CLERK,
Author of "The Antipodes and Round the World."
Crown 8vo. *[In the press.*

IN STRANGE COMPANY;
Or, The NOTE BOOK of a ROVING CORRESPONDENT.
By JAMES GREENWOOD,
"The Amateur Casual."
Crown 8vo. *[Preparing.*

THEOLOGY AND MORALITY.
BEING ESSAYS BY THE REV. J. LLEWELLYN DAVIES.
1 vol., 8vo. *[Preparing.*

THE RECONCILIATION OF RELIGION AND SCIENCE.

BEING ESSAYS BY THE REV. J. W. FOWLE, M.A.

1 vol., 8vo. [*In the press.*

A NEW VOLUME OF ACADEMIA ESSAYS.

EDITED BY THE MOST REVEREND ARCHBISHOP MANNING.

[*Preparing.*

THE FAYOUM; OR, ARTISTS IN EGYPT.

A TOUR WITH M. GÉRÔME AND OTHERS.

BY J. LENOIR. TRANSLATED BY MRS. CASHEL HOEY.

Crown 8vo, cloth. Illustrated. [*In the press.*

TENT LIFE WITH ENGLISH GYPSIES IN NORWAY. BY HUBERT SMITH.

In 8vo, cloth. Five full-page Engravings, and 31 smaller Illustrations, with Map of the Country, showing Routes. Price 21s.

THE GATEWAY TO THE POLYNIA;
OR, A VOYAGE TO SPITZBERGEN.

BY CAPTAIN JOHN C. WELLS, R.N.

In 8vo, cloth. Profusely illustrated. [*In the press.*

A WINTER IN MOROCCO.

BY AMELIA PERRIER.

Large crown 8vo. Illustrated. Price 10s. 6d. [*In the press.*

AN AUTUMN TOUR IN THE UNITED STATES AND CANADA.

BY LIEUT.-COLONEL JULIUS GEORGE MEDLEY.

Crown 8vo. Price 5s. [*In the press.*

65, Cornhill; & 12, Paternoster Row, London.

IRELAND IN 1872.
A TOUR OF OBSERVATION, WITH REMARKS ON IRISH PUBLIC QUESTIONS.
By Dr. JAMES MACAULAY.

Crown 8vo. 7s. 6d.

THE GREAT DUTCH ADMIRALS.
By JACOB DE LIEFDE.

Crown 8vo. Illustrated. Price 5s.

NEWMARKET AND ARABIA:
AN EXAMINATION OF THE DESCENT OF RACERS AND COURSERS.
By ROGER D. UPTON.

Crown 8vo. Illustrated. Price 9s.

FIELD AND FOREST RAMBLES OF A NATURALIST IN NEW BRUNSWICK.
WITH NOTES AND OBSERVATIONS ON THE NATURAL HISTORY OF EASTERN CANADA.

By A. LEITH ADAMS, M.A., &c.,
Author of "Wanderings of a Naturalist in India," &c., &c.

In 8vo, cloth. Illustrated. 14s.

BOKHARA: ITS HISTORY AND CONQUEST.
By Professor ARMINIUS VÀMBÈRY,
Of the University of Pesth, Author of "Travels in Central Asia," &c.

Demy 8vo. 18s.

"We conclude with a cordial recommendation of this valuable book. In former years, Mr. Vambery gave ample proofs of his powers as an observant, easy, and vivid writer. In the present work his moderation, scholarship, insight, and occasionally very impressive style, have raised him to the dignity of an historian."—*Saturday Review.*

"Almost every page abounds with composition of peculiar merit, as well as with an account of some thrilling event more exciting than any to be found in an ordinary work of fiction."—*Morning Post.*

"A work compiled from many rare, private, and unavailable manuscripts and records, which consequently cannot fail to prove a mine of delightful Eastern lore to the Oriental scholar."—*Liverpool Albion.*

OVER VOLCANOES;

Or, THROUGH FRANCE AND SPAIN IN 1871.

By A. KINGSMAN.

Crown 8vo. 10s. 6d.

"The writer's tone is so pleasant, his language is so good, and his spirits are so fresh, buoyant, and exhilarating, that you find yourself inveigled into reading, for the thousand-and-first time, a description of a Spanish bull-fight."—*Illustrated London News.*

"The adventures of our tourists are related with a good deal of pleasantry and humorous dash, which make the narrative agreeable reading."—*Public Opinion.*

"A work which we cordially recommend to such readers as desire to know something of Spain as she is to-day. Indeed, so fresh and original is it, that we could have wished that it had been a bigger book than it is."—*Literary World.*

ALEXIS DE TOCQUEVILLE.

CORRESPONDENCE AND CONVERSATIONS WITH NASSAU W. SENIOR FROM 1833 TO 1859.

EDITED BY MRS. M. C. M. SIMPSON.

2 vols., large post 8vo. 21s.

"Another of those interesting journals in which Mr. Senior has, as it were, crystallized the sayings of some of those many remarkable men with whom he came in contact."—*Morning Post.*

"A book replete with knowledge and thought."—*Quarterly Review.*

"An extremely interesting book, and a singularly good illustration of the value which, even in an age of newspapers and magazines, memoirs have and will always continue to have for the purposes of history."—*Saturday Review.*

JOURNALS KEPT IN FRANCE AND ITALY,

FROM 1848 TO 1852.

WITH A SKETCH OF THE REVOLUTION OF 1848.

By THE LATE NASSAU WILLIAM SENIOR.

Edited by his Daughter, M. C. M. SIMPSON.

In 2 vols., post 8vo. 24s.

"The present volume gives us conversations with some of the most prominent men in the political history of France and Italy . . . as well as with others whose names are not so familiar or are hidden under initials. Mr. Senior has the art of inspiring all men with frankness, and of persuading them to put themselves unreservedly in his hands without fear of private circulation."—*Athenæum.*

"The book has a genuine historical value."—*Saturday Review.*

"No better, more honest, and more readable view of the state of political society during the existence of the second Republic could well be looked for."—*Examiner.*

65, Cornhill; & 12, Paternoster Row, London.

A MEMOIR OF NATHANIEL HAWTHORNE,

WITH STORIES NOW FIRST PUBLISHED IN THIS COUNTRY.

BY H. A. PAGE.

Large post 8vo. 7s. 6d.

"The Memoir is followed by a criticism of Hawthorne as a writer; and the criticism, though we should be inclined to dissent from particular sentiments, is, on the whole, very well written, and exhibits a discriminating enthusiasm for one of the most fascinating of novelists."—*Saturday Review.*

"Seldom has it been our lot to meet with a more appreciative delineation of character than this Memoir of Hawthorne . . . Mr. Page deserves the best thanks of every admirer of Hawthorne for the way in which he has gathered together these relics, and given them to the world, as well as for his admirable portraiture of their author's life and character."—*Morning Post.*

"We sympathise very heartily with an effort of Mr. H. A. Page to make English readers better acquainted with the life and character of Nathaniel Hawthorne . . . He has done full justice to the fine character of the author of 'The Scarlet Letter.'"—*Standard.*

"He has produced a well-written and complete Memoir . . . A model of literary work of art."—*Edinburgh Courant.*

MEMOIRS OF LEONORA CHRISTINA,

DAUGHTER OF CHRISTIAN IV. OF DENMARK:

WRITTEN DURING HER IMPRISONMENT IN THE BLUE TOWER OF THE ROYAL PALACE AT COPENHAGEN, 1663—1685.

TRANSLATED BY F. E. BUNNETT,

Translator of Grimm's "Life of Michael Angelo," &c.

With an Autotype portrait of the Princess. Medium 8vo. 12s. 6d.

"A valuable addition to history."—*Daily News.*

"This remarkable autobiography, in which we gratefully recognize a valuable addition to the tragic romance of history."—*Spectator.*

LIVES OF ENGLISH POPULAR LEADERS.

No. 1. STEPHEN LANGTON.

BY C. EDMUND MAURICE.

Crown 8vo. 7s. 6d.

"Mr. Maurice has written a very interesting book, which may be read with equal pleasure and profit."—*Morning Post.*

"The volume contains many interesting details, including some important documents. It will amply repay those who read it, whether as a chapter of the constitutional history of England or as the life of a great Englishman."—*Spectator.*

65, Cornhill; & 12, Paternoster Row, London.

ECHOES OF A FAMOUS YEAR.
By HARRIET PARR,
Author of "The Life of Jeanne d'Arc," "In the Silver Age," &c.

Crown 8vo. 8s. 6d.

"A graceful and touching, as well as truthful account of the Franco-Prussian War. Those who are in the habit of reading books to children will find this at once instructive and delightful."—*Public Opinion*.

"Miss Parr has the great gift of charming simplicity of style; and if children are not interested in her book, many of their seniors will be."—*British Quarterly Review*.

NORMAN MACLEOD, D.D.,
A CONTRIBUTION TOWARDS HIS BIOGRAPHY.
By ALEXANDER STRAHAN.

Crown 8vo, sewed. Price One Shilling.

⁎ Reprinted, with numerous Additions and many Illustrations from Sketches by Dr. Macleod, from the *Contemporary Review*.

CABINET PORTRAITS.
BIOGRAPHICAL SKETCHES OF LIVING STATESMEN.
By T. WEMYSS REID.

1 vol. crown 8vo. 7s. 6d.

"We have never met with a work which we can more unreservedly praise. The sketches are absolutely impartial."—*Athenæum*.

"We can heartily commend his work."—*Standard*.
"The 'Sketches of Statesmen' are drawn with a master hand."—*Yorkshire Post*.

THE ENGLISH CONSTITUTION.
By WALTER BAGEHOT.

A New Edition, revised and corrected, with an Introductory Dissertation on recent changes and events. Crown 8vo. 7s. 6d.

"A pleasing and clever study on the department of higher politics."—*Guardian*.
"No writer before him had set out so clearly what the efficient part of the English Constitution really is."—*Pall Mall Gazette*.
"Clear and practical."—*Globe*.

REPUBLICAN SUPERSTITIONS.
ILLUSTRATED BY THE POLITICAL HISTORY OF THE UNITED STATES.
INCLUDING A CORRESPONDENCE WITH M. LOUIS BLANC.
By MONCURE D. CONWAY.

Crown 8vo. 5s.

"Au moment où j'écris ceci, je reçois d'un écrivain très distingué d'Amérique, M. Conway, une brochure qui est un frappant tableau des maux et des dangers qui résultent aux Etats Unis de l'institution présidentielle."—*M. Louis Blanc*.
"A very able exposure of the most plausible fallacies of Republicanism, by a writer of remarkable vigour and purity of style."—*Standard*.

65, Cornhill; & 12, Paternoster Row, London.

THE GENIUS of CHRISTIANITY UNVEILED, BEING ESSAYS BY WILLIAM GODWIN.

AUTHOR OF "POLITICAL JUSTICE," ETC.

Never before published. 1 vol. crown 8vo. 7s. 6d.

"Interesting as the frankly expressed thoughts of a remarkable man, and as a contribution to the history of scepticism."—*Extract from the Editor's Preface.*

"Few have thought more clearly and directly than William Godwin, or expressed their reflections with more simplicity and unreserve."—*Examiner.*

"The deliberate thoughts of Godwin deserve to be put before the world for reading and consideration."—*Athenæum.*

THE PELICAN PAPERS.

REMINISCENCES AND REMAINS OF A DWELLER IN THE WILDERNESS.

By JAMES ASHCROFT NOBLE.

Crown 8vo. 6s.

"Written somewhat after the fashion of Mr. Helps' 'Friends in Council.'"—*Examiner.*

"Will well repay perusal by all thoughtful and intelligent readers."—*Liverpool Leader.*

"The 'Pelican Papers' make a very readable volume."—*Civilian.*

SOLDIERING AND SCRIBBLING.

By ARCHIBALD FORBES,

Of the *Daily News*,

Author of "My Experience of the War between France and Germany."

Crown 8vo. 7s. 6d.

"All who open it will be inclined to read through for the varied entertainment which it affords."—*Daily News.*

"There is a good deal of instruction to outsiders touching military life, in this volume."—*Evening Standard.*

"There is not a paper in the book which is not thoroughly readable and worth reading."—*Scotsman.*

BRIEFS AND PAPERS.

BEING SKETCHES OF THE BAR AND THE PRESS.

By TWO IDLE APPRENTICES.

Crown 8vo. 7s. 6d.

"They are written with spirit and knowedge, and give some curious glimpses into what the majority will regard as strange and unknown territories."—*Daily News.*

"This is one of the best books to while away an hour and cause a generous laugh that we have come across for a long time."—*John Bull.*

65, Cornhill; & 12, Paternoster Row, London.

THE INTERNATIONAL SCIENTIFIC SERIES.

MESSRS. HENRY S. KING & CO. have the pleasure to announce that under this title they are issuing a SERIES of POPULAR TREATISES, embodying the results of the latest investigations in the various departments of Science at present most prominently before the world.

Although these Works are not specially designed for the instruction of beginners, still, as they are intended to address the non-scientific public, they will be, as far as possible, explanatory in character, and free from technicalities. The object of each author will be to bring his subject as near as he can to the general reader.

The volumes will all be crown 8vo size, well printed on good paper, strongly and elegantly bound, and will sell in this country at a price *not exceeding Five Shillings.*

☞ Prospectuses of the Series may be had of the Publishers.

Already published,

THE FORMS OF WATER IN RAIN AND RIVERS, ICE AND GLACIERS.

By J. TYNDALL, LL.D., F.R.S.

With 26 Illustrations. Crown 8vo. 5s.

"One of Professor Tyndall's best scientific treatises."—*Standard.*

"The most recent findings of science and experiment respecting the nature and properties of water in every possible form, are discussed with remarkable brevity, clearness, and fullness of exposition."—*Graphic.*

"With the clearness and brilliancy of language which have won for him his fame, he considers the subject of ice, snow, and glaciers."—*Morning Post.*

"Before starting for Switzerland next summer every one should study 'The forms of water.'"—*Globe.*

"Eloquent and instructive in an eminent degree."—*British Quarterly.*

PHYSICS AND POLITICS;

Or, Thoughts on the Application of the Principles of "Natural Selection" and "Inheritance" to Political Society.

By WALTER BAGEHOT.

Crown 8vo. 4s.

"On the whole we can recommend the book as well deserving to be read by thoughtful students of politics."—*Saturday Review.*

"Able and ingenious."—*Spectator.*

"The book has been well thought out, and the writer speaks without fear."—*National Reformer.*

"Contains many points of interest both to the scientific man and to the mere politician."—*Birmingham Daily Gazette.*

The Volumes now preparing are—

PRINCIPLES OF MENTAL PHYSIOLOGY. With their applications to the Training and Discipline of the Mind, and the Study of its Morbid Conditions. By W. B. CARPENTER, LL.D., M.D., F.R.S., &c. Illustrated.

ANIMAL MECHANICS; or, WALKING, SWIMMING, and FLYING. By Dr. J. BELL PETTIGREW, M.D., F.R.S. 125 Illustrations.

MIND AND BODY: THE THEORIES OF THEIR RELATIONS. By ALEXANDER BAIN, LL.D., Professor of Logic at the University of Aberdeen. Illustrated.

ON FOOD. By Dr. EDWARD SMITH, F.R.S. Profusely Illustrated.

THE STUDY OF SOCIOLOGY. By HERBERT SPENCER.

65, Cornhill; & 12, Paternoster Row, London.

STREAMS FROM HIDDEN SOURCES.
By B. MONTGOMERIE RANKING.
Crown 8vo. 6s.

THE SECRET OF LONG LIFE.
DEDICATED BY SPECIAL PERMISSION TO LORD ST. LEONARDS.
Second Edition. Large crown 8vo. 5s.

"A charming little volume, written with singular felicity of style and illustration."—*Times.*

"A very pleasant little book, which is always, whether it deal in paradox or earnest, cheerful, genial, scholarly."—*Spectator.*

"The bold and striking character of the whole conception is entitled to the warmest admiration."—*Pall Mall Gazette.*

"We should recommend our readers to get this book . . . because they will be amused by the jovial miscellaneous and cultured gossip with which he strews his pages."—*British Quarterly Review.*

CHANGE OF AIR AND SCENE.
A PHYSICIAN'S HINTS ABOUT DOCTORS, PATIENTS, HYGIÈNE, AND SOCIETY;
WITH NOTES OF EXCURSIONS FOR HEALTH IN THE PYRENEES, AND AMONGST THE WATERING-PLACES OF FRANCE (INLAND AND SEAWARD), SWITZERLAND, CORSICA, AND THE MEDITERRANEAN.

By Dr. ALPHONSE DONNÉ.
Large post 8vo. Price 9s.

"A very readable and serviceable book. . . . The real value of it is to be found in the accurate and minute information given with regard to a large number of places which have gained a reputation on the continent for their mineral waters."—*Pall Mall Gazette.*

"Not only a pleasant book of travel but also a book of considerable value."—*Morning Post.*

"A popular account of some of the most charming health resorts of the Continent; with suggestive hints about keeping well and getting well, which are characterised by a good deal of robust common sense."—*British Quarterly.*

"A singularly pleasant and chatty as well as instructive book about health."—*Guardian.*

"A useful and pleasantly-written book, containing many valuable hints on the general management of health from a shrewd and experienced medical man."—*Graphic.*

MISS YOUMANS' FIRST BOOK OF BOTANY.
DESIGNED TO CULTIVATE THE OBSERVING POWERS OF CHILDREN.
From the Author's latest Stereotyped Edition.
New and Enlarged Edition, with 300 Engravings. Crown 8vo. 5s.

It is but rarely that a school-book appears which is at once so novel in plan, so successful in execution, and so suited to the general want, as to command universal and unqualified approbation, but such has been the case with Miss Youmans' First Book of Botany. Her work is an outgrowth of the most recent scientific views, and has been practically tested by careful trial with juvenile classes, and it has been everywhere welcomed as a timely and invaluable contribution to the improvement of primary education.

65, Cornhill; & 12, Paternoster Row, London.

AN ESSAY ON THE CULTURE OF THE OBSERVING POWERS OF CHILDREN,

ESPECIALLY IN CONNECTION WITH THE STUDY OF BOTANY.

By ELIZA A. YOUMANS,

Edited, with Notes and a Supplement

By JOSEPH PAYNE, F.C.P.,

Author of "Lectures on the Science and Art of Education," &c.

Crown 8vo.   2s. 6d.

"The little book, now under notice, is expressly designed to make the earliest instruction of children a mental discipline. Miss Youmans presents in her work the ripe results of educational experience reduced to a system, wisely conceiving that an education—even the most elementary—should be regarded as a discipline of the mental powers, and that the facts of external nature supply the most suitable materials for this discipline in the case of children. She has applied that principle to the study of botany. This study, according to her just notions on the subject, is to be fundamentally based on the exercise of the pupil's own powers of observation. He is to see and examine the properties of plants and flowers at first hand, not merely to be informed of what others have seen and examined."—*Pall Mall Gazette.*

THE HISTORY OF THE NATURAL CREATION:

BEING A SERIES OF POPULAR SCIENTIFIC LECTURES ON THE GENERAL THEORY OF PROGRESSION OF SPECIES;

WITH A DISSERTATION ON THE THEORIES OF DARWIN, GOETHE, AND LAMARCK: MORE ESPECIALLY APPLYING THEM TO THE ORIGIN OF MAN, AND TO OTHER FUNDAMENTAL QUESTIONS OF NATURAL SCIENCE CONNECTED THEREWITH.

By Professor ERNST HÆCKEL, of the University of Jena.

8vo. With Woodcuts and Plates.   [*Preparing.*

AN ARABIC AND ENGLISH DICTIONARY OF THE KORAN.

By Major J. PENRICE, B.A.   4to.

[*Just ready.*

MODERN GOTHIC ARCHITECTURE.

By T. G. JACKSON.

Crown 8vo. Price 7s. 6d.   [*In the press.*

65, Cornhill; & 12, Paternoster Row, London.

A LEGAL HANDBOOK FOR ARCHITECTS.
By EDWARD JENKINS and JOHN RAYMOND.

Crown 8vo. Price 5s. [*Nearly ready.*]

CONTEMPORARY ENGLISH PSYCHOLOGY.
From the French of Professor TH. RIBOT.

AN ANALYSIS OF THE VIEWS AND OPINIONS OF THE FOLLOWING METAPHYSICIANS, AS EXPRESSED IN THEIR WRITINGS.

| JAMES MILL, | JOHN STUART MILL. | HERBERT SPENCER. |
| A. BAIN. | GEORGE H. LEWES. | SAMUEL BAILEY. |

Large post 8vo. [*Preparing.*]

PHYSIOLOGY FOR PRACTICAL USE.
BY VARIOUS EMINENT WRITERS.

Edited by JAMES HINTON.

With 50 Illustrations. [*Preparing.*]

HEALTH AND DISEASE
AS INFLUENCED BY
THE DAILY, SEASONAL, AND OTHER CYCLICAL CHANGES IN THE HUMAN SYSTEM.
By Dr. EDWARD SMITH, F.R.S.

A New Edition. 7s. 6d.

PRACTICAL DIETARY
FOR FAMILIES, SCHOOLS, & THE LABOURING CLASSES.

By Dr. EDWARD SMITH, F.R.S.

A New Edition. Price 3s. 6d.

CONSUMPTION IN ITS EARLY AND REMEDIABLE STAGES.
By Dr. EDWARD SMITH, F.R.S.

A New Edition. 7s. 6d.

65, *Cornhill;* & 12, *Paternoster Row, London.*

A TREATISE ON RELAPSING FEVER.

By R. T. LYONS,
Assistant-Surgeon, Bengal Army.

Small post 8vo. 7s. 6d.

"A practical work thoroughly supported in its views by a series of remarkable cases."—*Standard.*

IN QUEST OF COOLIES.

A South Sea Sketch.   By JAMES L. A. HOPE.

Second Edition. Crown 8vo, with 15 Illustrations from Sketches by the Author. Price 6s.

"Mr. Hope's description of the natives is graphic and amusing, and the book is altogether well worthy of perusal."—*Standard.*

"Lively and clever sketches."—*Athenæum.*
"This agreeably written and amusingly illustrated volume."—*Public Opinion.*

THE NILE WITHOUT A DRAGOMAN.

By FREDERIC EDEN.

Second Edition. In one vol. Crown 8vo, cloth. 7s. 6d.

"Should any of our readers care to imitate Mr. Eden's example, and wish to see things with their own eyes, and shift for themselves, next winter in Upper Egypt, they will find this book a very agreeable guide."—*Times.*
"We have in these pages the most minute description of life as it appeared on the banks of the Nile; all that could be seen or was worth seeing in nature or in art is here pleasantly and graphically set down. . . . It is a book to read during an autumn holiday."—*Spectator.*
"Gives, within moderate compass, a suggestive description of the charms, curiosities, dangers, and discomforts of the Nile voyage."—*Saturday Review.*

ROUND THE WORLD IN 1870.

A VOLUME OF TRAVELS, WITH MAPS.

By A. D. CARLISLE, B.A.,
Trin. Coll., Camb.

Demy 8vo. 16s.

"Makes one understand how going round the world is to be done in the quickest and pleasantest manner, and how the brightest and most cheerful of travellers did it with eyes wide open and keen attention all on the alert, with ready sympathies, with the happiest facility of hitting upon the most interesting features of nature and the most interesting characteristics of man, and all for its own sake."—*Spectator.*
"We can only commend, which we do very heartily, an eminently sensible and readable book."—*British Quarterly Review.*

65, *Cornhill;* & 12, *Paternoster Row, London.*

Military Works.

THE FRONTAL ATTACK OF INFANTRY.
By Capt. LAYMANN, Instructor of Tactics at the Military College, Neisse. Translated by Colonel EDWARD NEWDIGATE. Crown 8vo, limp cloth. Price 2s. 6d.

"This work has met with special attention in our army."—*Militarin Wochenblatt.*

THE FIRST BAVARIAN ARMY CORPS IN
THE WAR OF 1870-71, UNDER VON DER TANN. Compiled from the Official Records by Capt. HUGO HELVIG. Translated by Capt. G. SALIS SCHWABE. Demy 8vo. With 5 large Maps.

History of the Organisation, Equipment, and War Services of
THE REGIMENT OF BENGAL ARTILLERY.
Compiled from Published Official and other Records, and various private sources, by Major FRANCIS W. STUBBS, Royal (late Bengal) Artillery. Vol. I. will contain WAR SERVICES. The Second Volume will be published separately, and will contain the HISTORY of the ORGANISATION and EQUIPMENT of the REGIMENT. In 2 vols. 8vo. With Maps and Plans. [*Preparing.*

THE ABOLITION OF PURCHASE AND THE
ARMY REGULATION BILL OF 1871. By Lieut.-Col. the Hon. A. ANSON, V.C., M.P. Crown 8vo. Price One Shilling.

THE STORY OF THE SUPERSESSIONS.
By Lieut.-Col. the Hon. A. ANSON, V.C., M.P. Crown. 8vo. Price Sixpence.

ARMY RESERVES AND MILITIA REFORMS.
By Lieut.-Colonel the Hon. C. ANSON. Crown 8vo. Sewed. Price One Shilling.

ELEMENTARY MILITARY GEOGRAPHY,
RECONNOITRING, AND SKETCHING. Compiled for Non-Commissioned Officers and Soldiers of all Arms. By Lieut. C. E. H. VINCENT, Royal Welsh Fusileers. Small crown 8vo. 2s. 6d.

65, *Cornhill;* & 12, *Paternoster Row, London.*

MILITARY WORKS—*continued*.

VICTORIES AND DEFEATS.
An Attempt to explain the Causes which have led to them. An Officer's Manual. By Col. R. P. ANDERSON. Demy 8vo. 14*s*. [*In preparation.*

STUDIES IN THE NEW INFANTRY
TACTICS. Parts I. & II. By Major W. VON SCHEREFF. Translated from the German by Col. LUMLEY GRAHAM. [*Shortly.*

THE OPERATIONS OF THE FIRST ARMY
TO THE CAPITULATION OF METZ. By Major VON SCHELL, with Maps, including one of Metz and of the country around. Translated by Capt. E. O. HOLLIST. In demy 8vo. [*In preparation.*

⁂ The most important events described in this work are the battles of Spichern, those before Metz on the 14th and 18th August, and (on this point nothing authentic has yet been published) the history of the investment of Metz (battle of Noisseville).

This work, however, possesses a greater importance than that derived from these points, because it represents for the first time from the official documents the generalship of Von Steinmetz. Hitherto we have had no exact reports on the deeds and motives of this celebrated general. This work has the special object of unfolding carefully the relations in which the commander of the First Army acted, the plan of operations which he drew up, and the manner in which he carried it out.

THE OPERATIONS OF THE FIRST ARMY
IN NORTHERN FRANCE AGAINST FAIDHERBE. By Colonel COUNT HERMANN VON WARTENSLEBEN, Chief of the Staff of the First Army. Translated by Colonel C. H. VON WRIGHT. In demy 8vo. Uniform with the above.

[*In preparation.*

THE OPERATIONS OF THE FIRST ARMY,
UNDER GEN. VON GOEBEN. Translated by Col. C. H. VON WRIGHT. With Maps. Demy 8vo.

TACTICAL DEDUCTIONS FROM THE WAR
OF 1870–1. By Captain A. VON BOGUSLAWSKI. Translated by Colonel LUMLEY GRAHAM, late 18th (Royal Irish) Regiment. Demy 8vo. Uniform with the above. Price 7*s*.

"Major Boguslawski's tactical deductions from the war are, that infantry still preserve their superiority over cavalry, that open order must henceforth be the main principles of all drill, and that the chassepot is the best of all small arms for precision. . . . We must, without delay, impress brain and forethought into the British Service; and we cannot commence the good work too soon, or better, than by placing the two books ('The Operations of the German Armies' and 'Tactical Deductions') we have here criticised, in every military library, and introducing them as class-books in every tactical school."—*United Service Gazette.*

MILITARY WORKS—*continued*.

THE OPERATIONS OF THE GERMAN ARMIES IN FRANCE, FROM SEDAN TO THE END OF THE WAR OF 1870-1.
With Large Official Map. From the Journals of the Head-quarters Staff, by Major WM. BLUME. Translated by E. M. JONES, Major 20th Foot, late Professor of Military History, Sandhurst. Demy 8vo. Price 9s.

"The book is of absolute necessity to the military student. . . . The work is one of high merit and . . . has the advantage of being rendered into fluent English, and is accompanied by an excellent military map."—*United Service Gazette.*

"The work of translation has been well done; the expressive German idioms have been rendered into clear, nervous English without losing any of their original force; and in notes, prefaces, and introductions, much additional information has been given."—*Athenæum.*

"The work of Major von Blume in its English dress forms the most valuable addition to our stock of works upon the war that our press has put forth. Major Blume writes with a clear conciseness much wanting in many of his country's historians, and Major Jones has done himself and his original alike justice by his vigorous yet correct translation of the excellent volume on which he has laboured. Our space forbids our doing more than commending it earnestly as the most authentic and instructive narrative of the second section of the war that has yet appeared."—*Saturday Review.*

THE OPERATIONS OF THE SOUTH ARMY IN JANUARY AND FEBRUARY, 1871.
Compiled from the Official War Documents of the Head-quarters of the Southern Army. By COUNT HERMANN VON WARTENSLEBEN, Colonel in the Prussian General Staff. Translated by Colonel C. H. VON WRIGHT. Demy 8vo, with Maps. Uniform with the above. Price 6s.

HASTY INTRENCHMENTS.
By Colonel A. BRIALMONT. Translated by Lieutenant CHARLES A. EMPSON, R.A. Demy 8vo. Nine Plates. Price 6s.

"A valuable contribution to military literature."—*Athenæum.*

"In seven short chapters it gives plain directions for performing shelter-trenches, with the best method of carrying the necessary tools, and it offers practical illustrations of the use of hasty intrenchments on the field of battle."—*United Service Magazine.*

"It supplies that which our own text-books give but imperfectly, viz., hints as to how a position can best be strengthened by means . . . of such extemporised intrenchments and batteries as can be thrown up by infantry in the space of four or five hours . . . deserves to become a standard military work."—*Standard.*

"A clever treatise, short, practical and clear."—*Investor's Guardian.*

"Clearly and critically written."—*Wellington Gazette.*

THE ARMY OF THE NORTH-GERMAN CONFEDERATION.
A Brief Description of its Organisation, of the different Branches of the Service and their 'Rôle' in War, of its Mode of Fighting, &c. By a PRUSSIAN GENERAL. Translated from the German by Col. EDWARD NEWDIGATE. Demy 8vo. 5s.

*** The authorship of this book was erroneously ascribed to the renowned General von Moltke, but there can be little doubt that it was written under his immediate inspiration.

65, *Cornhill;* & 12, *Paternoster Row, London.*

MILITARY WORKS—*continued.*

CAVALRY FIELD DUTY.

By Major-General VON MIRUS. Translated by Captain FRANK S. RUSSELL, 14th (King's) Hussars. Crown 8vo, limp cloth. 5s.

*** This is the text-book of instruction in the German cavalry, and comprises all the details connected with the military duties of cavalry soldiers on service. The translation is made from a new edition, which contains the modifications introduced consequent on the experiences of the late war. The great interest that students feel in all the German military methods, will, it is believed, render this book especially acceptable at the present time.

STUDIES IN LEADING TROOPS.

By Colonel VON VERDY DU VERNOIS. An authorised and accurate Translation by Lieutenant H. J. T. HILDYARD, 71st Foot. Parts I. and II. Demy 8vo. Price 7s. [*Now ready.*

*** General BEAUCHAMP WALKER says of this work:—"I recommend the first two numbers of Colonel von Verdy's 'Studies' to the attentive perusal of my brother officers. They supply a want which I have often felt during my service in this country, namely, a minuter tactical detail of the minor operations of the war than any but the most observant and fortunately-placed staff-officer is in a position to give. I have read and re-read them very carefully, I hope with profit, certainly with great interest, and believe that practice, in the sense of these 'Studies,' would be a valuable preparation for manœuvres on a more extended scale."—Berlin, June, 1872.

THE FRANCO-GERMAN WAR, 1870-71.

FIRST PART:—HISTORY OF THE WAR TO THE DOWNFALL OF THE EMPIRE. FIRST SECTION:—THE EVENTS IN JULY. Authorised Translation from the German Official Account at the Topographical and Statistical Department of the War Office, by Captain F. C. H. CLARKE, R.A. First Section, with Map. Demy 8vo. 3s.

DISCIPLINE AND DRILL.

Four Lectures delivered to the London Scottish Rifle Volunteers. By Captain S. FLOOD PAGE. A New and Cheaper Edition. Price 1s.

"One of the best-known and coolest-headed of the metropolitan regiments, whose adjutant moreover has lately published an admirable collection of lectures addressed by him to the men of his corps."—*Times.*

"The very useful and interesting work. . . . Every Volunteer, officer or private, will be the better for perusing and digesting the plain-spoken truths which Captain Page so firmly, and yet so modestly, puts before them; and we trust that the little book in which they are contained will find its way into all parts of Great Britain."—*Volunteer Service Gazette.*

THE SUBSTANTIVE SENIORITY ARMY

LIST. Majors and Captains. By Captain F. B. P. WHITE, 1st W. I. Regiment. 8vo, sewed. 2s. 6d.

65, *Cornhill;* & 12, *Paternoster Row, London.*

Books on Indian Subjects.

THE EUROPEAN IN INDIA.
A HAND-BOOK OF PRACTICAL INFORMATION FOR THOSE PROCEEDING TO, OR RESIDING IN, THE EAST INDIES,

RELATING TO OUTFITS, ROUTES, TIME FOR DEPARTURE, INDIAN CLIMATE, ETC.

By EDMUND C. P. HULL.

WITH A MEDICAL GUIDE FOR ANGLO-INDIANS.

BEING A COMPENDIUM OF ADVICE TO EUROPEANS IN INDIA, RELATING TO THE PRESERVATION AND REGULATION OF HEALTH.

By R. S. MAIR, M.D., F.R.C.S.E.,
Late Deputy Coroner of Madras.

In 1 vol. Post 8vo. 6s.

"Full of all sorts of useful information to the English settler or traveller in India."—*Standard*.

"One of the most valuable books ever published in India—valuable for its sound information, its careful array of pertinent facts, and its sterling common sense. It is a publisher's as well as an author's 'hit,' for it supplies a want which few persons may have discovered, but which everybody will at once recognise when once the contents of the book have been mastered. The medical part of the work is invaluable."—*Calcutta Guardian*.

EASTERN EXPERIENCES.
By L. BOWRING, C.S.I.,
Lord Canning's Private Secretary, and for many years the Chief Commissioner of Mysore and Coorg.

In 1 vol. Demy 8vo. 16s. Illustrated with Maps and Diagrams.

"An admirable and exhaustive geographical, political, and industrial survey."—*Athenæum*.

"The usefulness of this compact and methodical summary of the most authentic information relating to countries whose welfare is intimately connected with our own, should obtain for Mr. Lewin Bowring's work a good place among treatises of its kind."—*Daily News*.

"Interesting even to the general reader, but more especially so to those who may have a special concern in that portion of our Indian Empire."—*Post*.

"An elaborately got up and carefully compiled work."—*Home News*.

A MEMOIR OF THE INDIAN SURVEYS.
By CLEMENT R. MARKHAM.
Printed by order of Her Majesty's Secretary of State for India in Council.

Imperial 8vo. 10s. 6d.

65, *Cornhill;* & 12, *Paternoster Row, London.*

BOOKS ON INDIAN SUBJECTS—*continued.*

WESTERN INDIA BEFORE AND DURING THE MUTINIES.

PICTURES DRAWN FROM LIFE.

By MAJOR-GEN. SIR GEORGE LE GRAND JACOB, K.C.S.I., C.B.

In 1 vol. Crown 8vo. 7s. 6d.

"The most important contribution to the history of Western India during the Mutinies which has yet, in a popular form, been made public."—*Athenæum.*

"The legacy of a wise veteran, intent on the benefit of his countrymen rather than on the acquisition of fame."—*London and China Express.*

"Few men more competent than himself to speak authoritatively concerning Indian affairs."—*Standard.*

EXCHANGE TABLES OF STERLING AND INDIAN RUPEE CURRENCY,

UPON A NEW AND EXTENDED SYSTEM,

EMBRACING VALUES FROM ONE FARTHING TO ONE HUNDRED THOUSAND POUNDS, AND AT RATES PROGRESSING, IN SIXTEENTHS OF A PENNY, FROM 1s. 9d. TO 2s. 3d. PER RUPEE.

By DONALD FRASER,

Accountant to the British Indian Steam Navigation Co., Limited.

Royal 8vo. 10s. 6d.

A CATALOGUE OF MAPS OF THE BRITISH POSSESSIONS

IN INDIA AND OTHER PARTS OF ASIA.

Published by order of Her Majesty's Secretary of State for India in Council.

Royal 8vo, sewed. 1s.

A continuation of the above, sewed, price 6d., is now ready.

☞ *Messrs. Henry S. King & Co. are the authorised agents by the Government for the sale of the whole of the Maps enumerated in this Catalogue.*

65, *Cornhill;* & 12, *Paternoster Row, London.*

Juvenile Books.

LOST GIP. By HESBA STRETTON, Author of "Little Meg," "Alone in London." Square crown 8vo. Six Illustrations. Price 1s. 6d.

BRAVE MEN'S FOOTSTEPS. A Book of Example and Anecdote for Young People. By the Editor of "MEN WHO HAVE RISEN." With Four Illustrations. By C. DOYLE. 3s. 6d.

"The little volume is precisely of the stamp to win the favour of those who, in choosing a gift for a boy, would consult his moral development as well as his temporary pleasure."—*Daily Telegraph.*

"A readable and instructive volume."—*Examiner.*
"No more welcome book for the schoolboy could be imagined."—*Birmingham Daily Gazette.*

THE LITTLE WONDER-HORN. By JEAN INGELOW. A Second Series of "Stories told to a Child." Fifteen Illustrations. Cloth, gilt. 3s. 6d.

"Full of fresh and vigorous fancy: it is worthy of the author of some of the best of our modern verse."—*Standard.*

"We like all the contents of the 'Little Wonder-Horn' very much."—*Athenæum.*
"We recommend it with confidence."—*Pall-Mall Gazette.*

STORIES IN PRECIOUS STONES. By HELEN ZIMMERN. With Six Illustrations. Crown 8vo. 5s.

"A series of pretty tales which are half fantastic, half natural, and pleasantly quaint, as befits stories intended for the young."—*Daily Telegraph.*

"Certainly the book is well worth a perusal, and will not be soon laid down when once taken up."—*Daily Bristol Times.*

GUTTA-PERCHA WILLIE, THE WORKING GENIUS. By GEORGE MACDONALD. With Illustrations. By ARTHUR HUGHES. Crown 8vo. 3s. 6d.

THE TRAVELLING MENAGERIE. By CHARLES CAMDEN, Author of "Hoity Toity." Illustrated by J. MAHONEY. Crown 8vo. 3s. 6d.

PLUCKY FELLOWS. A Book for Boys. By STEPHEN J. MACKENNA. With Six Illustrations. Crown 8vo. Price 3s. 6d.

65, Cornhill; & 12, Paternoster Row, London.

JUVENILE BOOKS—*continued.*

THE DESERTED SHIP. A Real Story of the Atlantic. By CUPPLES HOWE, Master Mariner. Illustrated by TOWNLEY GREEN. Crown 8vo. 3s. 6d.

GOOD WORDS FOR THE YOUNG. The Volume for 1872, gilt cloth and gilt edges, 7s. 6d. Containing numerous Contributions by popular authors, and about One Hundred and Fifty Illustrations by the best artists.

New Edition.

THE DESERT PASTOR, JEAN JAROUSSEAU. Translated from the French of EUGENE PELLETAN. By Colonel E. P. DE L'HOSTE. In fcap. 8vo, with an Engraved Frontispiece. Price 3s. 6d.

"There is a poetical simplicity and picturesqueness; the noblest heroism; unpretentious religion; pure love, and the spectacle of a household brought up in the fear of the Lord. . . . The whole story has an air of quaint antiquity similar to that which invests with a charm more easily felt than described the site of some splendid ruin."—*Illustrated London News.*

"This charming specimen of Eugène Pelletan's tender grace, humour, and high-toned morality."—*Notes and Queries.*

"A touching record of the struggles in the cause of religious liberty of a real man."—*Graphic.*

HOITY TOITY, THE GOOD LITTLE FELLOW. By CHARLES CAMDEN. Illustrated. Crown 8vo. 3s. 6d.

SEEKING HIS FORTUNE, AND OTHER STORIES. Crown 8vo. Six Illustrations. [*Preparing.*

THE "ELSIE" SERIES, 3s. 6d. *each.*

ELSIE DINSMORE. By MARTHA FARQUHARSON. Crown 8vo. Illustrated.

ELSIE'S GIRLHOOD. A Sequel to "Elsie Dinsmore." By the same Author. Crown 8vo. Illustrated.

ELSIE'S HOLIDAYS AT ROSELANDS. By the same Author. Crown 8vo. Illustrated.

65, *Cornhill;* & 12, *Paternoster Row, London.*

Poetry.

POT-POURRI. Collected Verses. By AUSTIN DOBSON. Crown 8vo.

IMITATIONS FROM THE GERMAN OF SPITTA AND TERSTEGEN. By Lady DURAND. Crown 8vo. 5s. [*In the press.*

EASTERN LEGENDS AND STORIES IN ENGLISH VERSE. By Lieutenant NORTON POWLETT, Royal Artillery. Crown 8vo. 5s.

EDITH; or, LOVE AND LIFE IN CHESHIRE. By T. ASHE, Author of the "Sorrows of Hypsipylé," etc. Sewed. Price 6d.

"A really fine poem, full of tender, subtle touches of feeling."—*Manchester News.*

"Pregnant from beginning to end with the results of careful observation and imaginative power."—*Chester Chronicle.*

THE GALLERY OF PIGEONS, AND OTHER POEMS. By THEO. MARZIALS. Crown 8vo. 4s. 6d. [*In the press.*

A NEW VOLUME OF SONNETS. By the Rev. C. TENNYSON TURNER. Crown 8vo. [*In the press.*

ENGLISH SONNETS. Collected and Arranged by JOHN DENNIS. Small crown 8vo. [*In the press.*

GOETHE'S FAUST. A New Translation in Rime. By the Rev. C. KEGAN PAUL. Crown 8vo. 6s.

WILLIAM CULLEN BRYANT'S POEMS. Handsomely bound, with Illustrations. A Cheaper Edition. A Pocket Edition. [*Preparing.*

65, *Cornhill;* & 12, *Paternoster Row, London.*

POETRY—*continued.*

CALDERON'S DRAMAS.
THE PURGATORY OF ST. PATRICK.
THE WONDERFUL MAGICIAN.
LIFE IS A DREAM.
Translated from the Spanish. By DENIS FLORENCE MAC-CARTHY.

SONGS FOR SAILORS. By Dr. W. C. BENNETT.
Dedicated by Special Request to H.R.H. the Duke of Edinburgh. Crown 8vo. 3s. 6d. With Steel Portrait and Illustrations.
An Edition in Illustrated paper Covers. Price 1s.

DR. W. C. BENNETT'S POEMS will be shortly
Re-issued, with additions to each part, in Five Parts, at 1s. each.

WALLED IN, AND OTHER POEMS. By the
Rev. HENRY J. BULKELY. Crown 8vo. 5s.

THE POETICAL AND PROSE WORKS OF
ROBERT BUCHANAN. Preparing for publication, a Collected Edition in 5 vols.
CONTENTS OF VOL. I.—
DAUGHTERS OF EVE.
UNDERTONES AND ANTIQUES.
COUNTRY AND PASTORAL POEMS. [*In the Press.*

SONGS OF LIFE AND DEATH. By JOHN
PAYNE, Author of "Intaglios," "Sonnets," "The Masque of Shadows," etc. Crown 8vo. 5s. [*Just out.*

SONGS OF TWO WORLDS. By a NEW WRITER.
Fcap. 8vo, cloth, 5s. Second Edition.

"The 'New Writer' is certainly no tyro. No one after reading the first two poems, almost perfect in rhythm and all the graceful reserve of true lyrical strength, can doubt that this book is the result of lengthened thought and assiduous training in poetical form. . . . These poems will assuredly take high rank among the class to which they belong."—*British Quarterly Review, April 1st.*

"If these poems are the mere preludes of a mind growing in power and in inclination for verse, we have in them the promise of a fine poet. . . . The verse describing Socrates has the highest note of critical poetry."—*Spectator, February 17th.*

"No extracts could do justice to the exquisite tones, the felicitous phrasing and delicately wrought harmonies of some of these poems." — *Nonconformist, March 27th.*

"Are we in this book making the acquaintance of a fine and original poet, or of a most artistic imitator? And our deliberate opinion is that the former hypothesis is the right one. It has a purity and delicacy of feeling like morning air."—*Graphic, March 16th.*

65, Cornhill; & 12, Paternoster Row, London.

POETRY—*continued.*

THE INN OF STRANGE MEETINGS, AND OTHER POEMS. By MORTIMER COLLINS. Crown 8vo. 5s.

"Abounding in quiet humour, in bright fancy, in sweetness and melody of expression, and, at times, in the tenderest touches of pathos."—*Graphic*.

"Mr. Collins has an undercurrent of chivalry and romance beneath the trifling vein of good humoured banter which is the special characteristic of his verse. . . . The 'Inn of Strange Meetings' is a sprightly piece."—*Athenæum*.

EROS AGONISTES. By E. B. D. Crown 8vo. 3s. 6d.

"The author of these verses has written a very touching story of the human heart in the story he tells with such pathos and power, of an affection cherished so long and so secretly. . . . It is not the least merit of these pages that they are everywhere illumined with moral and religious sentiment suggested, not paraded, of the brightest, purest character."—*Standard*.

THE LEGENDS OF ST. PATRICK & OTHER POEMS. By AUBREY DE VERE. Crown 8vo. 5s.

"Mr. De Vere's versification in his earlier poems is characterised by great sweetness and simplicity. He is master of his instrument, and rarely offends the ear with false notes. Poems such as these scarcely admit of quotation, for their charm is not, and ought not to be, found in isolated passages; but we can promise the patient and thoughtful reader much pleasure in the perusal of this volume."—*Pall-Mall Gazette*.

"We have marked, in almost every page, excellent touches from which we know not how to select. We have but space to commend the varied structure of his verse, the carefulness of his grammar, and his excellent English. All who believe that poetry should raise and not debase the social ideal, all who think that wit should exalt our standard of thought and manners, must welcome this contribution at once to our knowledge of the past and to the science of noble life."—*Saturday Review*.

ASPROMONTE, AND OTHER POEMS. Second Edition, cloth. 4s. 6d.

"The volume is anonymous, but there is no reason for the author to be ashamed of it. The 'Poems of Italy' are evidently inspired by genuine enthusiasm in the cause espoused; and one of them, 'The Execution of Felice Orsini,' has much poetic merit, the event celebrated being told with dramatic force."—*Athenæum*.

"The verse is fluent and free."—*Spectator*.

THE DREAM AND THE DEED, AND OTHER POEMS. By PATRICK SCOTT, Author of "Footpaths between Two Worlds," etc. Fcap. 8vo, cloth, 5s.

"A bitter and able satire on the vice and follies of the day, literary, social, and political."—*Standard*.

"Shows real poetic power coupled with evidences of satirical energy."—*Edinburgh Daily Review*. . . .

65, *Cornhill;* & 12, *Paternoster Row, London.*

Fiction.

WHAT 'TIS TO LOVE. By the Author of "FLORA ADAIR," "THE VALUE OF FOSTERSTOWN." 3 vols.

CHESTERLEIGH. By ANSLEY CONYERS. 3 vols. Crown 8vo.

SQUIRE SILCHESTER'S WHIM. By MORTIMER COLLINS, Author of "Marquis and Merchant," "The Princess Clarice," &c. Crown 8vo. 3 vols.

"We think it the best (story) Mr. Collins has yet written."—*Pall Mall Gazette.*

SEETA. By Colonel MEADOWS TAYLOR, Author of "Tara," "Ralph Darnell," &c. Crown 8vo. 3 vols.

"The story is well told, native life is admirably described, and the petty intrigues of native rulers, and their hatred of the English, mingled with fear lest the latter should eventually prove the victors, are cleverly depicted."—*Athenæum.*

"We cannot speak too highly of Colonel Meadows Taylor's book. . . . We would recommend all novel-readers to purchase it at the earliest opportunity."—*John Bull.*
"Thoroughly interesting and enjoyable reading."—*Examiner.*

A New and Cheaper Edition, in 1 vol., *each Illustrated, price* 6s., *of*
COL. MEADOWS TAYLOR'S INDIAN TALES
is preparing for publication.

THE CONFESSIONS OF A THUG *is in the press.*

JOHANNES OLAF. By E. DE WILLE. Translated by F. E. BUNNETT. Crown 8vo. 3 vols.

The author of this story enjoys a high reputation in Germany; and both English and German critics have spoken in terms of the warmest praise of this and her previous stories. She has been called "The 'George Eliot' of Germany."

"The book gives evidence of considerable capacity in every branch of a novelist's faculty. The art of description is fully exhibited; perception of character and capacity for delineating it are obvious; while there is great breadth and comprehensiveness in the plan of the story."—*Morning Post.*

OFF THE SKELLIGS. By JEAN INGELOW. (Her First Romance.) Crown 8vo. In 4 vols.

"Clever and sparkling. . . . The descriptive passages are bright with colour."—*Standard.*
"We read each succeeding volume with increasing interest, going almost to the point of wishing there was a fifth."—*Athenæum.*
"The novel as a whole is a remarkable one, because it is uncompromisingly true to life."—*Daily News.*

65, *Cornhill;* & 12, *Paternoster Row, London.*

FICTION—*continued.*

HONOR BLAKE: The Story of a Plain Woman.
By Mrs. KEATINGE, Author of "English Homes in India," &c. 2 vols. Crown 8vo.

"One of the best novels we have met with for some time."—*Morning Post.*

"A story which must do good to all, young and old, who read it."—*Daily News.*

THE DOCTOR'S DILEMMA. By HESBA STRETTON, Author of "Little Meg," &c., &c. Crown 8vo. 3 vols.

THE PRINCESS CLARICE. A Story of 1871.
By MORTIMER COLLINS. 2 vols. Crown 8vo.

"Mr. Collins has produced a readable book, amusingly characteristic. There is good description of Devonshire scenery; and lastly there is Clarice, a most successful heroine, who must speak to the reader for herself."—*Athenæum.*

"Very readable and amusing. We would especially give an honourable mention to Mr. Collins's '*vers de société*,' the writing of which has almost become a lost art."—*Pall Mall Gazette.*

"A bright, fresh, and original book, with which we recommend all genuine novel readers to become acquainted at the earliest opportunity."—*Standard.*

A GOOD MATCH. By AMELIA PERRIER, Author of "Mea Culpa." 2 vols.

"Racy and lively."—*Athenæum.*
"As pleasant and readable a novel as we have seen this season."—*Examiner.*

"This clever and amusing novel."—*Pall Mall Gazette.*
"Agreeably written."—*Public Opinion.*

THE SPINSTERS OF BLATCHINGTON. By MAR. TRAVERS. 2 vols. Crown 8vo.

"A pretty story. Deserving of a favourable reception."—*Graphic.*

"A book of more than average merits, worth reading."—*Examiner.*

THOMASINA. By the Author of "DOROTHY," "DE CRESSY," etc. 2 vols. Crown 8vo.

"A finished and delicate cabinet picture, no line is without its purpose, but all contribute to the unity of the work."—*Athenæum.*
"For the delicacies of character-drawing,

for play of incident, and for finish of style, we must refer our readers to the story itself."—*Daily News.*
"This undeniably pleasing story."—*Pall Mall Gazette.*

65, Cornhill; & 12, Paternoster Row, London.

FICTION—*continued.*

THE STORY OF SIR EDWARD'S WIFE. By HAMILTON MARSHALL, Author of "For Very Life." 1 vol. Crown 8vo.

"A quiet graceful little story."—*Spectator.*
"There are many clever conceits in it."

... Mr. Hamilton Marshall can tell a story closely and pleasantly."—*Pall Mall Gazette.*

LINKED AT LAST. By F. E. BUNNETT. 1 vol. Crown 8vo.

"'Linked at Last' contains so much of pretty description, natural incident, and delicate portraiture, that the reader who once takes it up will not be inclined to relinquish it without concluding the volume."—*Morning Post.*
"A very charming story."—*John Bull.*

PERPLEXITY. By SYDNEY MOSTYN. 3 vols. Crown 8vo.

"Written with very considerable power ... original ... worked out with great cleverness and sustained interest."—*Standard.*
"Shows much lucidity—much power of portraiture."—*Examiner.*
"Forcibly and graphically told."—*Daily News.*
"Written with very considerable power, the plot is original and ... worked out with great cleverness and sustained interest."—*Standard.*
"Shows much lucidity, much power of portraiture, and no inconsiderable sense of humour."—*Examiner.*
"The literary workmanship is good, and the story forcibly and graphically told."—*Daily News.*

HER TITLE OF HONOUR. By HOLME LEE. Second Edition. 1 vol. Crown 8vo.

"With the interest of a pathetic story is united the value of a definite and high purpose."—*Spectator.*
"A most exquisitely written story."—*Literary Churchman.*

CRUEL AS THE GRAVE. By the Countess VON BOTHMER. 3 vols. Crown 8vo.

"*Jealousy is cruel as the Grave.*"

"An interesting, though somewhat tragic story."—*Athenæum.*
"An agreeable, unaffected, and eminently readable novel."—*Daily News.*

MEMOIRS OF MRS. LÆTITIA BOOTHBY. By WILLIAM CLARK RUSSELL, Author of "The Book of Authors." Crown 8vo, 7s. 6d.

"The book is clever and ingenious."—*Saturday Review.*
"One of the most delightful books I have read for a very long while. Very few works of truth or fiction are so thoroughly entertaining from the first page to the last."—*Judy.*
"This is a very clever book, one of the best imitations of the productions of the last century that we have seen."—*Guardian.*

65, Cornhill; & 12, Paternoster Row, London.

FICTION—*continued.*

LITTLE HODGE. A Christmas Country Carol. By EDWARD JENKINS, Author of "Ginx's Baby," &c. Illustrated. Crown 8vo. 5s. A Cheap Edition in paper covers price One Shilling.

"We shall be mistaken if it does not obtain a very wide circle of readers."—*United Service Gazette.*
"Wise and humorous, but yet most pathetic."—*Nonconformist.*
"The pathos of some of the passages is extremely touching."—*Manchester Examiner.*
"One of the most seasonable of Christmas stories."—*Literary World.*

GINX'S BABY; HIS BIRTH AND OTHER MISFORTUNES. By EDWARD JENKINS. Twenty-ninth Edition. Crown 8vo. Price 2s.

LORD BANTAM. By EDWARD JENKINS, Author of "Ginx's Baby." Sixth Edition. Crown 8vo. Price 2s.

HERMANN AGHA: An Eastern Narrative. By W. GIFFORD PALGRAVE, Author of "Travels in Central Arabia," &c. Second Edition. 2 vols. Crown 8vo, cloth, extra gilt. 18s.

"Reads like a tale of life, with all its incidents. The young will take to it for its love portions, the older for its descriptions, some in this day for its Arab philosophy."—*Athenæum.*
"The cardinal merit, however, of the story is, to our thinking, the exquisite simplicity and purity of the love portion. There is a positive fragrance as of newly-mown hay about it, as compared with the artificially perfumed passions which are detailed to us with such gusto by our ordinary novel-writers in their endless volumes."—*Observer.*

SEPTIMIUS. A Romance. By NATHANIEL HAWTHORNE. Author of "The Scarlet Letter," "Transformation," &c. Second Edition. 1 vol. Crown 8vo, cloth, extra gilt. 9s.

A peculiar interest attaches to this work. It was the last thing the author wrote, and he may be said to have died as he finished it.

The *Athenæum* says that "the book is full of Hawthorne's most characteristic writing."
"One of the best examples of Hawthorne's writing; every page is impressed with his peculiar view of thought, conveyed in his own familiar way."—*Post.*

PANDURANG HARI; Or, Memoirs of a Hindoo. A Tale of Mahratta Life sixty years ago. With a Preface, by Sir H. BARTLE E. FRERE, G.C.S.I., &c. 2 vols. Crown 8vo.

THE TASMANIAN LILY. By JAMES BONWICK, Author of "Curious Facts of Old Colonial Days," &c. Crown 8vo. Illustrated. [*Preparing.*

The Cornhill Library of Fiction.

3s. 6d. per Volume.

IT is intended in this Series to produce books of such merit that readers will care to preserve them on their shelves.

They are well printed on good paper, handsomely bound, with a Frontispiece, and are sold at the moderate price of 3s. 6d. each.

ROBIN GRAY. By CHARLES GIBBON. With a Frontispiece by HENNESSY.

KITTY. By Miss M. BETHAM-EDWARDS.

READY MONEY MORTI-BOY. A Matter-of-Fact Story.

HIRELL. By JOHN SAUNDERS, Author of "Abel Drake's Wife."

ONE OF TWO. By J. HAIN FRISWELL, Author of "The Gentle Life," etc.

GOD'S PROVIDENCE HOUSE. By Mrs. G. L. BANKS.

OTHER STANDARD NOVELS TO FOLLOW.

Forthcoming Novels.

BRESSANT. A Romance. By JULIAN HAWTHORNE. 2 vols. Crown 8vo. [*Preparing.*]

CIVIL SERVICE. By J. T. LISTADO, Author of "Maurice Reynhart." 2 vols.

VANESSA. By the Author of "THOMASINA," etc. 2 vols.

A LITTLE WORLD. By GEO. MANVILLE FENN, Author of "The Sapphire Cross," "Mad," etc.

TOO LATE. By Mrs. NEWMAN. 2 vols. Crown 8vo.

THE QUEEN'S SHILLING. By Capt. ARTHUR GRIFFITHS, Author of "Peccavi; or, Geoffrey Singleton's Mistake." 2 vols.

TWO GIRLS. By FREDK. WEDMORE, Author of "A Snapt Gold Ring." 2 vols. Crown 8vo.

MIRANDA: a Midsummer Madness. By MORTIMER COLLINS.

EFFIE'S GAME; How she Lost and how she Won. By CECIL CLAYTON. 2 vols.

HEATHERGATE. In 2 vols.

65, *Cornhill*; & 12, *Paternoster Row, London.*

Religious.

HYMNS AND VERSES, Original and Translated. By the Rev. HENRY DOWNTON. Small crown 8vo.

THE ETERNAL LIFE. Being Fourteen Sermons. By the Rev. JAS. NOBLE BENNIE, M.A. Crown 8vo. 6s.

MISSIONARY ENTERPRISE IN THE EAST. By the Rev. RICHARD COLLINS. Illustrated. Crown 8vo. [*Preparing.*]

THE REALM OF TRUTH. By Miss E. CARNE. Crown 8vo. [*Preparing.*]

HYMNS FOR THE CHURCH AND HOME. By the Rev. W. FLEMING STEVENSON, Author of "Praying and Working." [*Preparing.*]

THE YOUNG LIFE EQUIPPING ITSELF FOR GOD'S SERVICE. Being Four Sermons Preached before the University of Cambridge in November, 1872. By the Rev. J. C. VAUGHAN, D.D., Master of the Temple. Third Edition. Crown 8vo. Price 3s. 6d.

WORDS & WORKS IN A LONDON PARISH. Edited by the Rev. CHARLES ANDERSON, M.A. Demy 8vo. 6s.

LIFE: Conferences delivered at Toulouse. By the Rev. PÈRE LACORDAIRE. Crown 8vo. 6s.

THOUGHTS FOR THE TIMES. By the Rev. H. R. HAWEIS, M.A., "Author of Music and Morals," etc. Third Edition. Crown 8vo. 7s. 6d.

CATHOLICISM AND THE VATICAN. With a Narrative of the Old Catholic Congress at Munich. By J. LOWRY WHITTLE, A.M., Trin. Coll., Dublin. Second Edition. Crown 8vo. 7s. 6d.

"A valuable and philosophic contribution to the solution of one of the greatest questions of this stirring age."—*Church Times.*
"We cannot follow the author through his graphic and lucid sketch of the Catholic movement in Germany and of the Munich Congress, at which he was present; but we may cordially recommend his book to all who wish to follow the course of the movement."—*Saturday Review.*

RELIGIOUS—*continued.*

NAZARETH: ITS LIFE AND LESSONS. By the REV. G. S. DREW, Vicar of Trinity, Lambeth. Second Edition. In small 8vo, cloth. 5*s*.

"*In Him was life, and the life was the light of men.*"

"A singularly reverent and beautiful book; the style in which it is written is not less chaste and attractive than its subject."—*Daily Telegraph.*
"Perhaps one of the most remarkable books recently issued in the whole range of English theology. . . . Original in design, calm and appreciative in language, noble and elevated in style, this book, we venture to think, will live."—*Churchman's Magazine.*

SCRIPTURE LANDS IN CONNECTION WITH THEIR HISTORY. By G. S. DREW, M.A., Vicar of Trinity, Lambeth, Author of "Reasons of Faith." Second Edition. Bevelled boards, 8vo. Price 10*s*. 6*d*.

"Mr. Drew has invented a new method of illustrating Scripture history—from observation of the countries. Instead of narrating his travels, and referring from time to time to the facts of sacred history belonging to the different countries, he writes an outline history of the Hebrew nation from Abraham downwards, with special reference to the various points in which the geography illustrates the history. The advantages of this plan are obvious. Mr. Drew thus gives us not a mere imitation of 'Sinai and Palestine,' but a view of the same subject from the other side. . . . He is very successful in picturing to his readers the scenes before his own mind. The position of Abraham in Palestine is portrayed, both socially and geographically, with great vigour. Mr. Drew has given an admirable account of the Hebrew sojourn in Egypt, and has done much to popularise the newly-acquired knowledge of Assyria in connection with the two Jewish Kingdoms."—*Saturday Review.*

MEMORIES OF VILLIERSTOWN. By C. J. S. Crown 8vo. With Frontispiece. 5*s*.

SIX PRIVY COUNCIL JUDGMENTS—1850-1872. Annotated by W. G. BROOKE, M.A., Barrister-at-Law. Crown 8vo. 9*s*.

THE DIVINE KINGDOM ON EARTH AS IT IS IN HEAVEN. By the Author of "Nazareth: its Life and Lessons." In demy 8vo, bound in cloth. Price 10*s*. 6*d*.

[*Now ready.*

"*Our Commonwealth is in Heaven.*"

"A high purpose and a devout spirit characterize this work. It is thoughtful and eloquent. . . . The most valuable and suggestive chapter is entitled 'Fulfilments in Life and Ministry of Christ,' which is full of original thinking admirably expressed."—*British Quarterly Review.*
"It is seldom that, in the course of our critical duties, we have to deal with a volume of any size or pretension so entirely valuable and satisfactory as this. Published anonymously as it is, there is no living divine to whom the authorship would not be a credit. . . . Not the least of its merits is the perfect simplicity and clearness, conjoined with a certain massive beauty, of its style."—*Literary Churchman.*

65, *Cornhill; & 12, Paternoster Row, London.*

Life & Works of the Rev. Fred. W. Robertson.
NEW AND CHEAPER EDITIONS.

LIFE AND LETTERS. Edited by STOPFORD BROOKE, M.A., Chaplain in Ordinary to the Queen.
In 2 vols., uniform with the Sermons. Price 7s. 6d.
Library Edition, in demy 8vo, with Two Steel Portraits. 12s.
A Popular Edition, in 1 vol. Price 6s.

SERMONS. FOUR SERIES. 4 vols. small crown 8vo, price 3s. 6d. per vol.

EXPOSITORY LECTURES ON ST. PAUL'S EPISTLE TO THE CORINTHIANS. Small crown 8vo. 5s.

AN ANALYSIS OF MR. TENNYSON'S "IN MEMORIAM." (Dedicated by permission to the Poet-Laureate.) Fcap. 8vo. 2s.

THE EDUCATION OF THE HUMAN RACE. Translated from the German of GOTTHOLD EPHRAIM LESSING. Fcap. 8vo. 2s. 6d.

LECTURES & ADDRESSES ON LITERARY AND SOCIAL TOPICS. Small crown 8vo. 3s. 6d. [*Preparing.*

A LECTURE ON FRED. W. ROBERTSON, M.A. By the Rev. F. A. NOBLE, delivered before the Young Men's Christian Association of Pittsburgh, U.S. 1s. 6d.

Sermons by the Rev. Stopford A. Brooke, M.A.,
Chaplain in Ordinary to Her Majesty the Queen.

CHRIST IN MODERN LIFE. Sermons Preached in St. James's Chapel, York Street, London. Third Edition. Crown 8vo. 7s. 6d.

"Nobly fearless and singularly strong. . . . carries our admiration throughout."—*British Quarterly Review.*

FREEDOM IN THE CHURCH OF ENGLAND. Six Sermons suggested by the Voysey Judgment. Second Edition. In 1 vol. Crown 8vo, cloth. 3s. 6d.

"A very fair statement of the views in respect to freedom of thought held by the liberal party in the Church of England."—*Blackwood's Magazine.*

"Interesting and readable, and characterised by great clearness of thought, frankness of statement, and moderation of tone."—*Church Opinion.*

SERMONS Preached in St. James's Chapel, York Street, London. Sixth Edition. Crown 8vo. 6s.

"No one who reads these sermons will wonder that Mr. Brooke is a great power in London, that his chapel is thronged, and his followers large and enthusiastic.

"They are fiery, energetic, impetuous sermons, rich with the treasures of a cultivated imagination."—*Guardian.*

THE LIFE AND WORK OF FREDERICK DENISON MAURICE: A Memorial Sermon. Crown 8vo, sewed. 1s.

65, *Cornhill;* & 12, *Paternoster Row, London.*

THE DAY OF REST.

Weekly, price ONE PENNY, *and in* MONTHLY PARTS, *price* SIXPENCE.

On the 1st of January, 1873, was published No. I. of the above, a new Illustrated Magazine for Sunday Reading.

Among the leading Contributions to the First Year's Issue may be mentioned:—

WORDS FOR THE DAY. By C. J. VAUGHAN, D.D., Master of the Temple.

LABOURS OF LOVE: Being further Accounts of what is being done by Dr. WICHERN and others. By the Rev. W. FLEMING STEVENSON, Author of "Praying and Working."

OCCASIONAL PAPERS. By the Rev. THOMAS BINNEY.

SUNDAYS IN MY LIFE. By the Author of "Episodes in an Obscure Life."

SONGS OF REST. By GEORGE MACDONALD.

TO ROME AND BACK: A Narrative of Personal Experience. By One who has made the Journey.

⁎ The late Dr. Norman Macleod, during the last few months of his life, frequently urged the preparation of a series of Popular Papers, by a thoroughly competent person, on the Church of Rome as it really is to-day. "To Rome and Back" is the result of his suggestion.

THE BATTLE OF THE POOR: Sketches from Courts and Alleys. By HESBA STRETTON, Author of "Jessica's First Prayer," and "Little Meg's Children."

Illustrated by the best Artists. Large Folio.

Price One Penny Weekly.   Monthly Parts, Price Sixpence.

THE CONTEMPORARY REVIEW.

THEOLOGICAL, LITERARY, AND SOCIAL.

Price Half-a-Crown Monthly.

THE SAINT PAULS MAGAZINE.

LIGHT AND CHOICE.

Price One Shilling Monthly.

GOOD THINGS FOR THE YOUNG OF ALL AGES.

EDITED BY GEORGE MACDONALD,

And Illustrated by the best Artists.

Price Sixpence Monthly.

Bradbury, Agnew, & Co., Printers, Whitefriars.

www.ingramcontent.com/pod-product-compliance
Lightning Source LLC
Chambersburg PA
CBHW022103300426
44117CB00007B/563